Speaking Freely

Speaking Freely

TRIALS OF THE FIRST AMENDMENT

Floyd Abrams

LARGE PRINT

This large print edition published in 2005 by
RB Large Print
A division of Recorded Books
A Haights Cross Communications Company
270 Skipjack Road
Prince Frederick, MD 20678

Published by arrangement with Viking Books,
a division of Penguin Putnam

Publisher's Cataloging In Publication Data
(Prepared by Donohue Group, Inc.)

Abrams, Floyd.
    Speaking freely : trials of the First Amendment / Floyd Abrams.

        p. (large print) ; cm.

    Includes bibliographical reference.
    ISBN: 1-4193-3955-9

1. Trials—United States. 2. Freedom of speech—United States. 3. Large type books. I. Title.

KF226.A27 2005b
342.7308/53

Printed in the United States of America

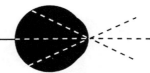

**This Large Print Book carries the
Seal of Approval of N.A.V.H.**

For Efrat, Daniel and Ronnie

The security of the Nation is not at the ramparts alone. Security also lies in the value of our free institutions. A cantankerous press, an obstinate press, a ubiquitous press must be suffered by those in authority in order to preserve the even greater values of freedom of expression and the right of the people to know.

JUDGE MURRAY GURFEIN,
June 1971

CONTENTS

INTRODUCTION

A few years ago, I was asked to write an introduction for a book entitled *Political Censorship*, a collection of *New York Times* articles that had been published on that topic throughout the twentieth century. My task was as fascinating as it was depressing. Here, in one place, were 549 pages of journalism about censorship, almost all of it displaying (sometimes inadvertently) its dangers and occasional lunacy.

Here was the loathsome Joseph Goebbels, brought to life again as only characters in faded newspaper articles can be, strutting about in 1937 as Germany's Minister of Popular Enlightenment and Propaganda, characterizing the press as a piano for him to play on. Touting the virtues of Nazi-style free expression, he insisted that the duty of a newspaper was "not to inform, but to shake up and spur onward." Here was a Soviet spokesman explaining a decade later that "liberty and objectivity of the press—these are fictions. Information is the means of class struggle, not a mirror to reflect events objectively." More often, censorship abroad was justified in more euphemistic language. Terms like "responsibility" and "accountability," "values" and "honor," and even "democracy" itself were used to support the suppression of speech not only in ruthlessly totalitarian states such as Nazi Germany and the Soviet Union but in far less authoritarian nations as well.

The more interesting entries for me, however, were not from foreign nations but from our own. In the United States, the law had been far from clear until well into the second half of the twentieth century about just what meaning should be given to the First Amendment's sweeping provision that Congress could pass "no law abridging the freedom of speech or of the press." Did "no law" literally mean no law at all? If not, what laws could pass constitutional muster? What degree of interference with freedom of speech and freedom of the press constituted an "abridgment"? And even more fundamentally, exactly what was meant by the words "freedom of speech" and "freedom of press"?

From a distance of two centuries, the intentions of those who drafted the First Amendment are not at all obvious. It is, as Thomas I. Emerson has observed, "by no means clear exactly what the colonists had in mind, or just what they expected from the guarantee of freedom of speech, press, assembly and petition." The truth, as Zechariah Chafee astutely observed, may well be "that the framers had no very clear idea as to what they meant."

What we do know, however, is that the framers

of the Constitution were deeply divided about the wisdom of adding any amendments at all to the Constitution at the time of its adoption. The Constitution itself described how the new national government would work. Hamilton and others argued that adding a Bill of Rights that would set forth individual liberties with which the national government could not interfere was not only "unnecessary" but "dangerous." Why, Hamilton asked, "declare that things shall not be done which there is no power to do? Why, for instance, should it be said that the liberty of the press shall not be restrained when no power is given by which restrictions may be imposed?"

To articulate in so many words such restrictions to congressional power, Hamilton argued, might suggest that the delegates at the Constitutional Convention of 1787 who drafted the Constitution believed that Congress had such power in the first place, a notion that was not only false but could lead a future Congress to act as if it were indeed so empowered.

Jefferson's answer and that of his followers was blunt: Deeply suspicious about the new powers being granted to the federal government, they would not support any Constitution that did not include a Bill of Rights setting forth a list of liberties upon which Congress could not impinge. "What I do not like" about the new Constitution, Jefferson wrote to Madison from France, was "the omission of a bill of rights providing clearly and without the aid of sophisms for freedom of religion, freedom of the press," and a number of other specified subjects.

Faced with this serious Republican opposition, the proponents of the new Constitution agreed to the addition of the first ten amendments. As the Supreme Court later observed, adoption of the Bill of Rights was the sine qua non for the adoption of the Constitution itself.

As for the First Amendment, the extraordinary breadth of its language—"no law abridging"—is unmistakable. It is clear that the framers at least meant to embody in law the great victory for freedom that England had recognized almost a century before in banning direct censorship or licensing of the press. But whether the First Amendment was intended simply to embody the same guarantees as English law or to provide far more protection for speech was an issue that remained a matter of debate for many years in the Supreme Court.

The failure of the framers to agree precisely how broadly the First Amendment was intended to be read in protecting free speech made it a far weaker instrument in the early days of the nation than it would later become. Less than a decade after the ratification of the Bill of Rights, the Sedition Act of 1798 was adopted by President John Adams's Federalist government. Passed at a time when war with France seemed likely and aimed at stifling criticism by Adams's Republican opponents of the conduct of the Federalist regime, the Sedition Act made it a criminal offense to "write, print, utter, or publish" any "false, scandalous, and malicious writing" about the president, Congress, or "the government of the United States." (Revealingly, criticism of the vice president was left unregulated, since it was Jefferson, the Republican leader, who held that position.) Republican newspaper editors, sometimes chosen by Adams himself, were duly charged, convicted, and imprisoned, and none of Jefferson's complaints about living under a "reign of witches" had any legal impact; not until he succeeded Adams as president in 1801 were all those convicted under the act pardoned.

In other areas as well the First Amendment initially offered little protection to speakers whose views displeased those in power. When a number of Southern states adopted legislation banning abolitionist speech in the 1830s, no federal judicial review of the constitutionality of the laws was even possible, since the First Amendment had been held to limit only the conduct of the federal government, and not that of the states, from abridging speech. Not until 1925 did the Supreme Court first indicate that the Fourteenth Amendment, adopted in the aftermath of the Civil War, provided protection against state suppression of free speech; only in the 1930s did the Court start to provide any serious First Amendment protection against violations by the states.

At the beginning of the twentieth century, then, little of what we now accept as being protected by the First Amendment actually received significant legal protection, and my reading of turn-of-the-century articles from the *New York Times* only confirmed the real-world impact of that state of affairs. A 1904 dispatch reported laconically on the action of the Boston police in stopping the sale of copies of a comic publication on which the word "Judge" was printed across a likeness of the American flag. Two years later, an article described the indictment of three St. Paul newspapers for reporting on the hanging of a criminal, notwithstanding a law that forbade "publication of details of a hanging" and that permitted newspapers simply "to announce the fact of the execution." Three years after that, Spokane authorities were reported to have seized every copy of the *Industrial Worker*, the house organ of the International Workers of the World, for publishing an article describing the "alleged experience" of a prisoner in the county jail. "The papers," the *Times* reported without comment, "will be burned." A year later, the *Times* reported on the jailing of the general manager of a Salt Lake City newspaper and the entry of fines against the paper itself and its editors for printing a confession made by an individual accused of murder, the publication of which, as a Utah judge concluded, had led to "great difficulty in obtaining a jury."

The apparently boundless degree of official authority reflected in the articles about what might and might not be said around the turn of the last century was startling. In New York City in 1908, the police barred jokes told in dialect, and while they permitted "acting," "vaudeville" was barred. The reporting about the impact of those rules reads like a Mack Sennett comedy routine. The *Times* duly described the police watching a quartet perform. Between two of their songs, the reader learned, the baritone struck the second tenor with a newspaper. "Cut that out," yelled a policeman, "that's vaudeville."

How was censorship actually carried out in the United States? It was used to bar films that were viewed as suggestive, to jail journalists who told too much truth, and ultimately to ban books. I was especially struck by a 1921 article under the headline "Improper Novel Costs Women $100." In its entirety, the article reported this:

> Margaret C. Anderson and Jane Heap, publisher and editor respectively of *The Little Review*, at 27 West Eighth Street, each paid a fine of $50 imposed by Justices McInerney, Kernochan and Moss in Special Sessions yesterday, for publishing an improper novel in the July and August, 1920, issues of the magazine. John S. Summer, Secretary of the New York Society for the Prevention of Vice, was the complainant. The defendants were accompanied to court by several Greenwich Village artists and writers. John Quinn, counsel for the women, told the

court that the alleged objectionable story, entitled *Ulysses*, was the product of one Joyce, author, playwright and graduate of Dublin University, whose work had been praised by noted critics. "I think that this novel is unintelligible," said Justice McInerney.

Mr. Quinn admitted that it was cast in a curious style, but contended that it was in similar vein to the work of an American author with which no fault was found, and he thought it was principally a matter of punctuation marks. Joyce, he said, didn't use punctuation marks in this story, probably on account of his eyesight. "There may be found more impropriety in the displays in some Fifth Avenue show windows or in a theatrical show than is contained in this novel," protested the attorney.

Assistant District Attorney Joseph Forrester said that some of the chief objections had to do with a too frank expression concerning a woman's dress when the woman was in the clothes described. The court held that parts of the story seemed to be harmful to the morals of the community.

Pause for a moment to reflect on that period piece. Imagine what Justice McInerney would have thought if he had understood the novel by "one Joyce." Or what Joyce himself must have made of Justice McInerney's difficulty with his prose, or of the defender of his book explaining away Joyce's lack of punctuation as being rooted in his poor eyesight.

It is the last line in the article, however, that is most telling. Because "parts of the story seemed to be harmful to the morals of the community," the story (and the book) were suppressed. Not for another dozen years was *Ulysses* permitted into the country.

The censors in the *Ulysses* case were judges. Other forms of censorship were imposed by Congress, by mayors, even by jurors. One striking lesson of the *Times* collection is that there always seemed to be plausible-sounding reasons to stop publication of a controversial work or to punish it when it occurred. Suppression of speech with which one differed, as Justice Oliver Wendell Holmes had sagely written, always seemed "perfectly logical." Another lesson was that the risks of harm from unfettered speech were invariably overstated while the benefits of freedom were invariably minimized. Justice Louis Brandeis had said it best: "Men feared witches and burned women."

By the time I began to practice First Amendment law in the late 1960s, the Supreme Court had decided only a few cases upon which a First Amendment legal defender could rely. There were the sublime dissenting and concurring opinions of Justices Holmes and Brandeis from the 1920s and early 1930s in cases commenced against socialists and anarchists in the aftermath of World War I, which remain among the most luminous defenses of free speech ever written. There was as well the 1931 ruling of the Supreme Court in *Near v. Minnesota*, all but prohibiting prior restraints—injunctions—on the press, a case that would be of central importance in the Pentagon Papers case forty years later. Several cases from the 1940s significantly limited the power of judges to hold journalists in contempt of court for what they wrote and published about the courts, including a spectacularly important one, *Bridges v. California*, written by Justice Hugo Black (and released exactly one day after Pearl Harbor), which sought to answer the still-disputed historical questions about the intended breadth of the First Amendment: "No purpose in ratifying the Bill of Rights was clearer," Black wrote, "than that of securing for the people of the United States much greater freedom of religion, expression, assembly and petition than the people of Great Britain had ever enjoyed." And there was the crown jewel of First Amendment law, the 1964 ruling of the Supreme Court in *New York Times Co. v. Sullivan*, strictly limiting the entry of libel judgments against the press and broadly articulating, in Justice William J. Brennan's memorable voice, the core First Amendment proposition "that debate on public issues should be uninhibited, robust and wide open and that it may well include vehement, caustic, and sometimes unpleasantly sharp attacks."

As of the late 1960s no Supreme Court cases had

yet been decided about how the First Amendment right of the press to print or broadcast was affected when national security issues were involved. The Court had yet to rule in any case involving efforts to prevent the press from publishing confessions or other potentially prejudicial material prior to the commencement of a criminal trial. Little had been decided about when, if ever, the press could be held criminally liable for publishing truthful material that, for one public policy reason or other, state or federal law prohibited. Few libel cases had been decided that applied the new protections afforded the press in 1964 by the *New York Times v. Sullivan* case.

Likewise, as of the late 1960s little case law existed about subjects as diverse as what limits a city, state, or federal government could place on its granting of funds to a cultural institution based upon the views expressed in works of art shown by those institutions, and what limits could be placed on the amount of money that could be spent on election-related advocacy.

The 1960s, then, was a time when the degree of First Amendment protection available to the press was still uncertain. It was also a time when the country began to suffer a sort of nervous break-down, with the assassinations of President John F. Kennedy, Reverend Martin Luther King, and Senator Robert Kennedy overlapping a civil rights revolution in the South and the ever-increasing impact on the nation of the doomed war in

Vietnam. At this historic moment I was an unlikely champion of the First Amendment.

Like most people, I had always been "for" freedom of speech—who seriously believes that he or she is against it?—but it was not until I began to defend the First Amendment in court in the late 1960s that I came to the view that the need for what Justice Brennan had characterized in *New York Times Co. v. Sullivan* as "uninhibited, robust and wide open" speech should outweigh all but the most vital competing societal interests, and even then only in the narrowest of circumstances.

My views about the First Amendment began to take shape when I was an undergraduate at Cornell University. I was sixteen when I began my college life in 1952, but my youth did not lead me to any exuberant adoption of libertarian principles. I had, as one professor remarked on one of my papers, the views of a liberal with the vocabulary of a conservative. In the area of freedom of speech, however, I seemed to have the views of a mid-1950s conservative as well.

Under the direction of Professor Robert E. Cushman, I wrote my senior thesis on the conflict between fair trial and free press. My approach was greatly influenced by the views of Supreme Court Justice Felix Frankfurter, whose opinions often treated the press more as an irresponsible and even dangerous nuisance than as an institution that could legitimately benefit society. Frankfurter's legal approach was in turn rooted in English law, and it was that law that I advocated adopting wholesale. Like England, I argued, America should make it criminal for the press to publish any information prior to a trial that could interfere with a defendant's right to a fair trial. Like England, I wrote, we should adopt a body of law that would result in the jailing of editors who published prior criminal records or pretrial confessions of defendants. That I would be arguing precisely the opposite in the United States Supreme Court twenty years later was unimaginable.

By the time I had graduated from Yale Law School, my views had been tempered but had not fundamentally changed. My political views were pronouncedly liberal, and I was generally more persuaded by and admiring of the liberal Supreme Court justices than the more conservative ones. But I had learned much from a new group of rather conservative scholars (as they were defined at Yale, at least) who began teaching at Yale in 1956, the year I arrived as a student. Foremost among them was Alexander M. Bickel, a startlingly brilliant young scholar. In my first year at Yale the curriculum had been changed to ensure that every entering student took part in a small seminar of about twenty students. The system was arranged alphabetically, which meant I was in especially close contact with my fellow students whose family names began with A, B, or C. The professor I came to know best was also first alphabetically—Bickel.

Born in Rumania, Bickel had emigrated to the United States with his family when he was fourteen, speaking little or no English. By the time I first saw him enter our seminar in constitutional law, he was thirty-one and already the stuff of student legend—an honored graduate of Harvard Law School, former law clerk to Justice Frankfurter, and author of a forthcoming book featuring previously unpublished drafts of opinions of Justice Brandeis. He was a formidable presence in the classroom, demanding and often irascible. His English not only was perfect but seemed specially crafted to deflate our (and all too often my) intellectual pretensions.

Bickel took particular joy in attacking the class's liberal judicial heroes, Justices Hugo Black and William O. Douglas, jurists who had engaged in an ongoing ideological conflict on the Court with Justice Frankfurter. I still remember his verbal assault on one of my fellow students who dared to answer his question asking what documents a court should look at in interpreting the Constitution by referring not to the text of the Constitution itself, nor to materials such as the Federalist Papers, but to the Declaration of Independence. I thought my classmate was right—not that Jefferson's stirring prose in the Declaration of Independence trumped the Constitution, but that in interpreting the latter it was entirely appropriate to consider the former. Years later, conservatives such as Clarence Thomas would turn anew to the Declaration of Independence as a source of natural law which, they argued, should be given great weight in constitutional adjudication. In my days in law school, however, at least under Professor Bickel's tutelage, the Declaration of Independence was treated as a mere revolutionary document, not one to look to for legal guidance.

Having taken none-too-supportive positions in college about the First Amendment, I found Bickel's (and Frankfurter's) less protective approach to First Amendment issues congenial with my own. What I found uncongenial—what I learned most from, that is—was Bickel's emphasis, often based on the writings of Justice Brandeis, on the need for judicial decision-making based upon the consistent application of legal standards, even when those standards led to the "wrong" side winning. Constitutional law, he argued, was not just politics under a different name but was—or at least was supposed to be—*law*. That did not mean that political or even judicial philosophy played no role in judicial decision-making; nor did it mean that I had to abandon my general personal preference for the liberal judicial icons of the day in favor of Bickel's mentor, Frankfurter. What it did mean, however, was that jurists could not (or at least should not) simply use their raw power to implement their ideologically driven desires.

I took a number of courses with Bickel, did well in the examinations he gave, and left Yale impressed with and a bit apprehensive of him. I was content to leave him behind in academia while I moved on to a different world.

My new world, after graduation from Yale, began at Princeton University, where I worked as a research associate for Professor Alpheus P. Mason in the Department of Politics. Mason was a political scientist who had written biographies of various members of the Supreme Court, including Justice Louis Brandeis and Chief Justice Harlan Fiske Stone. When I joined him, he had the idea of writing a book about the office and powers of the chief justice of the United States. I worked with him for about seven months, about the time it took for both of us to realize that although many chief justices had done interesting and important work while they served on the Court, there was too little to say about the position of chief justice itself to warrant a book-length study.

I moved on from Princeton a bit farther south and spent the next two years as a law clerk for Federal Judge Paul Leahy in Wilmington, Delaware. Leahy was a man of sparkling intelligence and charm who was a joy to work with. When he became ill during the second year of my clerkship, I spent a good deal of time working for Chief Judge Caleb Wright, a superb trial judge, from whom I learned much about the law that remains relevant to my practice four decades later.

I then returned to New York and accepted a position as an associate at the firm of Cahill

Gordon & Reindel. I worked entirely in the litigation area and through the 1960s did a growing amount of work for NBC, a client that increasingly found itself at odds with the government as it proceeded with its news-gathering efforts.

This book begins in 1967, when I had been working at Cahill Gordon for four years. With great difficulty and not a little pain at what I am excluding, I have chosen to describe a sampling of the First Amendment cases with which I have been involved in the ensuing thirty-seven years. Many were highly newsworthy, sometimes notoriously so; others were conducted virtually in secret. All of them reveal the way our courts dealt with competing claims and interests ranging from the right to publish against claims of harm to national security to the right of a museum to choose to display a controversial work of art against the claim of a city that it should not be obliged to fund that art. In each case, a First Amendment defense (or offense) was offered by me and my colleagues; in each, the opposing side urged that some other interest—national security, a defendant's fair-trial rights, an individual's reputation, a city's interest in not subsidizing art that offends, a nation's interest in having pure elections—should carry the day.

At the same time that I try to show how First Amendment law has developed in the years since I began to represent media-related clients, I seek as well to address a related subject that is rarely described with much candor—namely, how lawyers plan to and then actually try cases or argue appeals. I have read many books by or about lawyers. One difference between my life and those of such giants of the bar is that unlike almost all of them, I have lost as well as won cases, made errors as well as hit home runs. I like to think that I have learned from my losses. I know that I haven't forgotten them.

I have written *Speaking Freely* for people who care about our freedoms. While I hope the book will appeal to lawyers, journalists, and students who aspire to be either or both, my real intended audience is readers who live in this country and abroad who want to know more about just what we do protect and what we don't, and who are prepared to make their own judgments about how far our protection of free speech should go.

With that in mind, I begin in the first two chapters with the Pentagon Papers case, the 1971 ruling of the United States Supreme Court rebuffing efforts of the Nixon administration to bar the *New York Times* and other newspapers from publishing information made available by a confidential source who provided the newspaper with major portions of a highly classified analysis setting forth how the United States had become embroiled in the war in Vietnam. The government's effort to obtain a prior restraint—an injunction—barring the *Times* from publishing articles based upon that material led to a historic clash between the powers of the nation during wartime and the rights of the press to be free of governmental restrictions on what it may print. It was my first case that wound up in the Supreme Court, and was followed five years later with my first argument in that court, in a case involving another prior restraint against the press, this one barring the publication of information about a defendant in a sensational murder case.

In chapter 3, I describe two cases I argued a few years later in the Supreme Court, dealing with the issue of when, if ever, the press may be punished for publishing accurate information. The first involved the question of whether a statute could constitutionally make criminal the publication of the name of a judge at a time when he was under investigation by a confidential judicial fitness panel. The second concerned the constitutionality of a statute that made it criminal to publish the name of a juvenile who was then appearing before a juvenile court without first obtaining the permission of the judge. In both cases, the journalists published accurate information that they had lawfully acquired. In both, they had been convicted of crimes for doing so. The question in each was whether the First Amendment allowed the conviction to stand.

I chose three libel cases to describe in chapters 4, 5, and 6, each of which illustrates the new world of libel law brought into being by the Supreme Court's breathtaking 1964 ruling in

New York Times Co. v. Sullivan. The first case describes my surrealistic experience in defending NBC in Las Vegas against a libel suit commenced by Wayne Newton, the internationally recognized Las Vegas entertainer, who claimed that a number of NBC broadcast segments had falsely linked him to organized crime figures. The second was a libel action with a Perry Mason twist that had been commenced by a Turkish businessman who claimed that he had inaccurately been accused by *Newsday*, a New York newspaper, of having been a leading heroin dealer. The third was a litigation commenced by Victor Lasky, a well-known conservative journalist and author, who sued ABC for falsely claiming (as Lasky viewed it) that he was responsible for the McCarthy-like firing of a West Virginia professor.

The next two chapters, 7 and 8, relate to two enormously publicized cases. The first involved New York City Mayor Rudolph Giuliani's angry effort to strip the Brooklyn Museum of all city funding based upon his view that a painting it was about to display was sacrilegious. The last deals with my representation of Senator Mitch McConnell and the National Association of Broadcasters in an extremely controversial challenge to the constitutionality of the McCain-Feingold Act, the law that sought to limit or bar a variety of practices relating to political fund-raising and the expenditure of funds for advertisements during political campaigns. I conclude, in chapter 9, with a comparison of American free-speech law to that in effect in other democratic nations and the impact of the differences.

I know that some of my readers will take issue with various positions I took in the cases I describe. That is as it should be. The essence of the First Amendment, after all, is that we don't all have to agree.

CHAPTER 1

THE PENTAGON PAPERS CASE

In August 1967 I spent a few days in New Delhi, visiting a friend who had been a law school classmate seven years earlier. She was a princess—a genuine one, from a still-powerful regal family. In New York, when we were studying together, I had taken her to a Yankee game. In New Delhi she reciprocated by taking me to her fortune-teller—not just hers, but that of a bevy of Indian leaders, including former Prime Minister Jawaharlal Nehru and his daughter and successor as prime minister, Indira Gandhi. The fortune-teller, who looked to be seventy or so, stood about five feet tall and had a gnarled face and half-closed eyes. He spoke no English, only Hindi. Clad in what looked to be the tattered remains of an aged and discolored white sheet, he sat in a storefront on a solitary chair behind a small, battered wooden table. Mice ran about the wooden floor of the room, often crossing his bare feet. I stood across the table from him, my friend at my side. The fortune-teller glanced at me briefly (I could not tell if he ever actually saw me), asked the date and time of my birth (my friend translated), and then

1

quickly started speaking. He told me a number of things that I soon forgot and one that I remembered: Before I was thirty-five, he said, I would go to my country's capital to work on something that was important. The work, he said, would make me famous. It was not the sort of prediction that one entirely forgets. I was then thirty-one.

A bit less than four years later, I found myself spending a good deal of time in Washington, D.C., working with my former law school professor Alexander Bickel on one of the great challenges to freedom of the press in the nation's history. By the time the Pentagon Papers case ended—nine days before my thirty-fifth birthday—with an emphatic victory for our client, the *New York Times*, legal history had been made and my own life transformed.

I had seen Bickel only a few times between my graduation from Yale Law School and our sudden involvement together in 1971 as the lawyers for the *Times*. I had written to him once from Wilmington, Delaware, where I was serving as a law clerk, to complain about a Delaware state court ruling that upheld the whipping post as a means of punishment. It was cruel and unusual punishment, I insisted—an example of judges being unwilling to do their job properly. Bickel disagreed, writing that it was left to the state to decide how to punish its own prisoners. After I returned to New York and joined the law firm of Cahill Gordon & Reindel as an associate, we stayed in touch but spoke rarely.

In 1970 we renewed our contact, this time professionally. In the late 1960s journalists had been repeatedly subpoenaed to appear before grand juries in an effort to require them to reveal details about their news gathering. Cahill Gordon represented NBC, and in the two-and-a-half-year period from 1969 through July 1971, NBC and CBS alone had received 122 such subpoenas. Many of them sought to require the two networks to identify their confidential sources, individuals who provided, at considerable risk to themselves, information that was critical to the reporting of news. Other subpoenas required testimony about matters that were not inherently confidential—what a journalist, say, heard and saw at a press conference—but which forced the journalist to become a witness to the exchanges she had engaged in with sources.

As the volume of and the intrusiveness of subpoenas increased, however, so did the willingness of the press to resist them. Claims were increasingly asserted by journalists that the First Amendment shielded them from being obliged to reveal their sources. Toward the end of 1971, three cases came before the Supreme Court that raised novel issues in this area. Did journalists actually have any First Amendment right not to disclose their confidential sources? If so, under what circumstances would such a right be applied?

When the Supreme Court decided to resolve these issues by agreeing to hear one of the cases,

Branzburg v. Hayes, James C. Goodale, general counsel of the *New York Times*, persuaded representatives of other large publications and broadcasters—including the *Chicago Sun-Times*, the *Chicago Daily News*, and the Associated Press, as well as the three major television networks, ABC, NBC, and CBS—to write a single brief seeking to persuade the Court to grant First Amendment protection to journalists regarding their sources.

It was obviously going to be a hard sell. Notwithstanding the strong policy arguments in favor of establishing this privilege and the serious harm that would be caused by its absence, no such protection had ever been held to exist. Not only was the concept that the judicial system was entitled to "every man's evidence" (as it was called in prefeminist America) itself deeply rooted in the Constitution, but merely determining the scope of the privilege (*when* would it apply?) and identifying *who* would receive it (only regularly employed journalists? freelancers? anyone?) were difficult matters at best.

Still, four members of the Court had expansive views of the Bill of Rights generally and of freedom of speech and press in particular, which had led them to take positions that we believed would likely result in their viewing our position with sympathy. Justices Hugo Black, William O. Douglas, William J. Brennan, and Thurgood Marshall all seemed to us to be likely votes. But who would (or might) the fifth vote be? And what could we do to persuade the Court that journalists should be granted suffi-cient First Amendment protection so that they could advise their sources—as I, cloaked with the attorney-client privilege, routinely advised my own clients before they spoke to me—that what they said was privileged and thus safe from officially compelled disclosure? We made the decision at the outset not to have any of the firms that represented media entities draft the supporting brief, but instead to retain a highly respected scholar. We looked for one with a conservative bent, one who might appeal to one or more of the justices who came less easily to broad views of First Amendment protection.

After many telephone conferences that I (on behalf of NBC), Goodale (on behalf of the *Times*), and a number of other lawyers representing other media entities participated in, we agreed to approach three scholars. Two of them were legendary, and the third had already broken out of the academic pack and been recognized as an original and highly creative scholar. Professor Paul Freund of the Harvard Law School was the nation's most renowned (and, so it seemed, most quoted) constitutional scholar, but he was too busy working on a manuscript to take the task on. Professor Herbert Wechsler of Columbia Law School was a constitutional scholar of enormous distinction who had represented the *New York Times* in 1964 in the most significant First Amendment case of its era, *New York Times v. Sullivan*, which rewrote American libel law to ensure that First Amendment interests were protected. He, too, was unavailable.

We turned next to my choice, Bickel, the youngest of the three scholars, who was on sabbatical leave at Stanford in 1971. When I called him there to ask him if he would author our friend-of-the-court brief, my own views about the press had changed radically since we had last spoken. In the late 1960s I had spent a good deal of time representing NBC and had learned much about the difficulties and sometime dangers of gathering news, as well as the frustrations of reporting on government conduct when those in power often acted in secrecy and then lied about what they had done. "Sunshine is a weather report," NBC News President Reuven Frank had told me; "a flood is news." But more and more, it seemed that the Johnson and then the Nixon administrations were dedicated to denying the existence of floods, even as the waters rose. When I studied with Bickel at Yale, I had never met a journalist, had never heard the case made for protecting confidential sources of journalists in order to avoid losing specific stories of value or compromising the safety of real people, and had never understood that while there are always arguments available in support of suppressing speech, society is almost always better served when those arguments are rejected.

I had no idea how Bickel would react when I called him; and after listening carefully to my description of the case and what we wanted from him, he made two comments. First, he reminded me that he was "no First Amendment voluptuary." I knew that well—I would have described myself in similar terms when I was in law school—and chose not to tell him that that was one of the reasons we were calling him in the first place.

Second, he said in a more relaxed tone, "I assume that you are not calling me to ask me to be your law clerk on this brief?"

"No," I said. He would write the brief, I would assist him and we could surely work out any areas of disagreement jointly. He agreed.

For months we worked together by telephone. Bickel wrote a first draft of the brief in California while I provided him from New York with whatever legal backup he asked for. On June 14, 1971, I hosted a lunch at the University Club to introduce Goodale, other lawyers representing the press, and a number of journalists, including *New York Times* national editor Gene Roberts, to Professor Bickel. Bickel made a dazzling presentation, outlining the brief and reading passages from it aloud. One section from the draft, as later incorporated without change into the final brief, is typical of his brilliance. Answering the argument that the press should not itself ask for the right to stand mute at the same time it claimed to do so for the purpose of revealing more information, Bickel wrote as follows:

There is not even a surface paradox in the proposition, as it might somewhat mischievously be put, that in order to safeguard a public right to receive information it is necessary to secure to reporters a right to withhold information. Clearly the purpose of protecting the reporter from disclosing the identity of a news source is to enable him to obtain and publish information which would not otherwise be forthcoming. So the reporter should be given a right to withhold some information—the identity of the source—because in the circumstances, that right is the necessary condition of his obtaining and publishing any information at all. Information other than the identity of the source may also need to be withheld in order to protect that identity. Obviously, something a reporter learned in confidence may give a clue to his source, or indeed pinpoint it. That may be the very reason why the source imposed an obligation of confidence on the reporter.

Yet off-the-record information obtained in confidence is of the utmost importance to the performance of the reporter's function. It very frequently constitutes the background that enables him to report intelligently. It affords leads to publishable news, and understanding of past and future events. News reporting in the United States would be devastatingly impoverished if the countless off-the-record and background contacts maintained by reporters with news sources were cut off.

Bickel read this and other passages from our forthcoming brief with verve, knowing full well how sparkling his prose was and thoroughly enjoying our admiration of his skill. There were a few words in Bickel's presentation I would have edited out—"mischievously" was a bit too precious a word for the judges before whom I practiced—but taken as a whole, the language was golden.

But even as he read the document, the focus of our discussion began to turn to another topic. The day before the lunch, a Sunday, the *Times* had published on its front page an article under a deliberately understated and rather bland headline that read:

VIETNAM ARCHIVE: PENTAGON STUDY TRACES
3 DECADES OF GROWING U.S. INVOLVEMENT

What followed on page one and on three full pages later in the newspaper was a description of what the article, in its first line, described as "a massive study of how the United States went to war in Indochina, conducted by the Pentagon three years ago," a study that "demonstrated that four administrations progressively developed a sense of commitment to a non-Communist Vietnam, a readiness to fight the North to protect the South, and an ultimate frustration with the effort—to a much greater extent than their public statements acknowledged at the time." Based as it was on the three-thousand-page-long top secret analysis offered by the study—soon to become known as the Pentagon Papers—and four thousand pages of equally highly classified documents accompanying the analysis, the *Times*'s article of June 13 and a second one a day later seemed to set the stage for a cosmic legal clash between the newspaper and the government.

At our lunch, Bickel warned the lawyers and journalists who were present that while we likely had four votes in the case involving confidential sources, it would be a difficult task to pick up the needed fifth vote.* As regards the *Times*'s ongoing publication of the Pentagon Papers, however, we both offered kudos on the story and reassurance that the government would likely not mount a legal challenge to the *Times*'s publication. "That's one," Bickel affirmed, "that you can't lose." Both of us were free with advice to Goodale and Gene Roberts about the articles. The government would not likely be so foolish, we told them, as to seek to restrain the *Times*

---

*He was right. The vote was 5-4 against the press, with the critical fifth vote of Justice Lewis Powell separately explained by him in a concurring opinion that was so murky that it remains a subject of dispute to this day.

from publishing since (in language both of us used) "we have never had a prior restraint on the publication of news in our country's history." Supremely confident of our views, as only lawyers without clients are, we told the representatives of the *Times* that if the government went to court, the newspaper would obviously win.

That night, my world changed. Shortly after one a.m. Goodale awakened me with a telephone call to my home. I barely knew him—we had met personally only twice before—and could barely make out what he was saying. The government had demanded that the *Times* cease publication of portions of the Pentagon Papers, he explained. Of course, the newspaper would not do that, he said. The *Times*'s regular counsel at Lord, Day & Lord, however, had refused to represent the newspaper. As Bickel was in town, and he and I had spoken so persuasively at lunch about the right of the *Times* to publish, would I and my firm join with Bickel in representing the *Times*?

It was all like a dream—the most cheering, fulfilling, and delightful dream imaginable. Except that it all seemed unimaginable. Was I really going to represent the *New York Times* against Richard Nixon's administration? Was I really going to do so in collaboration with Alexander Bickel, my own professor from Yale?

I spoke quickly. Of course I'd be glad to take on the case, I told Goodale, but I would need my firm's approval before I could do so. Since it was the middle of the night, I couldn't obtain the authorization until the following day. Why didn't I simply go with Bickel to my office immediately, I suggested, and work through the night? I would get back to Goodale in the morning to confirm that we would accept the case.

I picked Bickel up in a taxi and we sped to my office. We came to the Pentagon Papers with a good degree of knowledge of applicable law but none at all of the turmoil at the *Times* that preceded the decision to publish them, or that within the government that had preceded its decision to challenge the *Times*. In fact, we knew almost nothing about the documents themselves.

The Pentagon Papers had been initiated in 1967 with a decision by Secretary of Defense Robert S. McNamara unique in the history of warfare. In the midst of the United States' seemingly endless involvement in Vietnam, McNamara ordered a historical "study" of the conflict. The secretary, by this point dubious about the American role in the war, wanted answers to fundamental questions about the nature of the struggle. The study, McNamara insisted, should be "encyclopedic and objective." It was expected to require the labor of six full-time professionals and three months to complete. In fact, by the time thirty-six scholars finished the task eighteen months later, a new secretary of defense, Clark M. Clifford, was in place.

The study was ultimately severely attacked. Critics on the left, such as Professor Noam Chomsky, of the Massachusetts Institute of Technology, would charge that it reflected the "pro-Government bias" of its authors. At the other end of the political spectrum, Henry Kissinger, in his memoirs, described it as "selective" and "one-sided," reflecting an antiwar point of view. Some historians, noting that the study had been based entirely upon sources such as the Department of Defense and the Central Intelligence Agency, complained about the lack of White House participation. And since no interviews were permitted of the participants in the war's decision-making process, the result was fairly described by Leslie H. Gelb, director of the Study Task Force that prepared the Pentagon Papers, later the *Times*'s national security correspondent and then the director of the Council on Foreign Relations, as "not so much a documentary history as a history based solely on documents—checked and rechecked with antlike diligence."

Whatever its limitations as history, the Pentagon Papers, which covered the decades from World War II to 1968, amply fulfilled the mandate to be encyclopedic. Its seven thousand pages contained a total of 2.5 million words and weighed sixty pounds. The text was thoughtful, often persuasive, inevitably debatable. The supporting documents were devastating, demonstrating an extraordinary level of governmental duplicity based upon an unprecedented source—the very files of the government itself.

On August 7, 1964, both houses of Congress, at the urging of the Johnson administration, had passed a resolution endorsing "all necessary measures to repel any armed attack against the forces of the United States and to prevent any further aggression." As the Pentagon Papers documents revealed, the administration had long sought the added powers conferred by that kind of resolution, and President Johnson had seized upon one particular incident—the allegedly "unprovoked" attack on an American ship in Vietnam's Tonkin Gulf—as the means to get the measure through Congress. He had not shared the true nature of his desire with Congress, nor had he shared with it the fact that prior to the Tonkin incident, American soldiers had been engaged in clandestine warfare against the North Vietnamese.

From other documents, the reader could trace the path of increased American involvement in Vietnam—and of repeated government deception about it. Some of the material revealed in the Papers had been previously reported; some had not. But in many instances the documents themselves proved the truth of what had only been alleged. The Truman administration, for example, had "directly involved" the United States in Vietnam by giving military aid to France in her war against the Vietminh. The Eisenhower administration's efforts to rescue South Vietnam from a

Communist takeover had played an important role in the final breakdown of the 1954 Geneva accords. The Kennedy administration had turned minor American involvement in Vietnam into a "broad commitment." The Johnson administration had consistently dissembled about American military plans and activities in the nation.

Such revelations, however, had never been intended for public eyes. When the study was delivered to Secretary Clifford on January 15, 1969, it carried a top secret classification. It was filed away, and the war continued to drag on—a circumstance that one of the study's authors, Daniel Ellsberg, soon came to consider intolerable.

A former Marine, and later a consultant in the departments of Defense and State, Ellsberg had started out as a fervent supporter of an American role in the Vietnam War. While assigned there from 1965 to 1967, though, he came to conclude that there was no hope of American success, and upon his return he became increasingly radicalized and increasingly distressed that the newly elected administration was not taking what he viewed as its opportunity to extricate the United States from the folly—and, he would conclude, its criminal conduct—in Vietnam.

As a consultant at the Rand Corporation, a California defense research organization, Ellsberg had access to one of the fifteen copies of the study. Starting in 1969, he tried to interest congressional committees in subpoenaing the study. When all such efforts failed, Ellsberg made a copy of the study available to Neil Sheehan, a *New York Times* reporter. For three months, in complete secrecy, a team of *Times* journalists pored over the text, checking it for accuracy and deciding if any portions of the materials could compromise national security. While the *Times* did not have the three most sensitive volumes of the Pentagon Papers—the so-called "negotiating" volumes, dealing with efforts until 1968 to resolve the war diplomatically—what it did have nonetheless presented the newspaper with a soul-wrenching set of decisions.

A century earlier, in the summer of 1871, the *Times* had printed another set of secret internal government documents; in that instance, it had exposed the criminal transgressions of the Tweed Ring in New York City. This time, the stakes were much higher. On the face of it, this sober, respectable paper had to decide whether or not it was going to print top secret documents that dealt with a war in which the nation was still engaged.

The debate within the *Times* was long, exhaustive, and acrimonious. Some disputes were tactical in nature. Should it print any of the classified documents themselves or only portions of the commentary? Should it publish everything in one day (as Goodale urged) to avoid even the risk of a prior restraint, or publish according to its own schedule (as Abe Rosenthal, the newspaper's executive editor, insisted)? Other questions required deeper analysis of the role of journalism in a free society. What should the role of a newspaper be during wartime? When should highly classified documents be published? Executives, editors, reporters, and attorneys argued over the meaning of patriotism and journalistic ethics and over the risks that publication, or nonpublication, of the Papers held for the profession and for the *Times* itself. At one point, Rosenthal, who personally supported the nation's war effort but whose sense of journalistic commitment ultimately led him to be the indispensable journalistic advocate of publication within the newspaper, seriously considered resigning if the *Times* did not publish. At another, James Reston, the *Times*'s legendary Washington columnist, who had won three Pulitzer Prizes and had directed the *Times*'s Washington bureau, and who was (as I would shortly learn) a man of the most extraordinary connections throughout the world, threatened to publish the Pentagon Papers himself in his own newspaper—the tiny *Vineyard Gazette*, on Martha's Vineyard—if the *Times* did not publish.

But the *Times* was, at its core, an establishment newspaper, one that ten years earlier would likely have agreed with the observation Chief Justice Warren Burger later made in the Pentagon Papers case itself that "one of the basic and simple duties of every citizen with respect to the discovery or possession of secret government documents" was "to report forthwith to responsible public officers." For a newspaper that had become a national institution, the decision to publish extensive portions, during wartime, of highly classified documents was a painful one. But for the fact that the journalists and editors of the paper had been lied to so often by the government about the war, the outcome might well have been different.

Another reason why the decision to publish was so difficult was that the *Times* had received the sternest warnings from its own outside counsel about the legal consequences of doing so. For over six decades the paper had been represented by the venerable New York law firm of Lord, Day & Lord. Lewis J. Loeb, the firm's partner who had advised the *Times* since 1929, and his senior partner Herbert Brownell, formerly the attorney general under President Eisenhower, had informed the newspaper that its publication of the Pentagon Papers would violate the Espionage Act. Likewise, the *Times*'s publisher, Arthur O. Sulzberger, was advised by them that he could well be jailed as a result of publishing the top secret documents in the paper's possession. Brownell went so far as to announce to Sulzberger (who, as James Reston later wrote, was not amused to hear it) that his father and grandfather, both of whom had been publishers of the *Times*, would never have considered such a course of action. Brownell and Loeb's view was staunchly opposed by Goodale, the *Times*'s general counsel and himself a former associate at Lord, Day & Lord. Goodale had reviewed the case law independently, prepared legal memoranda rejecting the counsel of Lord, Day & Lord, and repeatedly, at considerable personal risk, urged the *Times* to publish.

Eventually, Sulzberger, then in London, rejecting the views of some of his colleagues in senior management as well as the dire warnings of his outside counsel, made the call to accept the risks of publication rather than those of silence. On Sunday, June 13, the *Times* published the first in a series of seven articles about the Pentagon Papers. In retrospect, the decision may seem obvious, but it was by no means an easy one at the time, and it remains one for which Sulzberger deserves enormous credit.

As for the government's response, Bickel and I met many journalists who covered the case in the days shortly after we were retained. Many of them, like us, had wrongly predicted that the government would not sue. Almost all agreed (once again, incorrectly) that since the Pentagon Papers reflected badly on Kennedy and especially Johnson, and since they ended in 1968 and thus did not tarnish Nixon's reputation, the Nixon administration would not press the case vigorously. That conventional wisdom was conventionally wrong except in one respect. Nixon did, in fact, initially characterize to White House confidants the first *Times* article as having been "really tough on Kennedy, McNamara and Johnson" rather than on himself. But by Monday morning, June 14, after an emotional telephone conversation with Kissinger, his national security advisor, in which Kissinger warned Nixon that permitting continued publication would "show you're a weakling" and that such "leaks are slowly and systematically destroying us," Nixon was filled with fury at the *Times*. "The two of them are in a frenzy," Bob Haldeman said to John Ehrlichman about a Nixon-Kissinger meeting on Monday evening. By the end of that evening, the government was well on the way to seeking a court order barring the *Times* from any further articles based on the Pentagon Papers.

The story of the Nixon administration's decision-making process has been well documented in a number of accounts, including Harrison Salisbury's book about the *Times*, entitled *Without Fear or Favor*, David Rudenstine's *The Day the Presses Stopped*, and Richard Reeves's *President Nixon: Alone in the White House*. Most recently, *Inside the Pentagon Papers*, by John Prados and Margaret Pratt Parker, is filled with transcripts of telephone conversations between President Nixon and his aides and other data from which, as Prados and Parker conclude, it is now plain the case was brought "based on factors that were only incidentally about protection of classified information," and that there is no reason for "confidence that the government's specific assertions of what was secret in the Pentagon Papers ought to be taken at face value."

When we were retained, however, Bickel and I knew nothing of what had occurred within either the *Times* or the White House. In our late-night call

Goodale had told me only that the *Times* had received a telegram earlier that evening from Attorney General John Mitchell demanding that the *Times* cease publication and that Lord, Day & Lord had—miraculously, I thought—refused to represent the paper. Mitchell's telegram to the *Times* was unequivocal: the secretary of defense, Mitchell stated, had advised him that some of the documents quoted by the paper in its articles contained "information relating to the national defense" that was classified top secret. Section 793 of the Espionage Act, Mitchell continued, barred such a publication, and "irreparable injury" would result if the *Times* continued publication. The attorney general thus "respectfully request[ed]" that the *Times* publish "no further information of this character." The *Times* responded later that evening, "respectfully declining" to cease its publication "for the same reasons that led us to publish the articles in the first place."

As for Lord, Day & Lord's refusal to represent the *Times*, I knew little at that point other than that, after the *Times* had received the Mitchell telegram and Goodale called the firm to ask it to handle the case, Brownell had told him that it could not do so, in light of the fact that the documents at issue were all classified, and that Brownell, as President Eisenhower's attorney general, had drafted the executive order establishing the system that was still in effect in 1971. To those at the *Times* with whom I spoke in the days that followed, Brownell's explanation sounded ludicrous, for the reason he had given to recuse himself was nowhere near what the law considers a conflict of interest. In fact, Brownell's own role in drafting the classification guidelines could only have helped the *Times*, not hurt it, since his prior knowledge of the area, not to say his personal stature, would surely have added greater weight to the paper's arguments in court.

Not until 2004, when I read the Prados and Parker book, did I learn that Attorney General Mitchell had in fact telephoned Brownell and personally admonished him not to represent the *Times* in the case. At the time, I had assumed that Brownell's decision was either political, in the sense that Brownell, a national Republican leader for decades, had no stomach for a case against a Republican president, or personal and ideological, in that he and his colleagues were frustrated and angered at the *Times*'s persistent refusal to follow their advice and believed the paper's conduct to be so un-*Times*-like, so wrong, and ultimately so unpatriotic, that the firm could not bring itself to represent it. Whatever its motivation, the late-evening pronouncement by Lord, Day & Lord that it would not represent its client of over sixty years left the nation's most prestigious newspaper, as one author put it, like a church elder nabbed in a vice raid obliged to embark on a midnight manhunt for legal counsel. Bickel and I had been exuberantly optimistic at lunch—a bit excessively so, perhaps—and so, off we went to my office at 2 a.m. to begin our representation of the *Times*.

We arrived at my office at 2:30 a.m. and immediately headed for the library. Attorney General Mitchell had cited section 793 of the Espionage Act in his telegram, and we had to determine exactly what it said.

Spread over three pages of the red-bound *United States Code Annotated*, the language of the statute was all but incomprehensible. The only part of it that seemed even possible to apply to the *Times*, section 793(e), made it criminal for

[W]hoever having unauthorized possession of, access to, or control over any document, writing, code book, signal book, sketch, photograph, photographic negative, blueprint, plan, map, model, instrument, appliance, or note relating to the national defense, or information relating to the national defense which information the possessor has reason to believe could be used to the injury of the United States or to the advantage of any foreign nation, willfully communicates, delivers, transmits or causes to be communicated, delivered, or transmitted, or attempts to communicate, deliver, transmit or cause to be communicated, delivered or transmitted the same to any person not entitled to receive it, or willfully retains the

23

same and fails to deliver it to the officer or employee of the United States entitled to receive it.

And so we began. On our first middle-of-the-night reading, we supposed that the *Times* could be considered to have "unauthorized possession of, [or] access to" a "document"—twenty-four volumes of them, in fact. The documents, we supposed, could be said to "relat[e] to the national defense," although surely these words could not be read as expansively in a criminal statute as in common parlance. Was every foreign policy article that appeared in the *Times* one "relating to the national defense"? Whether the paper had "reason to believe" that its publication of portions of the Pentagon Papers "could be used to the injury of the United States or to the advantage of any foreign nation" seemed even more problematic. If the *Times*'s motivation was to educate the public, if it believed (but did the belief have to be reasonable?) that publication would help, not injure, the nation, was that a defense? Would the public at large, the readers of the *Times*, be considered "a person not entitled to receive" the articles?

And then there was what the statute did *not* say. It contained no reference to "publication," no explicit bar to a newspaper's printing any such documents. It contained no reference to classified information, no support for Mitchell's reliance on the top secret status of the documents as a basis for justifying a prior restraint. And it provided no statutory authority for a prior restraint on the publication of *anything*.

That was our preliminary reading of the statute. But were we looking in the right place? Because the case the government was about to bring was not a criminal case, how relevant was the statute, anyway? Shouldn't we focus first (and maybe last) on the case as a pure First Amendment challenge? Prior restraints on the press—bans, in advance, on publication—were, as we had so confidently proclaimed at lunch, all but unthinkable. As early as 1907, Justice Oliver Wendell Holmes himself, writing for the Court, had characterized the "main purpose" of the First Amendment as being "to prevent all such previous restraints upon publications as had been practiced by other governments." In 1931 the Court had concluded that only under the narrowest circumstances— the publication of the dates of the departures of ships during wartime, for example—could any prior restriction on speech be countenanced. As recently as 1969, Justice John Marshall Harlan, the Court's most distinguished conservative member after Felix Frankfurter's retirement, had noted that the Supreme Court had consistently "rejected all manner of prior restraint on publication." Given those imposing precedents, shouldn't we deal later (or maybe only in passing) with the statute and argue primarily that as a matter of First Amendment law, the relief the government was seeking—a bar on publication—was simply unavailable?

There was a third possible approach. We could take an even broader view of First Amendment law, one that would focus not so much on the fact that the government was seeking a prior restraint as on the impact of a victory of the government in such a case on life in a democratic society. We could argue that publication of just such materials as the *Times* was releasing—an exposé of governmental misjudgments and misconduct of the highest importance—was precisely what the First Amendment existed to protect.

From the start, Bickel wanted to take the first route, emphasizing the inapplicability of the Espionage Law, Congress's decision not to criminalize the publication of any information under section 793(e), and the absence of any statutory provision authorizing a prior restraint on publication. While he viewed as useful existing First Amendment law making prior restraints extremely difficult to obtain, he regarded it as insufficient in itself to persuade the courts to rule in our favor. We needed more, he thought, and congressional refusal to enact legislation explicitly criminalizing behavior like the *Times*'s or, at the least, permitting it to be enjoined was central to his vision of the case.

My own view that night was more oriented to the second alternative. Given what appeared to be a near-absolute ban on prior restraints on the publication of news, I thought we should ride that horse right up the steps of the Supreme Court. At the same time I was well aware that Bickel, a recognized constitutional expert of the highest repute, not only knew First Amendment law far better than I, but could assess better what might appeal to the Supreme Court. And I had no illusions regarding the fact that, while Bickel might well have been retained without me, there was never a chance that I—thirty-four years old and the youngest partner in a law firm the *Times* had never before used—could conceivably have been retained without him. We were co-counsel to the *Times*, but he was chief counsel, and that arrangement satisfied both of us.

We wound up working all night, reading both Espionage Act and First Amendment cases, and prepared a brief memorandum summarizing our views. At about eight a.m., unshaven and tieless, I went to the office of my senior litigation partner, Lawrence J. McKay, to ask for the firm's authorization to take the case. "You look like hell," McKay told me. "Well," I said, "I've been working through the night on a new client." I pointed to the headline in that morning's *New York Times*. McKay beamed, and I brought Bickel down to his office to introduce them. It was a good moment, so good that I forgot to tell Goodale that the decision had been made that we could proceed.

An hour later, we proceeded to the *Times* for our

first meeting with the client. Goodale and Rosenthal were present, as was Harding F. Bancroft, the *Times*'s executive vice president, who was, we quickly sensed, cool to the decision to publish in the first place. (He had actually opposed it.) In the course of the morning, one after another journalist with a byline well known to me came to meet us. James Greenfield, the *Times*'s foreign editor, who had previously served as undersecretary of state in the Johnson administration and was therefore well aware of what sort of disclosures of classified information could really threaten national security, arrived. Tom Wicker, formerly chief of the Washington bureau and then a columnist for the paper, introduced himself, as did Seymour Topping, the associate national editor, and Sydney Gruson, the assistant to the publisher and himself formerly a distinguished foreign correspondent for the *Times*.

Bickel addressed the group, emphasizing the need for us to articulate legal positions that could attract the same critical fifth vote on the Supreme Court that we had the day before told media lawyers and journalists at lunch we would have difficulty attracting in the case involving confidential sources of journalists. Black, Douglas, Brennan, and Marshall should be safely on our side, Bickel said, but to pick up a decisive fifth vote we would need to avoid any sign of First Amendment absolutism. We should concede, he argued, that the strong presumption against prior restraints was not conclusive and instead emphasize the failure of Congress to pass legislation either criminalizing behavior comparable to what the *Times* had done or permitting a prior restraint against it.

As Bickel was speaking, a message was handed to me: Michael Hess, the chief of the Civil Division of the United States Attorney's Office in Manhattan, was phoning. I stepped out of the room to take the call, and Hess told me that the government was going to court seeking a temporary restraining order barring the *Times* from further publication of the Pentagon Papers and that it would be appearing shortly before federal judge Murray Gurfein. I spoke briefly with Hess, thinking as I did that while my litigation experience was sound and my First Amendment knowledge substantial, I had never even seen an argument before the Supreme Court. As for Bickel, I surmised correctly that he had never appeared in *any* court as counsel. It was a sobering thought. Here, I thought, was a landmark case, an enormous threat to the press and, more broadly, to the First Amendment, being litigated by an academic with no courtroom experience, accompanied by a lawyer who had never even watched a Supreme Court argument. I hoped the thought would not occur to the executives, lawyers, and journalists at the *Times*.

At noon Bickel, Goodale, and I appeared before Judge Gurfein. New cases were assigned at random, and chance had sent this particular one to a judge so new that it was literally the first one he was deciding. (Years later, another judge sworn in on the same day as Judge Gurfein, Lawrence Pierce, told me that every night since that day in June 1971 when Gurfein drew the Pentagon Papers case, he got down on his knees to thank God that it had not happened to him.)

When we entered Judge Gurfein's courtroom he greeted us grimly. We had checked on him in the brief time before we left for court and learned that he was one of "Tom Dewey's boys," a former prosecutor in New York who had worked as a lawyer with former New York governor and two-time Republican presidential candidate Dewey, and then at the Nuremberg war-crime trials. We also learned that he had a significant background in military intelligence, which we knew would likely prove to be an important factor. But would it make him more hostile to the *Times*'s conduct or more inclined to be skeptical of the government's case?

Of course, the government had done its own checking on Judge Gurfein, whom Nixon had just appointed to his lifetime position. He was, Attorney General Mitchell told Nixon, "a good judge" who had been Dewey's counsel. "I know him well," Nixon responded. "Smart as hell." There was something else, Mitchell said. "He's new and he's appreciative." "Good," laughed Nixon.

Gurfein turned first to Hess, since it was the government that was seeking judicial intervention. Hess argued that publication of the Pentagon Papers violated section 793 and that the statute therefore authorized the entry of a prior restraint against the *Times*. Relying on Secretary of State William Pierce Rogers's statement, reported earlier that day, that a number of nations had already expressed "concern" about publication of the Papers and on an affidavit of Fred Buzhardt, general counsel of the Navy, alleging "irreparable injury" if the articles continued to appear, Hess asked the judge to enter a temporary restraining order barring publication. Bickel responded that principles of separation of powers barred the court from doing so, since no statute authorized that relief. Bickel also argued that since the relief sought was a prior restraint, and that since none of the exceptions to the general unavailability of that relief applied, the court should deny the application.

At the conclusion of the brief argument in open court, Gurfein asked us all to join him in his chambers. Sternly addressing us all (but particularly the *Times*'s representatives), Gurfein asserted that "we are all patriotic Americans" and that in the service of the nation the *Times* should voluntarily maintain the status quo by ceasing publication of the Pentagon Papers for a few days to permit him to review them. Bickel responded, to Gurfein's evident dismay, that if the judge entered a prior restraint enjoining the publication of news, he would be the first judge in American history ever to do so. As respected Gurfein's request, Bickel stated that he would consult with our client.

Gurfein, looking grimmer still, urged us to convince the *Times* to cease publication of the Papers temporarily.

It was a painful moment. On one level, the request was eminently reasonable. How could the judge do his job if we would not give him the time to do it? And how could any legitimate national security interests be protected if the *Times* was free to publish top secret documents before Gurfein even reviewed them?

But in its own way that approach was dangerous. The status quo, under the First Amendment, involves the right to print, not the suppression of speech. And if the *Times* was right in deciding that it did not compromise national security to publish in the first place, how could we agree to Gurfein's request? That reasoning led to the answer the *Times* had given Attorney General Mitchell when he asked it to cease publication: no, "for the same reasons that led us to publish the articles in the first place."

Bickel told Gurfein that he would let him know our decision within twenty minutes. After Goodale, Bickel, and I quickly conferred—we all opposed any voluntary cessation of publication—Goodale commandeered a telephone in the courthouse (there were no cell phones then) and, well after twenty minutes, obtained the negative answer he was seeking. Gurfein promptly and obviously unhappily entered an order granting the government's demand, setting a hearing for Friday, June

18, three days later, preceded by the submission of papers the day before.

We returned to the *Times*. While Bickel met with Bancroft, Goodale, and others, I gathered with the journalists who had been present that morning plus two other men whose names I knew well from their bylines but had never met. Max Frankel, the *Times*'s Washington bureau chief, had arrived, as had James Reston, whom I had last seen as an undergraduate at Cornell when he spoke to two thousand enraptured students. There was one topic on the agenda of this meeting, which was run by Rosenthal: how could the journalists help?

I told them that I would like to start the process of soliciting affidavits from renowned experts asserting that they had read what the *Times* had already published and that they were confident that national security had not been compromised—and may even have been advanced—by publication. "Who do you want?" Rosenthal asked. If I could choose, I said, I would pick former secretary of defense Robert McNamara. The Pentagon Papers had, after all, been prepared at his request. They were often referred to as the "McNamara Papers." If he asserted that publication would do no harm, how could we lose?

The journalists looked at one another. "Who knows McNamara best?" Rosenthal asked. After a pause, Reston spoke. "I'll call Bob," he said. (Only years later did I learn that Reston was dining in McNamara's home in Washington when Bancroft read to him on the telephone a draft of the *Times*'s response to Mitchell's telegram demanding that the *Times* cease publication, that McNamara actually helped to draft the *Times*'s response, and that he urged that it be tougher than as originally drafted.)

Asked for other names, I shot for the top of the military. General Lauris Norstad, formerly supreme Allied commander in Europe, would be good, I said, as would General Maxwell Taylor, former chairman of the Joint Chiefs of Staff. Again the journalists looked at one another, were briefly silent, and again Reston spoke, saying that he had just spoken with the first and had a date to see the second. In the end, Reston agreed to call well over half the people on my A-list. We didn't get them all—McNamara, steeped in depression and despair over the failure of his Vietnam policies, told Reston that he would testify for the *Times* at any criminal trial but not before, and the generals said no—but we did get a good many.

When we finally put our papers in on June 17, we included affidavits not only from Sulzberger and various *Times* reporters but from diplomats and historians such as Theodore Sorensen, James MacGregor Burns, Francis Plimpton, Eric F. Goldman, and Barbara Tuchman. And we included an extraordinary affidavit from Max Frankel, which answered many of the questions that my partner Bill Hegarty, who would handle the cross-examination of witnesses at the June 18 hearing, and I had repeatedly asked him. If the material was secret (and classified top secret), how could we justify the paper's decision to publish it? How does the paper decide what sort of "secret" material to print? Why does it print such material at all?

Frankel explained inside Washington to outsiders in a new way. "A small and specialized corps of reporters and a few hundred American officials regularly make use of classified, secret and top secret information," he wrote. They did it in "a cooperative, competitive, antagonistic and arcane relationship." Without such use of "secrets," Frankel wrote, "there could be no adequate diplomatic, military and political reporting of the kind our people take for granted." The fourteen-page-long document described a sort of reality that generally went undisclosed:

Presidents make "secret" decisions only to reveal them for the purposes of frightening an adversary nation, wooing a friendly electorate, protecting their reputations. The military services conduct "secret" research in weaponry only to reveal it for the purpose of enhancing their budgets, appearing superior or inferior to a foreign army, gaining the vote of a congressman or the favor of a contractor. The Navy uses secret information to run down the weaponry of the Air Force. The Army passes on secret information to prove its superiority to the Marine Corps. High officials of the government reveal secrets in the search for support of their policies, or to help sabotage the plans and policies of rival departments. Middle-rank officials of government reveal secrets so as to attract the attention of their superiors or to lobby against the orders of those superiors. Though not the only vehicle for this traffic in secrets—the Congress is always eager to provide a forum—the press is probably the most important.

Frankel's affidavit was a tour de force, one worthy of publication on its own. Filled with examples of the inner workings of the previously "secret" relationship between the press and those in government, it offered a view that could not only countenance the publication of much classified material but affirm it.

By now, we had also put together a serious team of lawyers at my firm, consisting of three partners and nine associates. In addition to Bill Hegarty, who was working on a full-time basis on the case, Lawrence McKay had become involved, offering sound advice from the moment I first discussed it with him. McKay, the toughest of litigators, had achieved a special sort of fame in a case he had argued in Washington, D.C., in which we represented a detergent company that was selling its product in a container that looked markedly—"suspiciously," the Federal Trade Commission said—like an orange-juice container. In an appearance before the three-judge court of appeals in Washington, McKay calmly told the astonished panel that even if a child did drink a bit of detergent, it would do him no harm—whereupon he poured himself a glass of detergent in court, mixed it with a pencil, drank it, and returned to his seat. We lost the case, but McKay had the solace of a *Washington Post* story recounting his feat.

McKay came to the Pentagon Papers with no particular First Amendment views at all. He had no pretensions about having firmly held positions on constitutional issues, no hero in the choice between Justices Black and Frankfurter. He tried cases for clients, and whatever their cause was, was his—and he usually won. He was, in short, a trial lawyer, and the sort of hard-edged trial lawyer who had given my firm the reputation of being a bunch of tough Irish gut-fighters who never avoided a conflict. He was also intensely, devotedly loyal to his clients and his partners, a characteristic that endeared him to all the junior partners and associates. Attending a board meeting of his largest client early in the Pentagon Papers case, McKay was asked by the company's far-right-wing president: "Since when does your firm represent traitors?" To which McKay, without letting a second pass, replied, "What the fuck do you know about the First Amendment?"

I had my own encounters with various angry observers of the case. On the way to court on Tuesday I passed a corporate partner heading to the office. His query was similar to the one McKay had encountered. "What's it like representing traitors?" I stared at my "partner" and moved on.

On Thursday, June 17, after working all through the night, we submitted our brief opposing the entry of a preliminary injunction to Judge Gurfein. It was consistent with Bickel's first-night views, containing much about the Espionage Act, much less about the First Amendment. After a brief section recounting the facts, which emphasized that thus far the government had offered nothing but the bare assertion that irreparable injury would befall the country if further publication was permitted, we offered a brief introductory section on First Amendment law generally and the "disfavored" status of prior restraints specifically. We then turned to the core of the brief: the failure of the government to demonstrate that the *Times* had violated any statute, and the need for such a demonstration before a prior restraint could be issued. Thirty-nine pages of our sixty-three-page brief, far too much in retrospect, were devoted to that subject.

The government wanted to inspect and duplicate the *Times*'s own copy of the Pentagon Papers and any other classified documents in its possession. According to the government, it needed to examine the documents in order to determine precisely what was at issue in the case.

Our view of the matter was different. The government's motion to inspect the doc, I had argued in an affidavit submitted to Judge Gurfein, was a thinly disguised effort to discover the *Times*'s source. If the government could inspect the original or even a copy of the *Times*'s copy of the Pentagon Papers, I argued, it could learn who the *Times*'s source was by means of an FBI examination of his fingerprints. That being so, we should not be obliged to turn the materials over.

Hess argued first, maintaining that it was ironic that the *Times* was "coming into court stating that they want openness, they want freedom for the right of the people to know, and yet they are refusing to let the people or the government or that Court know exactly what documents they have in their possession." When I responded that turning over the documents could reveal the paper's source, Judge Gurfein offered a solution: why not compile some sort of list of the documents the *Times* had obtained? That would give the government what it claimed it needed—specific information about the scope of the leaked materials—while avoiding the problem that concerned us—source identification. Both parties agreed to that suggestion, and we turned over a summary of documents in the *Times*'s possession.

I have always regarded Judge Gurfein's simple-sounding resolution of this issue as a signal example of judicial statesmanship, and one that, for us, avoided a potential disaster. Had the court ordered the *Times* to turn over the Pentagon Papers, covered as they were with Ellsberg's fingerprints, the paper almost certainly would have refused. The *Times* would, I believe, have concluded that it had no other choice, given its promise of confidentiality to him. Had the order been disobeyed, the court could have sanctioned the *Times* severely, possibly limiting its ability to defend itself in the action. Had there been sanctions, the nature of the case as it reached the Supreme Court would have been entirely different, with the *Times* accused of arrogantly viewing itself as entitled not only to make national security determinations contrary to those of the Department of Defense but to ignore binding court orders. While the Supreme Court might let the *Times* decide what to print, it would never allow the newspaper to decide which court orders to obey. Worse yet, merely by defying a court order of Judge Gurfein, the *Times* would have given considerable impetus to persuading the courts that it could not be relied upon to decide what to print, either.

The possibility of disobeying an order of Judge Gurfein was one we had to address from the start. The *Times*'s response to Attorney General Mitchell's telegram had promised (in an eerie fore-shadowing of later language used by President Nixon when he said he would obey any "lawful court order") to "abide by the final decision of the court." But what about nonfinal orders? We had our first meeting with the *Times*'s publisher Arthur Sulzberger when he returned from London on Wednesday, June 16, Judge Gurfein having entered the temporary restraining order against publication the day before. At a meeting chaired by Sulzberger and attended by senior journalistic and corporate management, Bickel reported on Judge Gurfein's action and his setting of Friday, June 18, as the date for the hearing in the case. When Sulzberger announced that the *Times* would obey the order, Tom Wicker softly interjected: "I thought that's what we were meeting to discuss." Sulzberger responded that he was glad to hear any views, and Wicker expressed concern about validating any order that would bar publication by obeying it. While he did not go so far as to urge defiance to the order, he was nonetheless deeply troubled by acquiescing to it. I spoke up, arguing that from any sort of strategic point of view—taking into account how Judge Gurfein would react, and how the appellate courts, including the Supreme Court, would react—disobedience would be self-destructive. Bickel viewed the issue more broadly. "What we are all about," he said, "the reason we are here, is to vindicate the rule of law." The *Times*, Bickel stated, must obey the court's order. After a pause, Sulzberger reaffirmed that the *Times* would obey the order. There was no dissent.

On Friday, June 18, after Bickel, Hegarty, and I spent another sleepless night in our office, Judge

41

Gurfein conducted a full hearing on the merits of the issues before him. The hearing went well, in large part because of the stellar performances of both Bickel and Hegarty. Hegarty's withering cross-examination of the government's witnesses (all conducted without preparation, since we did not know who they would be or what they would say) left little doubt that while there might be something of a diplomatic flap as a result of publication, the government could offer little to no proof of any genuine military harm it would cause. The key events of the day occurred in a session of the court that was closed, so that the government could make its case that national security interests of the highest order would be compromised by continued publication and by the use of classified information in doing so. Only counsel, witnesses, and Max Frankel (who was present to assist Hegarty in the cross-examination of government witnesses) were permitted to attend. By the end of the long day, we felt good about our chances.

The critical witness was Vice Admiral Francis J. Blouin, deputy chief of naval operations for plans and policy. In his direct examination, he had spoken broadly of the harm continued publication would do:

> Q: Do you have present information available which would indicate to you whether the public disclosure of the contents of that study would compromise the

military or defense plans of the United States or its intelligence operations?

A: I don't think it would be an overstatement to say that I think it would be a disaster to publish all of these other documents, let alone the ones that have already been published.

Q: Are you also in a position to explain to the Court how past publication by the *New York Times* and the stories which appeared earlier this week have already compromised the intelligence operations of the United States?

A: I would rather not get into detail because I think with the broad experience I have in the field that I can detect things in there that perhaps, as you noted yourself earlier, the ordinary layman would not detect, but I think as a matter of fact any intelligence organization will derive a great deal of benefit from the articles that have already been published and there is even more juicy material in the other volumes.

In the closed session it quickly became clear that his objections were so far-reaching and would affect so much of what routinely was published in the press that the government's reliance on his testimony asserting that particular portions of the Pentagon Papers could not be published was all but impossible. He referred to material that it "would be just better not to make public." He regretted that our withdrawal plans from Vietnam had been announced publicly by President Nixon, and concluded ruefully: "We just about live by the open book." He conceded that "maybe I am over-sensitive," and that his conclusion that the documents "are packed with highly sensitive material, not only straight military, but in the military-political field," rested on "just the quick look I took at these documents." More generally, as he reviewed articles already published in the *Times*, he said, "each article gave me the shivers." When the Court suggested to Blouin that much of what he objected to seeing published was in fact public knowledge, having been repeatedly revealed not only in numerous news reports but in memoirs and other books, the admiral could only reply: "I deplore much of what I read."

Throughout the hearing Judge Gurfein constantly urged the government witnesses to supply him with specific examples of material that would be dangerous to publish. A striking instance occurred in a late-afternoon colloquy between Gurfein and Dennis James Doolin, deputy secretary of defense for international security affairs, who was called by the government to testify as to the propriety of classifying the Pentagon Papers as top secret. Near the end of Doolin's cross-examination, Gurfein asked him: "I will give you one more chance, in this sense. Is there anything you would like to add to your testimony for the enlightenment of the court tying in with more specificity these dangers to security you mentioned arising from incidents that happened between 1945 and 1968 and that appear in these studies?" Doolin replied by alluding to an earlier reference to Thai operations in Laos, which it was the policy of the Thai government to deny (falsely), and on which the United States officially had no comment. Doolin went on: "I might add, Your Honor, that I called . . . the Pentagon at lunch and we asked that members of my staff go through the study again looking for one of these, but I didn't have time to come up with a list of, a lengthy list of, specifics." This testimony was offered by the official who over a period of six months, according to his testimony, had reviewed the classified study and recommended to Secretary of Defense Melvin Laird that it not be released, and who had also reviewed the documents since.

The most specific Doolin could get was to suggest what he called "an impact in terms of human intelligence" resulting from revealing to others that we had information and were "reading their traffic." No indication was made whether others were in fact already aware of our intelligence efforts, or how they could benefit in the present from knowledge of what we were doing at the time the documents originated, which at the latest was mid-1968 and for the most part was much earlier, even as long ago as two decades.

The very fact of disclosure—the gross fact of

a breach of security, presumably, the disclosure of *any* confidential document—"could have an impact," Doolin insisted, on countries like New Zealand and Thailand, which maintained forces in Vietnam. Publication of the Papers might cause them to accelerate their own withdrawal and thus impede our Vietnamization program. The Australians had already expressed, Doolin said, "their concern, great concern," and at another point he added that the Australian prime minister had said he was "appalled." But all the possible ramifications were plainly surmise, and as Doolin went on, Judge Gurfein gave every indication that he was losing respect for the seriousness of the government case.

Doolin also testified that the United States had been using other governments as intermediaries in attempting to negotiate the release of American prisoners held in North Vietnam, and that such governments would now refuse to undertake confidential missions on our behalf, knowing that perhaps in the future their communications with us might be revealed. This general point, obviously speculative but possibly accurate, recurred in the testimony of other witnesses as well. Bickel orally and Hegarty in the brief he later wrote about it conceded that this argument might have some substance, but not enough to overcome the First Amendment right to publish, especially because confidential diplomatic communications are in due course almost inevitably disclosed, whether

46

in memoirs, other historical writings, or news-paper reports, and they are indeed often made public quite contemporaneously.

Asked to be more specific concerning his fears that other governments would now refuse to be intermediaries in our efforts to release prisoners held in North Vietnam, Doolin said that he thought that the Swedish government would be unlikely to help us further. Asked whether there was any communication with the Swedish government in the documents in issue in the case that would support his contention, Doolin answered, "To the best of my knowledge, no."

Doolin approached any degree of specificity in only two other instances. The documents contained references, he said, "to certain SEATO operational plans, Plan 5 in particular, which is still in existence." In fact, nowhere in the record was there any indication of the original date of the plan, or an explanation of how a plan at least three years old could, while "still in existence," be considered current, so that its revelation would benefit an enemy or potential enemy, given the obvious enormous changes that had been taking place in the military posture of the United States and its allies in Southeast Asia. Nor, again, was there any indication that these plans, while no doubt classified, were not so general as to be obvious, or so old and frequently bruited about as to be familiar.

Doolin's remaining attempt at specificity was to

47

suggest that studies of the value of bombing targets in North Vietnam dating back not just three but four, five, or more years remained of interest and should not be revealed, because "some of them are still targets." When Gurfein remarked that he could not follow why it should still be of interest what targets were selected some years back, Doolin could only reply: "Again, Your Honor, and I am trying to be helpful, you have to look at all of this in the context of totality of the study, in terms of the decision process taking you into it, in terms of what we did in points of time as we went up in terms of our involvement, and it just gives the other side frankly just one hell of a jump ahead."

In our sealed brief later submitted to the court, we argued that while Doolin was the government witness who exhibited the most familiarity with the documents in issue in the case, nothing in his testimony came close to meeting the demanding tests established in First Amendment case law to justify a prior restraint.

By this point in the case, all the lawyers—and sometimes Judge Gurfein himself—were referring to the Supreme Court's leading decision on prior restraint, the 1931 ruling in *Near v. Minnesota*, in a sort of shorthand. *Near* had struck down as unconstitutional a Minnesota statute that permitted injunctions against publications that were "malicious, scandalous and defamatory." While Chief Justice Charles Evans Hughes's opinion emphasized that "the chief purpose" of the First Amendment was "to prevent previous restraints on publication," he did offer a few examples of what prior restraints *would* be allowed. "No one would question," he wrote, "but that a government might prevent the publication of the sailing dates of transports or the number and location of troops."

All sides quickly compressed the *Near* language into a single question critical to our case: was there an example of material in the Pentagon Papers akin to revelation of details about a "transport"? Or, as we distilled it still further, "Where's the troopship?" Judge Gurfein welcomed, as judges do, the apparent agreement of counsel on so central a legal issue in the case. "Everyone seems to agree," he said, on the law. "The issue is the balancing of what the facts are."

As Friday wore on, it became ever clearer that there was no troopship and, more important, that Judge Gurfein did not think so, either. Sitting behind our table in the courtroom as the evidence came in and our spirits lifted, Bickel and I both felt the increasingly angry stare of Robert Mardian, the assistant attorney general in charge of internal security, upon us. Mardian had been active in the case from the start, had drafted many of the government's papers, and had a fierce devotion to suppressing the *Times*'s, and by that time other newspapers', publication of stories based on the Pentagon Papers. "Every time he looks at me," Bickel whispered to me, "I think he wants to deport me back to Romania." Hegarty later phrased it in a more literary way to Harrison Salisbury: Mardian reminded him, he said, of the character of Judge Hathorne in Stephen Vincent Benét's "The Devil and Daniel Webster." Hathorne kept saying "Hang them . . . hang them all . . ."

On Saturday, June 19, we went to court to pick up Judge Gurfein's opinion. It was a stunning, total vindication of the *Times.* The government had failed even to produce enough facts to demonstrate a "sharp clash" between "vital security interests of the Nation and the compelling constitutional doctrine against prior restraint." The "*in camera* proceedings*,*" he wrote, "did not convince this Court that the publication of these historical documents would seriously breach the National security." As for the statute relied upon by the government, it did not, just as Bickel had argued, contain any language barring "publication" of anything. And then, the sublime conclusion:

> If there be some embarrassment to the Government in security aspects as remote as the general embarrassment that flows from any security breach we must learn to live with it. The security of the Nation is not at the ramparts alone. Security also lies in the value of our free institutions. A cantankerous press, an obstinate press, a ubiquitous press must be suffered by those in authority in

order to preserve the even greater values of freedom of expression and the right of the people to know. In this case there has been no attempt by the Government at political suppression. There has been no attempt to stifle criticism. Yet in the last analysis it is not merely the opinion of the editorial writer, or of the columnist, which is protected by the First Amendment. It is the free flow of information so that the public will be informed about the Government and its actions.

These are troubled times. There is no greater safety valve for discontent and cynicism about the affairs of Government than freedom of expression in any form. This has been the genius of our institutions through our history. It has been the credo of all our Presidents. It is one of the marked traits of our national life that distinguish us from other nations under different forms of government.

CHAPTER 2

TO THE SUPREME COURT AND AFTER

After we received Judge Gurfein's decision on the Pentagon Papers, the government quickly sought and obtained a stay from Judge Irving Kaufman of the U.S. Court of Appeals for the Second Circuit until that court decided the case. For the time being, publication continued to be barred. Argument was scheduled for the following Tuesday, June 22.

As had been our strategy in our brief to Judge Gurfein, our submission to the court of appeals was long on separation of powers, short on the First Amendment. David Rudenstine later observed in his book *The Day the Presses Stopped* that the inclusion in the brief of only three pages about the First Amendment and over forty-five to the argument that the government was not authorized to sue the *Times* was "extraordinary." There was, Rudenstine correctly observed, "no justification for devoting only three pages to the First Amendment issues."

In the end, the composition of our brief made little difference.

The argument was a disaster. United States

Attorney Whitney North Seymour contended that the case before Judge Gurfein had been handled in too rushed a fashion and that the government had not had sufficient time to assemble its proof of grave harm to the nation. The Pentagon Papers had been stolen, he asserted, and these stolen documents were precisely of the nature for which the "troopship" exception in *Near* provided. The government was nonetheless willing, he said, to separate out those portions of the Papers that were dangerous to disseminate, leaving the rest available for public disclosure.

Bickel was pounded mercilessly by Chief Judge Henry Friendly from the moment he rose to respond. The printed page cannot fully reflect the anger with which Friendly spoke, an anger that reminded me of that of my partner who had asked me how I felt representing traitors, and of McKay's client who had accused him of the same thing. It began—and for all practical purposes ended—this way:

MR. BICKEL: May it please the Court, Mr. Seymour, Your Honors, we hear a great deal about stolen documents. The word has been in this case from the very beginning. Just very briefly I would like to point out that there is no evidence anywhere in the record, certainly not, that the *Times* stole these documents or that anybody stole them.

JUDGE FRIENDLY: You know that someone gave them to the *Times* when he had no authority to do it, though?

MR. BICKEL: That is the allegation, Your Honor. But how he got them—

JUDGE FRIENDLY: Is there even the slightest doubt about that?

JUDGE KAUFMAN: You have not denied that, have you?

MR. BICKEL: We have not denied that the *Times* did not get the documents from a government source authorized—

JUDGE FRIENDLY: Why not just say the answer is the *Times* got them without authorization? Then we need not waste time quibbling about that.

MR. BICKEL: That, it seems to me, begs a certain question. I am not arguing that. I am only very briefly trying to get the word "stolen" out of this discourse.

JUDGE FRIENDLY: They received them from someone who had no authority to give it to them, and they knew perfectly well that was the fact, and according to Mr. Seymour they had known it for three months, is that right?

MR. BICKEL: I don't know who they received them from. They received them from somebody. I don't for a moment suggest it, but it could, for example, on this record be Mr. Clifford or Mr. McNamara, for all we know.

JUDGE FRIENDLY: You aren't serious. Why don't you face the facts?

MR. BICKEL: I am not a bit serious about that, of course. But I don't know where they were gotten and I am simply resisting the word "stolen."

JUDGE FRIENDLY: Nobody says the *Times* went into the Department of Defense with a chisel. It is equally clear that someone gave it to the *Times* when he had no authority to do so. We are all agreed on that. Why not go on from there?

MR. BICKEL: I was simply resisting, Your Honor, the word "stolen," which it does seem to me is a highly colored word.

JUDGE FRIENDLY: Let's say they received the goods in the process of embezzlement, then, if you prefer.

MR. BICKEL: Without dwelling further on the point, may I say I resist that as well.

JUDGE FRIENDLY: You may resist it.

After that introductory exchange, Bickel's voice, which had been penetratingly alive and vibrantly audible throughout Judge Gurfein's courtroom, was noticeably more subdued. He sounded beaten. By the end of the argument, which was followed by a briefer *in-camera* hearing on national security issues argued by Hegarty and Seymour, it was clear that we had considerable, but by no means total, opposition to our position in the court. It came as no surprise, then, when it ruled the next day, 5-3, that the case should be remanded to Judge Gurfein for further closed hearings. The court, which evidently accepted Seymour's argument that Judge Gurfein had rushed the proceedings in a manner that had potentially prejudiced the government, required Gurfein to determine by July 3 whether disclosure of any items put at issue by the government "pose such grave and immediate danger to the security of the United States as to warrant their being enjoined." Given Judge Friendly's sense of offense at our case (and, evidently, our client), someone suggested that we could have done worse—capital punishment for Sulzberger, perhaps.

But the Second Circuit ruling was no joke. To be forced to wait until early July for a ruling and then to appear in front of the same judges who had reversed Judge Gurfein's judgment in the first place seemed to place us on a tortuously long road. Prior restraints were supposed to be virtually banned, we told one another, yet on the basis of much claim of harm by the government but almost no proof of it, the *Times* had already been enjoined for nine days with at least another ten now facing it, and then maybe even more as the Supreme Court considered the case.

We spent the rest of Wednesday, June 23, discussing our response to the ruling. The obvious course of conduct was to file an immediate petition for a writ of certiorari—a written request that the United States Supreme Court hear the case. But that tactic, too, had its problems. The order of the court of appeals was interlocutory—that is, not final—and the Supreme Court rarely heard such cases. Beyond that, one could maintain (which is precisely what the government would do) that all the court of appeals had done was to give the government a few more days to prove that "grave and immediate" harm would befall the country if publication was allowed. What was the matter with that? Lots, we thought, but even so, the argument against the Court hearing the case immediately was not insubstantial.

At the same time that we were discussing whether to petition the Court, the *Washington Post* was in the throes of its own litigation with the government. Well aware of the *Times*'s thwarted efforts to publish, Ellsberg had made portions of the Pentagon Papers available to the *Post*, the *Chicago Sun-Times*, the *Christian Science Monitor*, and other newspapers. As one paper was enjoined from publishing, another would begin.

The *Washington Post* case had begun after ours had, since it had not received the documents and begun running its own series until late in the week of the *Times*'s initial publication. Their case had proceeded rapidly, with a victory for the paper in the district court, a quick reversal by the Court of Appeals of the District of Columbia calling for more hearings, and a new district court ruling in its favor. They, too, we saw, would likely be approaching the Supreme Court at about the same time we were.

We finally decided on June 23, with no little concern, to petition the Supreme Court for a writ of certiorari and I spent a good part of the night in our Washington office preparing the petition for filing the next day, June 24. Late on the twenty-third, the *Washington Post* won its case in the Court of Appeals for the District of Columbia, creating a direct conflict for the Court to resolve. Nonetheless, we could not be sure that the Supreme Court would take the case.

On the twenty-fourth, I checked into the Madison Hotel about 3 a.m. and woke up about 6:30 a.m. in preparation for a memorable breakfast with Frankel, Wicker, and Reston. I admired each of them from their writings and wanted to make the best possible impression. I had arrived at the Madison with my shaving items, a clean shirt and underwear, and some papers. When I awoke, groggy as I often was that week, I was confronted with a vexing problem: I could find only one sock of the two I had worn before I went to sleep. The room was empty, except for me and my few possessions. A sock cannot, I told myself, disappear. I searched for twenty minutes, then gave up, dressed without it, pulled my pants down as far as they could go to cover my bare ankle, put my shoes on, and departed. The *Times*'s journalists, either out of politeness or inattention, made no reference to my sockless foot, and I survived breakfast intact.

Photographers were waiting when we arrived at the Court, something we had come to expect and had learned, not unhappily, to live with. Also there was a most unlikely figure: the clerk of the Supreme Court itself, not in his office within the great marble palace in which the Court sits, but on its top step, waiting for us. "The justices were wondering when you would arrive," he told me. It occurred to me then that I should have understood earlier that this was no ordinary "civil action" or "litigation." It was an extravaganza, a mixture of law, politics and journalism that had always been bound for the Supreme Court. How could I have really feared, I asked myself, that the Court would forgo the chance to decide this case? How could I even have considered not going directly to the Supreme Court?

Bickel had flown back to Stanford for a brief break on June 23. There could, of course, be an emergency argument in his absence, he told me; if so, he said, I should handle it. On Friday, June 25, the Court agreed to hear the case and scheduled argument for the following day. Bickel flew back to Washington.

The most striking thing about the order granting our petition and scheduling argument was contained in the final paragraph. In addition to asking the Court to hear the case, we had also filed a motion asking the Court to vacate the ruling of the court of appeals that reversed Judge Gurfein. We had thus asked the Court for a total victory *without* any argument. Four members of the Court—Justices Black, Douglas, Brennan, and Marshall—had voted to do just that. They "would not continue the restraint upon the *New York Times*" for another moment.

So there we were again: we had four votes and were at no risk of losing any of them. From whom might the fifth come? What could we say to persuade him?

Saturday morning, after still another sleepless night, we filed our brief on the merits of the case. This time we started by focusing far more strongly than we had before on the prior restraint issue. We moved from there to the need for the government to have some basis set forth in a statute for the restraint, even if any prior restraint could otherwise be sustained. The brief summarized the facts, reviewed the rulings of Judge Gurfein and the court of appeals, and then began with a passage of legal poetry composed by Bickel that he would later include in his book *The Morality of Consent*, and that would then be adopted by the Supreme Court itself. It was his explanation of why prior restraints on speech were so intolerable:

> Prior restraints fall on speech with a brutality and a finality all their own. Even if they are ultimately lifted, they cause irremediable loss, a loss in the immediacy, the impact of speech. They differ from the imposition of

criminal liability in significant procedural respects as well, which in turn have their substantive consequences. The violator of a prior restraint may be assured of being held in contempt. The violator of a statute punishing speech criminally knows that he will go before a jury, and may be willing to take his chance, counting on a possible acquittal. A prior restraint therefore stops more speech, more effectively. A criminal statute chills. The prior restraint freezes.

The argument in the Supreme Court itself began with less of a flourish, but still in an encouraging fashion. First, Chief Justice Burger announced that the Court had denied a motion made by the government to conduct part of the argument involving national security matters in secret. Three justices—Burger, Harlan, and Blackmun—would, the Chief Justice announced, have granted "a limited *in camera* argument."

We knew two things from the Chief Justice's announcement. The first, which we tried to put aside to concentrate on matters at hand, was that the Solicitor General's Office had made a motion to the Court of which we—incredibly, inexcusably, and in violation of all accepted court practice—had not even been advised. The second, which was far more significant to our conduct of the case, was that the vote had been 6-3 against the motion, with Justices Potter Stewart and Byron White joining what we now viewed as "our" four votes. It was a good start, made better still by a weak opening argument for the government by Solicitor General Erwin Griswold.

Griswold was a distinguished scholar who had served as dean of the Harvard Law School. He had written a widely acclaimed book during the worst days of the McCarthy era defending the Fifth Amendment and the rights of those who claimed its protection. But this was not his day to defend civil liberties or even to advance his client's cause. Bickel had faltered in the court of appeals after Friendly's berating of him; Griswold faltered in the Supreme Court from the start by discussing the wrong subjects.

Griswold's argument started with the unexceptionable but not terribly relevant proposition that prior restraints were by no means always banned. For example, he said, they were permitted in copyright cases, in some other cases involving literary property, in labor cases and the like. He went on for over five minutes about these other areas of law until Justice Stewart—one of the two critical potential swing votes on the Court—interjected.

> Mr. Solicitor General, of course, the *Times* in this case, and there are no doubt others, I did not understand your brother counsel on the other side really questioned any of this. I thought at least for purposes of this case they

conceded that an injunction would be not violative of the First Amendment, or put it this way, that despite the First Amendment, an injunction would be permissible in this case if the disclosure of this material would in fact pose a grave and immediate danger to the security of the United States, that is, for purposes of this case they conceded that, but they have said that in fact disclosure of this material would not pose any such grave and immediate danger.

Griswold responded lamely that "if" we had "conceded" that—as we had from our first moment before Judge Gurfein—he would proceed on that basis.

Griswold did little better in sparring with Justice Stewart on other matters. The government had emphasized the classified nature of the documents in its written brief. But how important was that? Justice Stewart asked the question directly:

Q: As I understand it, Mr. Solicitor General, and you tell me, please, if I misunderstand it, your case does not really depend upon the classification of this material, whether it is classified or how it is classified. In other words, if the *New York Times* and the *Washington Post* had this material as a result of the indiscretion or irresponsibility of an

Under Secretary of Defense who took it upon himself to declassify all of this material and give it to the paper, you would still be here.

A: I would still be here. It will be one string off my bow.

Q: I did not understand it was a real string on your bow. That is why I am asking you the question.

A: Maybe it is not, but there are those who think it is, and I must be careful not to concede away in this court grounds which some responsible officers of the Government think are important.

Griswold's message could hardly have been clearer—or weaker. He had little use for the argument that the classified nature of the Pentagon Papers should on its own turn the tide in the government's favor. "Some responsible officers of the Government"—Attorney General Mitchell, perhaps, or Assistant Attorney General Mardian—believed it, but not the highly respected solicitor general himself.

Justice Stewart pursued the matter of how seriously Griswold took the questions of the classified nature of the documents, and how the *Times* had obtained them:

Q: Mr. Solicitor General . . . this brings me back to my original question of a few moments ago as to what the real basic issue in this case is. As I understand it, you are not claiming that you are entitled to an injunction simply or solely because this is classified material.

A: No.

Q: Nor do I understand it that you are claiming that you are entitled to an injunction because it was stolen from you, that it is your property. You are claiming rather and basically that whether or not it is classified or however it is classified, and however it was acquired by these newspapers, the public disclosure of this material would pose a grave and immediate danger to the security of the United States of America, period.

A: Yes, Mr. Justice.

I could imagine Mardian's red face becoming redder still.

Probably the highlight of Griswold's argument, at least for our side, was his clash with Justice Hugo Black. Black had long espoused the view that the First Amendment was an absolute and that when the framers had stated in the First Amendment that "Congress shall make no law . . . abridging the freedom of speech or of the press," it meant *no* law at all. While that view had never been shared by a majority of the Court, it remained Black's strongly, almost religiously held belief. Griswold, however, took issue with Black's reading of the amendment: "Now Mr. Justice," he said, looking at Black, "your construction of that is well known, and I certainly respect it. You say that 'no law' means 'no law,' and that should be obvious. I can only say, Mr. Justice, that to me it is equally obvious that 'no law' does not mean 'no law,' and I would seek to persuade the Court that that is true."

This was probably the least persuasive challenge to Justice Black's views ever publicly expressed, and Black listened to it with evident delight. Bickel, who himself had no use for First Amendment absolutism, could have made a more nuanced argument far more gracefully and persuasively. If textual support was required from the language of the First Amendment itself, it would be far easier to maintain that the word "abridging" has considerable room for inter-pretation, or even (as Justice Scalia has argued) that the words "*the* freedom of speech" must be interpreted historically and not as we might other-wise read it today. The one approach that Griswold should not have taken was the very one he did: arguing that "no law" does not mean "no law."

Griswold was followed by Bickel, who faced tougher questions from our "friends" on the bench (with whom he generally thoroughly disagreed) than those justices more likely to vote with the government. If anything, Bickel invited a rebuke from Justices Black and Douglas by once again offering his separation-of-powers theme—Congress never authorized this—far more vigorously than any defense rooted in the First Amendment. This time, there was no blurring his priorities. The argument based on the absence of a statute came first.

If I may, at this point, take up Mr. Justice Stewart's question to the Solicitor General, referring to our position, we concede, and we have all along in this case conceded for purposes of the argument, that the prohibition against prior restraint, like so much else in the Constitution, is not an absolute. But beyond that, Mr. Justice, our position is a little more complicated than that, nor do we really think that the case, even with the statute out of it, is a simple—presents indeed a simple question of fact. Rather, our position is twofold. First, on principles, as we view them, of the separation of powers, which we believe deny the existence of inherent Presidential authority on which an injunction can be based.

First on those, and secondly, on First Amendment principles, which are interconnected, and which involve the question of a standard before one reaches the facts, a standard on which we differ greatly from the Solicitor General. On both these grounds, we believe that the only proper resolution of the case is a dismissal of the complaint.

Justice Douglas took Bickel up on his first argument.

> Q: Why would the statute make a differ-ence, because the First Amendment provides that Congress shall make no law abridging freedom of the press. Do you read that to mean that Congress could make some laws abridging freedom of the press?
>
> A: No, sir. Only in that I have conceded, for purposes of this argument, that some limitations, some impairment of the absoluteness of that prohibition is possible, and I argue that, whatever that may be, it is surely at its very least when the President acts without statutory authority because that inserts into it, as well—
>
> Q: That is a very strange argument for The Times to be making. The Congress can make all this illegal by passing laws.
>
> A: I did not really argue that, Mr. Justice.
>
> Q: That was the strong impression that was left in my mind.

Bickel's answers to Justice Douglas were as interesting and also as irrelevant as Griswold's clash with Black. Both justices' votes were ours—both had voted in our favor before any oral argument and surely would not be changed by it—and nothing Bickel said could have lost them, just as nothing Griswold said could have won them. But what of Justices Stewart and White, the center of the Court in those days?

Bickel's most critical answers, which were central to winning the case, came in response to a hypothetical question put by Justice Stewart:

Q: Mr. Bickel, it is understandably and inevitably true that in a case like this, particularly when so many of the facts are under seal, it is necessary to speak in abstract terms, but let me give you a hypothetical case. Let us assume that when the members of the Court go back and open up this sealed record we find something there that absolutely convinces us that its disclosure would result in the sentencing to death of 100 young men whose only offense had been that they were 19 years old and had low draft numbers. What should we do?

A: Mr. Justice, I wish there were a statute that covered it.

Q: Well there is not. We agree, or you submit, and I am asking in this case what should we do.

A: I am addressing a case of which I am as confident as I can be of anything that Your Honor will not find that when you get back to your chambers. It is a hard case. I think it would make bad separation of powers law. But it is almost impossible to resist the inclination not to let the information be published, of course.

Justice Stewart pursued Bickel anew.

Q: As you know, and I am sure you do know, the concern that this Court has term after term with people who have been convicted and sentenced to death, convicted of extremely serious crimes in capital cases, and I am posing you a case where the disclosure of something in these files would result in the deaths of people who are guilty of nothing.

A: You are posing me a case, of course, Mr. Justice, in which that element of my attempted definition which refers to the chain of causation—

Q: I suppose in a great big global picture this is not a national threat. There are at least 25 Americans killed in Vietnam every week these days.

A: No, sir, but I meant it is a case in which

the chain of causation between the act of publication and the feared event, the death of these 100 young men, is obvious, direct, immediate.

Q: That is what I am assuming in my hypothetical case.

A: I would only say as to that that it is a case in which in the absence of a statute, I suppose most of us would say—

Q: You would say the Constitution requires that it be published, and that these men die, is that it?

A: No. I am afraid that my inclinations to humanity overcome the somewhat more abstract devotion to the First Amendment in a case of that sort.

There was much criticism of that answer in the civil liberties community and considerable concern expressed about it by post-argument *Times* journalists. The American Civil Liberties Union filed a rare postargument brief disowning Bickel's response and urging that the only danger that could justify a prior restraint would be to the nation itself, and not to some small subset of its population. In the years that have passed since the Pentagon Papers case, I have occasionally tried to formulate an answer that would fall somewhere between Bickel's and that of the ACLU. But looking back on it, I cannot escape the conclusion that Bickel's response was a required one.

For when the tally was taken and we won by a 6-3 vote—"our" four plus justices Stewart and White—our victory was so tenuous that any slight change in the judicial calibration of the case might have deprived us of the additional votes we so desperately needed.

The only opinion in favor of the *Times* issued by the Court that more than three jurists agreed upon was a laconic *per curiam* three-paragraph order stating that we had won. The government had a "heavy burden" of demonstrating that it needed a prior restraint, the Court said, and it had failed to meet that burden. It was the individual opinions of the justices—nine justices, nine opinions—that told the detailed story behind the judgment.

The opinions we savored most—the opinions I still reread most often—were from the four jurists that no lawyers for the *Times* could have lost. Justice Black, in an opinion joined by Douglas, was especially eloquent. With only a passing reference to the fact that what was in contention was a prior restraint, Black went to the heart of the First Amendment issue raised by the case. "Every moment's continuation of the injunctions against these newspapers," he wrote, "amounts to a flagrant, indefensible and continuing violation of the First Amendment." The press, he argued, was "left free" by the First Amendment "to publish news, whatever the source, without censorship, injunctions or prior restraints." And, in stirring language, Black wrote that

> the press was protected so that it could bare the secrets of government and inform the people. Only a free and unrestrained press can effectively expose deception in government. And paramount among the responsibilities of a free press is the duty to prevent any part of the government from deceiving the people and sending them off to distant lands to die of foreign fevers and foreign shot and shell. In my view, far from deserving condemnation for their courageous reporting, the *New York Times*, the *Washington Post*, and other newspapers should be commended for serving the purpose that the Founding Fathers saw so clearly. In revealing the workings of government that led to the Viet Nam war, the newspapers nobly did precisely that which the Founders hoped and trusted they would do.

Having admonished Bickel during his oral argument for even focusing on the absence of any statute authorizing the relief the government sought, Justice Douglas, joined by Black in his opinion, not only concluded that the First Amendment "leaves . . . no room for governmental restraint on the press" but relied on our argument that no statute barred the press from publishing the Pentagon Papers. As for the disclosures themselves, Douglas acknowledged that they "may have a serious impact" but noted that all of the matters raised in the in-camera brief of the government were "history, not future events," with none of it more recent than 1968. As for the prior-restraint issue, Douglas concluded that "the stays in these cases that have been in effect for more than a week constitute a flouting of the principles of the First Amendment" as set forth in *Near v. Minnesota*.

Justice Brennan's opinion in favor of the *Times* took aim at another aspect of the case: "The error which has pervaded these cases from the outset was the granting of any injunctive relief whatsoever, interim or otherwise." The government had argued, he said, that publication of the articles by the *Times* "could" or "might" or "may" prejudice the national interest. But such "surmise or conjecture," Brennan concluded, could never overcome the nearly total ban or prior restraints.

Justice Marshall's opinion was based, in its entirety, on the absence of any statutory authority supporting the government's application for injunctive relief. Twice, Marshall wrote, Congress considered giving the President "broad power to protect the Nation from disclosure of damaging state secrets"; twice Congress had not provided the President with such power. "It is not for this Court," Marshall concluded, "to fling itself into every breach perceived by some Government official nor is it for this Court to take on itself the burden of enacting law, especially law that Congress has refused to pass."

The four justices we had counted on had thus, to different degrees, relied upon all three of the themes Bickel and I had discussed in my office when we first spent the night there strategizing. Three of the four had cited the absence of statutory authority by the government (the Douglas-Black and Marshall opinions). Three of the four had focused on the fact that what was at issue was a prior restraint (the Douglas-Black and Brennan opinions). Finally, Black and Douglas had relied—far more than we ever had—on the notion that prior restraint aside, the whole purpose of the First Amendment was to protect the sort of speech that was at the heart of this case.

And what of the critical opinions of Justices Stewart and White? Each justice wrote his own opinion, and each joined in the opinion written by the other. Justice Stewart's opinion began by acknowledging a paradox. While it was in the area of national defense and international affairs that a "press that is alert, aware and free" was most needed, at the same time, Stewart wrote, "the successful conduct of international diplomacy and the maintenance of an effective national defense require both confidentiality and secrecy." The reconciliation of these opposing interests lay in the conclusion that "the responsibility must be where the power is." Thus, the executive branch was responsible for protecting the confidentiality of information within its control. But this case was different.

> We are asked, quite simply, to prevent the publication by two newspapers of material that the Executive Branch insists should not, in the national interest, be published. I am convinced that the Executive is correct with respect to some of the documents involved. But I cannot say that disclosure of any of them will surely result in direct, immediate, and irreparable damage to our Nation or its people. That being so, there can under the First Amendment be but one judicial resolution of the issues before us.

Justice White's opinion first disposed of, in a footnote, Griswold's effort to persuade the Court that since prior restraint was permitted in copyright and other commercial areas, the Court should be less troubled about permitting it here. All these situations, White pointed out, are different from one in which the government is seeking an injunction "against publishing information about the affairs of government, a request admittedly not based on any statute." White stated that he was "confident" that the government was correct in arguing that "revelation" of material that it characterized as the "most sensitive and destructive" would "do substantial damage to public interests." It was "not easy" in these circumstances, White concluded, "to deny relief based on the government's good-faith claims . . . that publication will work serious damage to the country." But the government had nonetheless, White concluded, failed to satisfy "the very heavy burden which it must meet to warrant an injunction against publication in these cases, at least in the absence of appropriately limited congressional authorization for prior restraints in circumstances such as these."

The Stewart and White opinions reveal just how close a case the Pentagon Papers case was. Both jurists believed publication would do "substantial damage" to the country. Both also concluded, as was stated in another part of White's opinion, that a *criminal* conviction of the *Times* for its publication would be constitutional. But the combination of the high level of protection afforded the press against prior restraint and the absence of any congressional warrant for the relief the government sought was sufficient—and just sufficient—to carry the day.

The three dissenting opinions of Chief Justice Burger and Justices Harlan and Blackmun raised concerns about what Burger characterized as "the frenetic haste" with which the case had been conducted. Burger objected to the *Times*'s behavior from beginning to end. Why had the newspaper not given the government the chance "to review the entire collection and determine whether agreement could be reached on publication?" While Black had concluded that the *Times* and the *Post* were deserving of commendation for their courageous reporting, Burger proclaimed (in language Herbert Brownell must have treasured) that "it is hardly believable that a newspaper long regarded as a great institution in American life would fail to perform one of the basic and simple duties of every citizen with respect to the discovery or possession of stolen property or secret government documents. That duty, I had thought—perhaps naively—was to report forthwith, to responsible public officers. This duty rests on taxi drivers, Justices and the *New York Times*."

Justice Harlan's opinion, joined by both Burger and Blackmun, was characteristically less emotionally charged than Burger's attack on the *Times* but was nonetheless filled with distress at the "almost irresponsibly feverish" pace of the proceedings. Harlan listed seven questions he believed should have been posed in the case, including whether an injunction should have been issued based on the harm done "simply from the demonstration of such a breach of secrecy"—a point not unlike Kissinger's to Nixon. At the least, Harlan concluded, the decision of the court of appeals should have been affirmed because its determination that the "Government had not been given an adequate time to present its case" to Judge Gurfein had not been an abuse of discretion. More broadly, Harlan argued that great deference should be shown by the courts to a determination by the executive branch that revelation of classified information would do substantial harm to the nation.

Justice Blackmun's dissenting opinion was even angrier than Burger's. He condemned both papers for their conduct, concluding with the following assault:

> I strongly urge, and sincerely hope, that these two newspapers will be fully aware of their ultimate responsibilities to the United States of America. Judge Wilkey, dissenting in the District of Columbia case, after a review of only the affidavits before his court (the basic papers had not then been made available by either party), concluded that there were a number of examples of documents that, if in the possession of the *Post* and if published, "could clearly result in great harm to the nation," and he defined "harm" to mean "the death of soldiers, the destruction of alliances, the greatly increased difficulty of negotiation with our enemies, the inability of our diplomats to negotiate . . ." I, for one, have now been able to give at least some cursory study not only to the affidavits, but to the material itself. I regret to say that, from this examination, I fear that Judge Wilkey's statements have possible foundation. I therefore share

his concern. I hope that damage already has not been done. If, however, damage has been done, and if, with the Court's action today, these newspapers proceed to publish the critical documents and there results therefrom "the death of soldiers, the destruction of alliances, the greatly increased difficulty of negotiation with our enemies, the inability of our diplomats to negotiate," to which list I might add the factors of prolongation of the war and of further delay in the freeing of United States prisoners, then the Nation's people will know where the responsibility for these sad consequences rests.

Rereading the pentagon Papers case today, it is difficult not to be struck by the degree to which the government succeeded in persuading the Court that great harm would befall the country if publication continued, yet still failed to win the case. Justices Douglas and Black, after all, conceded that the disclosures "may have a serious impact"; Justices White and Stewart concluded that publication "will do substantial damage to public interests"; Justice Blackmun said that further publication "'could clearly result in great harm to the nation'"; and there is no reason to doubt that other members of the Court—Burger and Harlan, surely—shared these sentiments.

How seriously did the Court take the government's representations of likely harm? One sign may be found in the first draft of Justice Marshall's concurring opinion: "If the Government believes the assertions it is making in this Court," he wrote, "then the newspapers, their publishers and some of their staff and editors could in good faith be prosecuted" under the Espionage Law. In fact, Marshall wrote, "given the announced intention of the newspapers to publish additional stories" based upon the Pentagon Papers, "it would appear that there is a conspiracy within the staffs of the *Washington Post* and *New York Times* to violate that statute."

With those chilling words as background, it is worth pausing to consider the specific allegations of harm made by the government which were so persuasive to members of the Court. An article in the *William & Mary Law Review* by Professor John Cary Sims thoughtfully and comprehensively analyzes each of these assertions, as presented by the government in its then-secret brief filed with the Supreme Court. One of them maintained:

There are specific references to the names and activities of CIA agents still active in Southeast Asia. There are references to the activities of the National Security Agency.

The items designated are specific references to persons or activities which are currently continuing. No designation has been made of any general references to CIA activities.

This may not be exactly equivalent to the disclosure of troop movements, but it is very close to it.

Sims's article pointed out in response that the secret brief offered

> no example to illustrate the nature of the harm that is feared. Not only [were] no details given to support the allegations being made, but the Secret Brief [did] not even allege that publication would impair the interests of the United States. The Supreme Court was apparently left to fill in for itself the dire consequences that might flow from references to CIA and NSA activities. The Secret Brief [did] not even contend that the names and activities referred to in the Pentagon Papers had previously been kept secret.

Another potentially troubling allegation was one that the solicitor general's brief referred to as: "SEATO Contingency Plan 5 dealing with the communist armed aggression in Laos." The brief stated: "This discloses what the military plans are. The SEATO plans are continuing plans. This involves not only the disclosure of military plans, but a breach of faith with other friendly nations."

Again, no details at all were provided, nor was any assessment offered of the degree to which the information was already in the public domain or of the sort of harm that could possibly result from publication. What is a court to do when confronted with such a submission? If Justice Harlan's dissenting opinion in the case had carried the day, the Court would have deferred to the assessment of harm made by the executive branch, so long as it was duly made by the highest-ranking official. But with the passage of time, and the opportunity it offers for hindsight, we can say with confidence, over thirty years after the fact, that all of the government's fears were overstated and that, in fact, none of them appear to have been accurate. None at all—not the solicitor general's representations to the Supreme Court; not the fears of the justices themselves; nothing. When the Prados and Parker book was published in 2004, the authors examined the claims of potential harm in great detail, concluding that there was no basis to credit any of the government's contentions.

Even ten years after their publication, in the course of preparing a magazine article reassessing the Pentagon Papers hearings, I called every government witness I could find who testified. Not one of them could cite a single published passage that had compromised national security. Not one.

In fact, as soon as a few months after the Supreme Court's ruling in the Pentagon Papers case, the Department of Justice itself had become acutely aware of the fact that the claims it had made of damage to national security interests were of the most dubious validity. One of the most powerfully phrased affidavits submitted by the United States in the case against the *Washington Post* had been that of Lieutenant General Melvin Zais of the Joint Chiefs of Staff. In it he had stated that publication had the potential of "causing exceptionally grave damage to the national security of the United States and grave damage to the well-being and safety of its deployed armed forces in Southeast Asia." When Daniel Ellsberg was indicted for, among other things, violating the Espionage Act in 1971, the Department of Justice asked the Defense Department to support General Zais's prediction by preparing a post-publication damage assessment setting forth the actual impact of the Papers' publication. The response of the Defense Department (in a November 1971 memorandum made available under the Freedom of Information Act to Professor Sims) dutifully concluded that publication had had "a severely adverse impact on the defense interests of the United States." Once again, little evidence was cited in support of that assessment. But this time, eager to prepare a credible case against Ellsberg, Assistant Attorney General Mardian cut through the haze of generalities he had been provided and in December 1971 dismissed the memorandum as "totally inadequate." The reasons he cited were the same as those that had plagued the government's case at the Pentagon Papers trial, and might well have been drafted by Bickel, Hegarty, or me:

> Although the assessment states that the compromise of the study "had a severely adverse impact on the defense interests of the United States," the injuries described therein primarily concern internal political matters in Vietnam and situations which are embarrassing to this country, but which cannot fairly be termed injuries to our defense interests. Furthermore, the injuries described are conjectural and highly speculative, and any causal relationship between the compromise of the study and such injuries is, at best, attenuated and probably incidental.

Another critical document that surfaced after the Pentagon Papers case was far more public: an op-ed written in 1989 for the *Washington Post* by Erwin Griswold. Notwithstanding that he had affirmed to the Supreme Court that further publication of the Papers would "irreparably" injure national security and "materially affect the security of the United States" and that it would "affect lives," "affect the process of the termination of the war," and "affect the process of recovering prisoners of war," Griswold now admitted that he had "never seen any trace of a threat to the national security from their publication" or "even seen it suggested that there was such an actual threat." The *Times* took special care to review each item Judge Gurfein had flagged before it resumed publication. Many had never been intended for publication; a few others were deleted.

Judge Gurfein himself had come upon a few documents out of the mass presented to him which had given him pause. As he had handed Hegarty a copy of the ruling in our favor, he had also given him what he explained was a list of documents contained in the Pentagon Papers that he had separately compiled as a "private citizen." The *Times* was free to publish them all, he said, but he wished the paper would give special consideration to them all before doing so.

Much did change as a result of the publication of the Pentagon Papers by the *Times* and the legal confrontation that followed. As regards the war itself, there seems little doubt that the revelations in the Papers strengthened public and congressional opposition to continued American participation. Charles Nesson, a Harvard Law School professor, concluded that publication "lent credibility to and finally crystallized the growing consensus that the Vietnam War was wrong and legitimized the radical critique of the war." Other observers give the Papers less credit for a fundamental shift in attitude, pointing out that the war did not in fact end for another four years, but as former secretary of state Cyrus Vance said in an interview, "Publication plainly had an effect on public opinion and public opinion had an effect on the duration of the war."

The Pentagon Papers may also have paved the way for the public's reaction to the Watergate transgressions. In this view, the disillusionment with the government aroused by the Papers made the public less trusting, less willing to accept government denials concerning Watergate.

Publication certainly had direct, if utterly unpredictable, effects on the Nixon White House. Apart from reinforcing Nixon's views of the press as his implacable enemy, it set into motion a subsequent crazy-quilt series of events. The "leak" of the Pentagon Papers led the president to establish the group that would later become known as the Watergate Plumbers. Assigned the task of gathering information for the purpose of discrediting Daniel Ellsberg, they engaged in the criminal break-in at the office of his former psychiatrist, which proved to be one of the events that finally led to the dismissal of the government's criminal case against Ellsberg for copying the Pentagon Papers. The illegal acts of the Plumbers would later figure importantly in the impeachment resolutions that brought on Nixon's ultimate resignation.

The effect of publication on the press was substantial. As Fred W. Friendly, the former president of CBS News, said, it "stiffened the spines of all journalists." It may have done more. Benno Schmidt, then a professor at Columbia University

Law School, noted that the papers "signaled the passing of a period when newspapers could be expected to play by tacit rules in treating matters that Government leaders deem confidential."

There are many who hold that, for better or worse, publication of the Pentagon Papers marked the beginning of a new period of press militancy, in which journalists would increasingly come to see their function as that of exposing wrongdoing rather than of merely reprinting officially sanctioned governmental statements. Harrison Salisbury, for example, argued that the reporting of Watergate would not have occurred but for the willingness of the press to publish the Pentagon Papers. An opposing view is that of McGeorge Bundy, who told me that the Pentagon Papers case had led the press, in one sense, to "change for the worse. One of the things that has happened is the growth of the notion that unless the relationship between the press and government is adversarial, it's not honest." Others charge that the pressure to produce investigatory journalism has led to a greater reliance by many publications on unnamed sources. (Ironically, both Richard Nixon and Daniel Ellsberg expressed suspicions that government leaks were increased by the publication of the Papers.)

Publication also underlined the absurdity of a classification system that barred from public view so much information that was ultimately of no security consequence. After a series of congressional hearings and debates over the course of several years, which included frequent references to the Pentagon Papers case, the Freedom of Information Act was strengthened to allow, for the first time, judicial scrutiny of documents that meet classification criteria.

But the most important effects of the Pentagon Papers relate neither to the war they described nor to the journalistic decision to publish them. The legal ramifications of the case dwarf all others. Up to that time prior restraints had historically been viewed as the single most intrusive and dangerous form of government conduct threatening freedom of expression. In the Pentagon Papers case, that notion was considered in the context of publication that a majority of the Supreme Court believed would do significant harm, yet still held was protected by the First Amendment.

Five years to the day after the Pentagon Papers ruling of the Supreme Court, in a matter arising in Nebraska, the Supreme Court unanimously struck down a series of prior restraints on publication that would have limited the right of the press to publish information about defendants in the midst of their criminal cases, such as the fact that they had confessed or had an extensive criminal record. This was the same topic that I had written about in my senior thesis at Cornell and, ironically, I was one of the two lawyers who appeared before the Court to contend that it should move still further away from the English mode that had so impressed me a score of years before. Arguing in the *Nebraska Press Association v. Stuart* case in 1976, I began:

> I appear here today on behalf of a variety of publishers, broadcasters and journalists from around the country to join with the Nebraska press and to urge upon you today a ruling which would be unthinkable in any nation in the world except ours. That it is in our view entirely consistent with American history makes it no less remarkable but simply points to the remarkable nature of that history. For what we would ask of you is nothing less than a renunciation of power, the conclusion by this Court that the Judiciary should not and indeed may not tell the press in advance what news it may print, save only in that rare national security situation, in that rare national security case adverted to by this Court in *Near v. Minnesota,* and in the Pentagon Papers case. And what we urge upon you is that that renunciation occurred two hundred years ago, that it has been reaffirmed by this Court since its formation and that you should reaffirm it today.

The judicial orders in question had been imposed by the courts in Nebraska for the stated purpose of ensuring a defendant a fair trial. Nonetheless, the prior restraints were unanimously held un-constitutional, even though the Court's ideological disagreements, which had been reflected in the many opinions in the Pentagon Papers case, persisted. Only three members of the Court (Justices Brennan, Stewart, and Marshall) were prepared to go as far as I had urged—supporting a rule flatly banning prior restraints in *all* cases involving claims that publication would interfere with a defendant's right to a fair trial; while two more (White and Stevens) indicated that they might go that far in the future, they joined an opinion of Chief Justice Warren Burger which, while making the issuance of such orders in the future extremely unlikely, did leave open that possibility.

Yet the practical effect of the *Nebraska* ruling, built in turn upon that in the Pentagon Papers case, has been virtually to end the issuance of prior restraints on publication. An occasional trial court has attempted to impose one, but in vir-tually all cases an appellate court has reversed that decision. The exception to this de facto end to the issuance of virtually all prior restraints has been in the very area around which the Pentagon Papers case revolved, national security.

It was in the midst of his most trying and least successful argument of the entire Pentagon Papers case that Bickel, sorely pressed by Judge Friendly and others on the Court of Appeals for the Second Circuit, had attempted to offer one example of material that, if published, could "possibly" justify the entry of a prior restraint. His example was a situation in which, as he put it, "the hydrogen bomb turns up." It was precisely that subject that would be involved eight years later in the only case since the Pentagon Papers in which the United States sought a prior restraint on publication. The *Progressive*, a small but influential left-liberal magazine whose publisher and editors believed that the dangers of nuclear proliferation were so grave that only promptly reached international agreements limiting the spread of such weapons could halt their threat to humanity, was about to publish an article entitled "The H-Bomb Secret," which included detailed instructions for the construction of a hydrogen bomb. Since all the information in the article was derived from public sources, the magazine claimed, it was not really adding to the risks of a nuclear holocaust, but only exposing those risks in a particularly acute manner.

I had no doubt that the decision to publish the article was made in complete good faith. At the same time, I thought (and think) that decision was both irresponsible and reckless. Even if the information in the article could be obtained from a variety of sometimes obscure public sources, the notion of making the point that an end had to be found to the increasing risks of a nuclear conflagration by "exposing" in detail just how easy it was to build a hydrogen bomb seemed to me folly.

Of course, the decision to publish the article was

not one with which I had any involvement. I was, however, deeply involved in the decision of much of the most powerful media in the nation about how to respond when the government went to court to enjoin its publication. At the district court level, the United States sought and obtained from the United States District Court in Wisconsin an order barring publication on the ground that the "right to life" trumped any First Amendment interest in the freedom to publish the article. It was a distressing ruling for two reasons. For all the irresponsibility exhibited in publishing the piece, most of the details in it were already freely available, and much of what the magazine did publish was sufficiently lacking in detail that it would likely not have been of critical assistance to a foreign nation fixed on building such a bomb. That being so, it may well have been that the *Progressive* would have won the case, if anything like the test set forth in the Pentagon Papers case by Justice Stewart— "direct, immediate and irreparable harm to the Nation or its people"—had been applied.

But that test was not applied. Instead, federal judge Robert W. Warren abandoned any requirement of immediacy in light of what he viewed as the obvious cataclysmic impact risked by publication. If affirmed by the court of appeals, such an approach would have gutted much of what we had won in the Pentagon Papers case.

The decision about how the leaders of the national press should respond to the case was not easy. Some thought that the *Progressive* should be fully supported, others that newspapers and broadcasters should submit a briefing stating that they disapproved of the decision to publish in the first place. I thought we should take another tack, articulating a strong pro-*Progressive* legal position based on the Pentagon Papers case while taking no position on what result the application of that test would be in the case itself.

Ultimately, the *New York Times*, the American Society of Newspaper Editors, the Association of American Publishers and other media organizations agreed to follow my advice, and my associate, Eugene R. Scheiman, drafted a brief for them urging the court of appeals to adhere to and apply Justice Stewart's opinion (including the "immediacy" requirement) and saying little else. "What is most important in this case," we argued, "is not which side ultimately prevails: it is that the 'virtually insurmountable barrier' against prior restraints remains just that for the future." Fortunately, during the pendency of the appeal of the *Progressive* case, information extremely similar to what was contained in its article was published elsewhere. To my relief, the government then dropped its effort to prevent publication. So far as we know, no harm ever resulted from the piece's appearance.

Taken together, the *Progressive* case and the Pentagon Papers case lead to one further conclusion: judicial bans on publishing seem all but totally ineffective.

In the Pentagon Papers matter, during the period in which the *Times* was enjoined from publishing the documents, Ellsberg made portions of them available to almost twenty other newspapers. The government brought actions for injunctive relief against three of them, but no action was taken against the others. The number of newspapers that published some portion of the Pentagon Papers led Judge Roger Robb of the United States Court of Appeals for the District of Columbia, while hearing a related case, to inquire of counsel for the government whether it was "asking us to ride herd on a swarm of bees."

Judge Robb's question underscored an inescapable dilemma regarding the issuance of *any* prior restraint on publication. Once information has been released, it is virtually impossible to stop its broader dissemination. All the prior restraints issued in the Pentagon Papers case failed to prevent Ellsberg from continuing his distribution. The *Nebraska* injunction was held unconstitutional five years after the Pentagon Papers case in part because of the Court's conclusion that events that occur in a small community will be passed on by rumors even if newspapers are barred from publishing. "Plainly," Chief Justice Burger observed, "a whole community cannot be restrained from discussing a subject intimately affecting life within it." The prior restraint issued in the *Progressive* case three years after that did not prevent the very material that the government sought to bar from the magazine from being printed elsewhere. Today, in a world transformed by the Internet, reliance on prior restraints to keep secrets seems an especially pointless endeavor. Ellsberg could (and probably would) now place the whole Pentagon Papers online and likely escape detection.

Though the press ultimately triumphed in the Pentagon Papers case, the victory was, it must be acknowledged, of a limited nature. A majority of the Supreme Court left open the possibility not only of prior restraints being issued in other cases but of criminal sanctions being imposed upon the press following publication of the Papers themselves. While restrictions in advance of publication have historically—and correctly—been viewed as the worst possible intrusions on press freedoms, the threat of criminal prosecution after publication was hardly one to encourage boldness among editors.

Even the fact that the United States had *sought*, however unsuccessfully, to bar publication was troubling. "Law," Bickel later wrote, "can never make us as secure as we are when we do not need it. Those freedoms which are neither challenged nor defined are the most secure." In this sense, he suggested, the very attempt by the government for the first time to censor the press was itself a kind of defeat. By doing so, a "spell was broken, and in a sense freedom was thus diminished."

But if the legal victory of the *Times* in the case

was limited, the effects of defeat would have been staggering. As Professor Thomas I. Emerson later wrote: "The result was certainly favorable to a free press. Put the other way, a contrary result would have been a disaster. It would have made the press subject to a very considerable extent of advance restriction. It would have changed the whole relationship between the press and Government."

In retrospect, the entire Pentagon Papers case was based on flawed premises. The law required the courts to assume that restraints on publication would be effective when, in fact, they were not and there was little reason to expect them to be. The law also required the courts to assume that they could predict the effects of publication when neither they nor anyone else could do so. The efforts at making such predictions were, particularly among some appellate judges, tilted in favor of the government on the basis of the view (as summarized by Justice Harlan) that the courts should defer to the executive branch of the Government in determining "the probable impact of disclosure on the national security."

What occurred during the last two weeks of June 1971 was thus a continuing series of restraints upon publications entered by the courts, despite the extraordinary frailty of the government's case. Assuming that under some circumstances in which claims of national security were asserted, pre-publication limits would be proper, Judge

Gurfein first restrained the *Times* from publishing so that he could consider the matter; so, in turn, did the court of appeals; so, too, did the Supreme Court itself in the *Washington Post* case, which the newspaper had won in the lower courts. It was all perfectly logical. But each delay violated the core principle that, as Justice Brennan put it, "the First Amendment tolerates absolutely no prior judicial restraints of the press predicated upon surmise or conjecture that untoward consequences may result."

There is a problem with Justice Brennan's argument—the same one we were forced to address when Judge Gurfein asked us to persuade the *Times* to cease publication voluntarily so that he could have the chance to study the matter. If prior restraints are to be permitted at all, how can a court not take enough time to study the matter thoroughly? And if the process of judicial consideration itself leads to interference with the immediacy of speech, is that not a price worth paying so as to avoid the "irresponsibly feverish" pace objected to by Justice Harlan? It is a serious argument to which there is a serious answer. There are worse demands than forcing judges to act quickly, particularly when weighed against the risks of a system of law that stops speech in its tracks simply because the government urges that result. Justice Brennan put it this way: unless and until the government demonstrates that publication "must inevitably, directly and immediately" bring about enormous national harm, no prior restraints on publication should be permitted for a moment.

Of course, another approach is one that would not garner a single vote on the Supreme Court today. If prior restraints on publication are often useless yet always dangerous, why not totally remove them from the arsenal of government attorneys? In this scheme criminal prosecutions could, if appropriate, still be commenced after publication; prior restraints before publication, so rarely even attempted in our history, could be avoided.

Views such as these were most often expressed in the Supreme Court by Justice Black. Rarely cited by the Supreme Court today, Justice Black is generally viewed by the Court (as he was by Bickel) as too "absolutist," too unyielding, too unresponsive to other societal needs. But the Pentagon Papers case may, even now, best be recalled in Justice Black's opinion, the last he would write on the Court:

> The press was to serve the governed, not the governors. The Government's power to censor the press was abolished so that the press would remain forever free to censure the Government. The press was protected so that it could bare the secrets of government and inform the people. Only a free and unrestrained press can effectively expose deception in government.

Black's approach, as I have said, was the third alternative Bickel and I outlined when we first sat down at my office at 2:30 a.m. on June 15, 1971, to discuss the case. We never really discussed that core principle to any extent in our briefs. But on my thirty-fifth birthday, nine days after the Supreme Court decided the case, my first toast was to Hugo Black.

CHAPTER 3

TRUTH AND THE FIRST AMENDMENT

Journalists understand better than most the limits of their craft. The "way we cover news," David Broder has written, "is to dig for facts, in hopes that they will yield an approximation of truth." Even when that approximation is offered by the best of journalists, its value is often transient and limited. "The press," Walter Lippmann elegantly observed, "is no substitute for institutions. It is like the beam of a searchlight that moves restlessly about, bringing one episode and then another out of darkness into vision. Men cannot do the work of this world by this light alone."

All these qualifications are true enough. When we add to them the fact that journalists sometimes provide something less than the truth and that much of what they print or broadcast is merely a recitation of what other people *say*, whether or not those statements are themselves true, members of the press should take care not to overstate the value of their calling. But there can be no overstating of the value of truth-telling by journalists, or of what the Supreme Court has characterized as the "overarching public interest . . . the dissemination of truth."

Despite this recognition, however, legal protection for the publication of truthful statements by the press is by no means total. Although truth is a complete defense in libel cases, many states allow recovery for the truthful disclosure of what are viewed as "private" facts of an individual's life. More troubling still, it remains unclear when, if ever, the publication of truthful statements may give rise to criminal liability. In a number of cases argued before the Supreme Court from the 1970s through the beginning of the twenty-first century, there has been a struggle over that very question. I argued two of those cases in 1978 and 1979 in my first two full arguments before the Supreme Court and wrote briefs in later cases concerning the same issue for many years afterward.

The 1978 case, *Landmark Communications v. Virginia*, arose out of the publication in the *Virginia Pilot*, a Norfolk newspaper, of an article about an investigation by a state judicial fitness panel that was considering whether or not to institute disciplinary action against a judge. H. Warrington Sharp sat on the Juvenile and Domestic Relations Court in Norfolk. A complaint had been filed by a citizen, claiming that he was incompetent, with the Virginia Judicial Inquiry and Review Commission, a state commission that assessed complaints filed by members of the public against the judiciary to determine if they raised serious enough issues for formal proceedings to be commenced. Under the Virginia statute, each complaint was initially considered in secret by the commission, and only if it was judged to be serious enough to require a hearing was it then made public; all aspects of the subsequent hearing were then also held in public. If the charges were not credible enough to require any further proceedings or were deemed too insignificant, they would be dismissed outright by the commission, with no public statement issued indicating that they had ever been filed.

Virginia was one of forty-seven states that provided some sort of mechanism for judicial inquiry and disciplinary procedures, and all of them provided for the confidentiality of the initial proceedings in which a panel was deciding whether the claim was strong enough to warrant a further consideration. But of all the states that mandated the confidentiality of such proceedings, only two, Virginia and Hawaii, provided for criminal sanctions to be imposed on the press or other non-participants in the commission process if they disclosed any confidential material of which they, by one means or another, had learned.

The article in the *Virginia Pilot* of October 4, 1975, was clear-cut. Under the headline "Hearing Held About Judge," the piece disclosed that a two-day hearing had been conducted by members of the state commission that "apparently stemmed from charges of incompetence against the 55-year-old judge." It noted that no formal complaint had been filed by the commission against Sharp, "indicating either that the five-man panel found insufficient cause for action or that the case is still under review." A picture of Judge Sharp, his eyes covered by sunglasses, accompanied the article.

A month after the story appeared, Landmark Communications, Inc., the owner of the *Virginia Pilot*, was indicted by the Commonwealth of Virginia for publishing the article. The indictment charged that the publisher "did unlawfully divulge the identity of a judge of a Court not of record, which said Judge was the subject of an investigation and hearing" by the commission. A trial was quickly held, and Landmark Communications was speedily convicted of a misdemeanor and fined fifty dollars.

For the publisher, being convicted of a crime for accurately reporting the name of a sitting judge then under investigation raised a major issue of principle. Landmark appealed to the Supreme Court of Virginia, which affirmed the conviction by a 6-1 vote. According to the court, the revelation of the judge's name had created a "clear and present danger" to "the orderly administration of justice." The "requirement of confidentiality in Commission proceedings," the court concluded, served three purposes: the protection of the reputation of an individual judge "by shielding him from publicity involving frivolous complaints"; protection of "public confidence in the judicial system by preventing a disclosure of a complaint" until "the Commission has determined the charge is well-founded"; and protection of complainants and witnesses "from possible recrimination" by keeping their names secret unless their complaint was deemed meritorious.

I was retained by Landmark Communications to file papers in the United States Supreme Court urging that body to rule that the newspaper's conduct was protected by the First Amendment and thus to set aside the criminal conviction. Our primary argument was straightforward: What the newspaper had published was true. It had not obtained the information illegally, and the essence of the alleged offense was nothing more or less than reporting the truth about complaints about how a public official performed his public role. How could that be a crime?

The case, our brief argued, raised "anew a question which penetrates to the core of our concept of self-government. It is nothing less than whether the press may be punished for printing the truth about a public official in connection with his public duties."

When the court granted a writ of certiorari, thus agreeing to hear the case, I began, with my partner, Dean Ringel, the task of preparing for oral argument. While I had worked closely with Professor Bickel on the Pentagon Papers case, he had made the oral argument for the *Times* in the Supreme Court.* And while I had shared the argument in

---

*Bickel had died, tragically young, of cancer in 1974.

105

the *Nebraska Press Association* case five years later with the distinguished Washington attorney Barrett Prettyman Jr. (he had argued for twenty minutes, I for ten), I had never before argued a Supreme Court case on my own. Since arguments in that court are thirty minutes in length per side, and since most of the time consumed in argument is taken up with responses to questions of the Court, Dean and I devoted most of our preparation to three overlapping issues, ones that have consumed my attention in every later Supreme Court argument as well. The first was jurisprudential in nature. What rule of law were we urging the Court to adopt? How would it apply in any future case? What would be its impact on First Amendment legal doctrine?

The second was tactical. Usually, members of the Court take up almost all the time counsel is allotted in spirited question-and-answer exchanges. What was my core message? If I only had a brief time to argue to the Court, what, above all, did I want the justices to bear in mind?

Third, what questions might the Court ask that might be especially difficult for me to respond to? What answers should I give to those questions?

The core jurisprudential question raised by the case was evident. The Virginia Supreme Court had concluded that the statute was designed to meet a "clear and present danger" to the administration of justice in that commonwealth. The term "clear and present danger" had been first used in the Supreme Court in a series of rulings and dissents written by the legendary justice Oliver Wendell Holmes in the immediate aftermath of World War I in cases involving prosecution of Socialists and anarchists who had opposed American entry into the war and had urged people not to register for the draft to fight in it. The first of these cases was *Schenck v. United States*, a criminal prosecution of a Socialist Party official who had published leaflets during the war urging people to "demand the repeal" of the Conscription Act, to oppose the draft, and to resist "cunning politicians of a merciless capitalist press" who were seeking "wrongly and untruthfully" to "mold your thoughts." For this speech, which now seems so tame that it is difficult to comprehend how Charles Schenck could even have been prosecuted at any time other than one of near hysteria, he was convicted of conspiracy to cause "insubordination" in the armed forces and to "obstruct" recruiting. Justice Holmes, writing an affirmance of the conviction for the Supreme Court in 1919, had rather casually observed that "the question in every case is whether the words used are used in such circumstances and are of such a nature as to cause a clear and present danger that they will bring about the substantive evils that Congress has a right to prevent." That Schenck's conviction should have been affirmed after such a statement of the "question" indicates how weak the protections of a clear-and-present-danger test could be. In later cases in this area, in which Holmes had dissented, he had transformed the clear-and-present-danger test into one that was far more protective of free speech. "It is only the present danger of an immediate evil or an intent to bring it about," he wrote later in 1919, "that warrants Congress in setting a limit to the expression of opinion." But even this articulation of the test in one of Holmes's most glowing dissenting opinions, *Abrams v. United States,* required the sort of balancing that might be necessary with regard to speech supposedly imperiling national security interests, but which I thought was hardly required with respect to truthful speech about the competence of sitting judges.

Certainly any clear and present danger test was far less protective than the rule that our briefs had urged upon the Court, and that I meant to focus on in argument. Our contention was that truthful speech about public officials in the course of their public duties should never give rise to criminal liability. That was the message, as well, that we wished most to leave with the Court, even if I had had the chance to say nothing else.

The article, I kept repeating to myself as I practiced for the argument, was all true; it concerned a public official and, more specifically, a challenge to his competence in office; the newspaper had done nothing inappropriate, not to say illegal, other than reporting the truth about the proceedings in which the public official was embroiled.

There was one other point that demanded attention. Virginia was virtually unique in concluding that it required criminal penalties to guarantee that its system of confidentiality remain effective. Every other state, with the exception of Hawaii, that had such a system simply relied upon the members of the judicial commission, and all personnel associated with it, to abide by the requirements imposed upon them regarding confidentiality. If they did not, criminal sanctions could be imposed against them, but not against a third or fourth or fifth party who had learned the confidential information from someone else. On what basis, I prepared to argue, could Virginia ever insist that criminal sanctions against the press were so required?

The third area to which Dean and I devoted most of our time was more difficult: What questions might the Court ask that would be especially problematic? What were the best answers we could provide to them? While there were a number of areas that we discussed, two seemed particularly troublesome. Suppose, we thought, a draft opinion of the Supreme Court itself had leaked to the press before it had been released to the public. Or suppose that some other internal document— a memorandum from one of the law clerks on the Court to his or her justice or, worse yet, one from one justice to another—had been leaked. Was I prepared to argue that the publication of that material as well *could* not be made criminal? Our answer was clear enough: of course, I would say, the publication of truthful information, lawfully acquired, about the activities of public officials could not be made criminal even if it came from the Supreme Court itself. But the thought of making that assertion to members of the Court itself was unappealing.

There was an even harder potential question on which we had to focus. Information submitted to grand juries has historically been kept secret, and it has long been a crime for prosecutors or others connected with the grand jury process to reveal such information publicly. Under current federal law, however, a witness before a grand jury can publicly disclose his or her own testimony, and the press is free to publish whatever it learns from that witness. Suppose, however, that a federal law did make criminal the disclosure by the press or others of the substance of grand jury testimony. Suppose the press received such information and published it. Would we take the same position that there, too, publication could not be made a criminal offense? Again, our answer was clear enough: absolutely. If we were going to take the position that truth-telling about public officials in the course of their public duties was fully protected by the First Amendment, we had to do so unequivocally. Nonetheless, I hoped to avoid dealing with that sensitive subject with the Court as well. The reputation of judges, sensitive as that topic might be, seemed far less a potential source of concern to the Court than the internal workings of the judiciary or the privacy of grand jury materials. But our approach to all of them had to be consistent.

ARGUMENT

Appearing before the Supreme Court as chief counsel in a significant case often reminds me of taking the field in a strangely transformed sort of baseball game. Counsel who is arguing walks to home plate, the podium in the Court which faces the nine justices. As in baseball (and baseball uniquely among our sports), the batter is alone, confronted by all nine fielders, in the Supreme Court, the fielders are also pitchers, each of them throwing questions at his or her own pace, sometimes one after another, sometimes nearly simultaneously. Balls thrown by each of the nine pass one another in the air, some pitched hard, fast, and straight; others high and inside, obviously designed to keep the lawyer/batter from digging in too comfortably at the plate. Some of the questions are curveballs, sinkers, or virtually unhittable knuckleballs. But the lawyer/batter must hit them all cleanly, and if he or she does not, the game may be lost on a single pitch alone. An added fillip is that the nine pitchers are also the *umpires*. As a result, however wild their pitches may be, they must be treated as strikes.

The argument for the Landmark hearing started

111

slowly. I outlined for the Court the central facts of the case—that the article was true and that, indeed, the truth of the article was the essence of the crime. I described the evidence offered by the commonwealth and Landmark's responses at both the trial court level and in the Supreme Court of Virginia. Justice William H. Rehnquist, ten years later appointed Chief Justice and already viewed as uncongenial to broad First Amendment arguments, posed the first question. Was there, he asked, "anything in the record of which we may properly take cognizance of how Landmark learned of the facts that it published?" I knew the answer but kicked myself mentally, not only because I had not predicted the question, but because we were potentially veering dangerously in the direction of rearguing the issue of the confidential sources of journalists, which the Court had decided (however ambiguously) in the *Branzburg* case six years earlier. The press had lost that one, feelings were still ruffled about it, and it would be of no possible value to me to proceed down that line, except for what was absolutely required in order to respond to Rehnquist's question. Accordingly, my answers were brief. Was there anything in the record? I answered, "No, there is nothing in the record whatsoever." Rehnquist pursued the point, observing, "I suppose only the editor of the paper knows that. Would that be a reasonable assumption?" Again, I offered the quickest possible response: "I think it is a reasonable assumption," I acknowledged, "that the editor and the journalists involved knew that."

I was then asked a more difficult question, although a far friendlier one, by Justice John Paul Stevens, a jurist generally sympathetic to claims rooted in the Bill of Rights but not a predictable First Amendment supporter. He had noticed in our briefs that neither side had mentioned the name of the judge referred to by the *Virginia Pilot*. Would Virginia's statute apply to me personally if I told the Supreme Court itself the name of the judge? Here was an absolutely no-lose question: the broader the statute, the less likely it was that it could withstand constitutional scrutiny. At the same time, however, the Court had, in earlier cases, decided that material in public court files could be freely reported, and Judge Sharp's name was certainly to be found there. I had to try to take advantage of the friendly question while avoiding an answer that took such an unpersuasively overbroad reading of the statute as to lose credibility with the Court. I tried this tactic:

> Mr. Justice Stevens, I think it would unless there was some other privilege which protected me because I was in this court-room. I have little doubt that it would apply to me if I were to walk outside and provide the name of the judge [to the

press], with one caveat, that this Court has decided, of course, that once papers are publicly filed in court, the press may print with impunity what is contained in them. So I suppose in this particular case, since there was a criminal prosecution . . . that I could with impunity speak. If there had been no prosecution, if the newspaper article had been printed and no prosecution had followed, it seems to me that the Virginia statute must apply by the terms of the opinion of the Virginia Supreme Court if I were to repeat to someone else the information contained in the article.

It was a long way around the barn, but there was no avoiding a complex answer. I could not go so far as to say that I could not even mention Judge Sharp's name, since it had been set forth in the public court records of this case itself. At the same time, however, that was the only reason that I was free to mention the name. Hence, the long, none-too-elegant response.

Chief Justice Burger then asked a more helpful question, demonstrating the extraordinary breadth of the statute. Our exchange, like an eighteenth-century minuet, went as follows:

Q: How would the statute apply, if it would apply, to the person who released the information?

A: It would apply to the person who released the information.

Q: He or she would be guilty of the same crime.

A: Yes, Your Honor.

Q: Even if it was the chairman of the Commission.

A: Indeed. There is no—

Q: Or a member of the Supreme Court of the State of Virginia, the commonwealth of Virginia?

A: Yes, Your Honor.

What bliss! Now the statute seemed so broad that it could not possibly pass First Amendment scrutiny. My argument had presupposed that it was constitutional to make criminal the release of Judge Sharp's name by any of the participants before the Virginia commission or anyone else connected with the commission. But the chief justice's question opened the door to a broader critique. What sort of statute would make it criminal for a state supreme court justice to disclose the name of the person who had publicly announced the identity of another judge?

The first genuine bit of trouble on the horizon surfaced when Justice Byron White asked me his first question. I cannot think of a single answer that I made in the years that I argued before the Court while Justice White sat on it that seemed to satisfy him. While I won a number of cases that I argued before him, and he voted for my side in most of them, I never had the sense that anything I said pleased him. White, a former all-American running back (whose much-repeated college nickname, Whizzer, was one that appalled him), was no fan of press claims for broad First Amendment protection. He invariably asked questions that were both pointed and powerful.

One of the issues on which the Court had not yet expressed any view at the time of the *Landmark* argument was whether the press should receive any additional or special protection under the First Amendment, given that that amendment itself made reference to protecting "the freedom of the press" in addition to "the freedom of speech." Justice Potter Stewart had made just that argument in a speech he had delivered at the Yale Law School in the immediate aftermath of the Watergate revelations by the *Washington Post*. The "institutional" press, he argued, was the only business referred to by name in the Constitution, and was therefore entitled to more protection than other speakers might receive. I agreed with that contention but knew it would find no favor with Justice White and most other members of the Court.

Our exchange reflected White's effort to test my theory of the case by seeing if it was in fact dependent upon the notion that the press ought to receive more protection than anyone else, and my own effort to avoid taking that uncomfortable position while still not abandoning the argument:

Q: Is your submission that the statute is unconstitutional as applied to anybody or just the press?

A: It is my submission today that it is unconstitutional as applied to anyone who is not the party before the Commission. We have a press case today. I think that has bearing on Your Honors' decision, but I do not argue to you today that the statute is unconstitutional as it applies to a participant before the Commission itself. It does seem to me that there may be some problems with that, but that is not the heart of my argument.

Q: Let's assume—so your argument is that even if it is wholly constitutional to forbid the participants from disclosing anything, nevertheless it is unconstitutional as applied to the press.

A: Yes, Your Honor.

At this, Justice Stewart, a committed defender of First Amendment press rights, intervened on my behalf, noting that all I needed to argue was that the statute was unconstitutional as applied to Landmark itself in the criminal case being heard by the Court. I quickly agreed and ran, once again, into Justice White, who immediately asked me if it was not true that my arguments did not "question the underlying validity of the statute as applied to participants" before the judicial commission. When I responded that I had not gone that far, Chief Justice Burger reentered the fray, asking if the judge who was the subject of the inquiry would violate the statute by calling a press conference and saying, "I welcome this inquiry and, of course, I will be vindicated swiftly."

Now I had the chance to clarify my earlier answer. "It seems to me," I said, "that the only way to read the statute is that the judge would have violated the provision of the statute; the newspaper, if it prints what the judge said, would have violated it; and any reader of the newspaper who repeats what the newspaper said would have violated it." That was the question I had wanted and the answer I had ached to give.

At this point, I was confronted with a question from Justice Rehnquist for which I was totally unprepared. Did I think, he asked, that my client's protection was "in any way diminished by the fact that it's a corporation"? At the time Rehnquist asked me the question, I did not know (as I should have) that the Court was focusing in another case dealing with the degree to which corporations have free-speech rights. I responded by first observing generally (as I contemplated, somewhere else in my brain, a better answer to the question) that I knew of no case that suggested that a corporation that owns a newspaper was not entitled to full First Amendment rights. When Justice Rehnquist observed, with too much pleasure for any comfort on my part, that I seemed to be saying that "corporations and individuals stand on an equal footing," I quickly responded that that was true. Again Justice Stewart came to my rescue, observing that that was true "so far as the protection of the press goes," a question/comment that I first repeated and then expanded upon: "At least so far as the press. Certainly it has never been suggested otherwise in any of your press decisions. In *New York Times v. Sullivan*"—the Court's great libel ruling of the 1960s providing sweeping protection for speech in libel cases—"there was no less protection because it was a corporation." When Justice White then returned again to the question of the degree to which I was relying on the notion that the *Virginia Pilot* was "press," as distinguished from any other speaker (a subject I was becoming increasingly uncomfortable dealing with), we had the following exchange:

Q: Is there any reason to think that if it is so as to the press, it's different as to freedom of expression?

A: As a general matter, Your Honor, it seems to me that this case could be decided as a freedom-of-expression case without necessarily relying on the press clause itself. As I suggested earlier, I do think that the statute is unconstitutional for many of the same reasons we urge under the press clause under the speech clause as well if I were charged with a violation of the statute for repeating what I were to read in a newspaper. We do have a press clause case today. I think we are bolstered even more by the fact that it is that kind of case and that this kind of statute strikes so directly, as we view it, at press freedom. But if that were not so, I think most of the arguments that I am making to you today would also apply.

The problem with that answer and the dangers of it were quickly made apparent by the chief justice's then asking me whether I was suggesting "the First Amendment protection reaches only to corporations which published newspapers." Once again, his articulation of the question allowed me to answer cleanly, stating, "No, Your Honor, but it certainly does reach corporations which publish newspapers."

At this point, the Court had apparently finished toying with me for a few moments and allowed me to return to my argument. Like a mouse freed from a tormenting cat, I returned to my prior path, arguing that truthful speech should not be criminally punished, and certainly not so when based upon the desire to protect the reputation of judges or for the other reasons articulated by the Virginia Supreme Court. As for the clear-and-present doctrine, I plunged ahead, arguing that it was not a test that should commend itself to the Court. Why not? Justice Rehnquist asked. I responded that more recent cases of the Court had provided more protection than any application of the clear-and-present-danger test could. Would I, Justice Rehnquist asked, take the same position with regard to Justice Holmes's initial formulation of the test in *Schenck*? Wondering how I had gotten into the position of arguing with Justice Holmes, I responded, yes, *Schenk* did provide inadequate protection, since on the face of that ruling it did not offer "anything like the kind of First Amendment protection which this Court has since come" to provide.

Suppose, Justice Stevens now asked me, that there existed proof that Judge Sharp (whose name was never actually mentioned in the argument) could not function effectively if his name were disclosed on the eve of a trial. Would that make any difference? When I responded that "that was a social price which the First Amendment requires us to pay," Justice Stevens told me that he, like Justice Rehnquist, was unclear as to precisely what legal test I was relying on. I responded that rather than utilize a loose and unpredictable clear-and-present-danger test, the Court should, so far as possible, consider speech categorically, asking first whether this was "the kind of area in which there can be any limits" on free expression at all. If the answer was no, the question was resolved. Here, I said, "at least with respect to truthful speech about public officials," there was no room for criminal sanctions at all. Back came Justice Rehnquist, observing that I seemed to disagree with the heart of Justice Holmes's landmark opinion in *Schenck*. That test, I pointed out again, had been much eroded through the years and should not be resuscitated by the Court.

Justice Thurgood Marshall, hero of the civil rights movement and the eloquent advocate who had argued *Brown v. Board of Education*, which had led to the end of segregated public schools, then offered a lifeline. What showing, he asked, had Virginia made that there was, in fact, clear and present danger resulting from publication? I breathed more easily. Here was an ideological ally, a sure vote, helping me by asking a question to which the answer could be crisp. "The State showed nothing," I said. As Justice Marshall nodded approvingly, Justice Lewis Powell, often the decisive vote on the Court and a man who had been a distinguished lawyer in private practice in Virginia for many years, responded by pointing out that the Supreme Court of Virginia had concluded that publication of the judge's name did pose a clear and present danger to the administration of justice. "Yes," I agreed, the court had said that, but it did not and could not base that opinion on the legislative history of the statute, since no such history existed. Chief Justice Burger, to whom I felt increasingly indebted as the argument proceeded, now intervened and asked if it would not be fair to say that the Supreme Court of Virginia had "indulged in a presumption" that the reason the Virginia legislature had enacted the statute was to protect the administration of justice. That, I responded, was very fair to say.

At this point, I took a fleeting glance at my watch. I had only a few minutes left. As I contemplated summing up, Justice White chose to attack on the very issue I had been most concerned about, grand juries.

Q: Are there State laws against the press publishing confidential information from grand juries?

A: There may be. There is none in Virginia or in New York. I don't know of any, but I could certainly—

Q: But anyway, I would take it that situation would be involved in the decision in this case.

Now I had to really address the most painful question in the case. Slipping into the conditional tense, I tried to answer this way: "It could be, Your Honor. It depends on whether, for one thing, the Court were to view the grand jury at least as possibly different because of the historic role of secrecy in grand jury proceedings. But I would say, Your Honor, that it would be our submission to you at least that a law which made it a crime to print a leak from a grand jury would be unconstitutional for some of the same reasons that we urge upon you in this case."

As Justice White listened and leaned back in his chair looking unsatisfied, Chief Justice Burger rejoined the roast, asking whether it was not true that a grand jury was concerned exclusively with criminal conduct, as opposed to the fitness of a judge for duty. Wasn't that an important difference?

"Yes," I said, "that is one very relevant difference."

The Ping-Pong game continued, with Justice White once again grasping the paddle and slamming:

Q: Which way does it cut?
A: Well, I think it would cut at least in favor of us in this case and make the grand jury case, if anything, a little bit harder.
Q: Do you think it would be hard for you to win this case and lose the grand jury case?
A: I hope so, Your Honor.
Q: You hope.

At this point what I hoped for most was a conclusion to the argument. I was sure I had a winning case, was confident that we would triumph, and simply trusted that the pummeling I was enduring was more for sport than because my case was actually imperiled. My face having flushed a bit when Justice White disparagingly repeated my "hope," I responded by saying "I think so." Now Justice Rehnquist reentered the game:

Q: I don't quite see why you responded to the Chief Justice and Justice White's question that the difference in the nature of the Commission as opposed to a grand jury cuts in your favor rather than the other way.

A: To the extent what is involved in the Commission is a determination of the fitness of public officials for their public service, it seems to us that, if anything, that cuts more in favor of fuller freedom to publish.

It was again White's turn:

Q: What about the facts presented to a grand jury that say a high public official or well-known private businessman is guilty of a crime?

At this point I could not restrain my admiration for Justice White, who had posed a superb question. Why, I asked myself ruefully, had I started down the road of saying that the grand jury case would be harder than mine, when the easier answer to defend would have been that they were the same, and that I should win on both? I knew the answer: I was so concerned about the grand jury hypothetical that I wanted to let the Court think that while perhaps some other year it *might* rule differently in that case, it didn't have to think about that today. But the price I was paying in being buffeted back and forth was enormous. I tried again, reminding the court that "the fact that President Nixon was an unindicted co-conspirator was printed in the press" before it was officially revealed. That was grand jury material, and yet surely that could not be made criminal. As for the question of which was a harder case for me—a grand jury leak or a leak about the identity of a judge—I repeated once again that *if* it was necessary to assess the relative degree of First Amendment protection of information about the fitness of public officials for their jobs, and about potential criminal culpability of some entity or person before a grand jury, more First Amendment protection should be afforded to the former.

With only a few minutes left before my time ran out, Justice Stevens asked me a number of brief questions, and I finally returned to my seat. It had been quite an introduction for me to arguing for a complete thirty minutes in the Supreme Court: fifty-four judicial questions and comments. Years later, when I saw Albert Brooks play a television journalist in *Broadcast News* who perspired so much when on the air that his shirt looked like he had just returned from a swim, I wondered if I had presented the same appearance after my *Landmark* argument.

But if I had had difficulties in dealing with all the potential First Amendment ramifications of the position I was asserting, Assistant Attorney General James E. Kulp of Virginia faced far more obstacles on the merits. Justice Marshall, who had been relatively quiet as I spoke, leapt to the chase:

> Q: Am I correct that Virginia is the only State that has this criminal provision—
> A: No, sir, the State of Hawaii.
> Q: —other than Hawaii.
> A: Yes, sir.
> Q: Those are the only two.
> A: Yes, sir. And there are three other—
> Q: So any broad statements you make about the other 48 States is just not true.

Well, I thought, Justice White may have mocked me for using the word "hope," but at least he had not said that anything I had said was untrue. And White himself was no less tough on my opponent:

> Q: General Kulp, I take it you are saying that the protection of the judge and the

protection of the legal system generally against insult are secondary justifications for this statute, that you are saying that it is necessary to have an effective system to offer confidentiality. Is that your submission?

A: Yes, sir.

Q: Would you defend that kind of a statute?

A: No, sir, I don't think that is what the Supreme Court of Virginia, as well as the statute, has indicated that it is merely drawn—

Q: If it was protection for the judge and protection for the judicial system generally that was involved, I would think you would defend that kind of a statute.

A: No, sir. I think the cases from this Court have been clear in that respect, that, in other words, a judge, as any public official, may certainly be criticized, the administration of justice may be criticized, and we don't have any argument about that.

But if that was so, Justice White then observed, the reason offered by the Virginia Supreme Court about protecting judicial reputation, or, indeed, insult to the judicial system generally, could hardly be credited. As Kulp agreed, I glowed.

The remainder of Kulp's argument was taken up with the scope of the statute. Chief Justice Burger observed that if a lawyer announced at a press conference that he was filing statements accusing a judge of misconduct with the commission and handed a copy of the statement to the press, that would violate the statute. If, on the other hand, he made the statement and did not file the charges, First Amendment protection would be available. He looked at Kulp, who unhappily agreed.

My time was almost up and I was, despite all the verbal horseplay with the Court, reasonably confident of victory. I chose to offer no rebuttal to Kulp.

THE DECISION

The decision of the Court was unanimous in our favor. Chief Justice Burger, writing for himself and five other members (Justices Brennan and Stevens having recused themselves from participating) concluded that, while it was unnecessary to adopt the categorical approach to the issue that I had urged (to the effect that truthful reporting about public officials in connection with their public duties was always insulated from the imposition of criminal sanctions by the First Amendment), "the publication Virginia seeks to punish under its statute lies near the core of the First Amendment." Acknowledging, for purposes of argument, that confidentiality of commission proceedings serves legitimate state interests, the Court rejected the notion that these interests were sufficient to justify the imposition of criminal sanctions on nonparticipants in proceedings such as *Landmark*.

Perhaps most satisfying to me, the Court not only questioned the relevance of the clear-and-present-danger test to Landmark's claims—even Holmes could not carry the day for Virginia—but noted, in language frequently quoted by the Supreme Court thereafter, that it was insufficient for the Virginia Supreme Court simply to defer to the legislative judgment that there was some sort of clear and present danger. "Properly applied," the Court's opinion concluded, "the test requires a court to make its own inquiry into the imminence and magnitude of the danger said to flow from the particular utterance and then to balance the character of the evil as well as its likelihood against the need for free and unfettered expression." Putting it more bluntly two paragraphs later, the Court concluded that "deference to a legislative finding cannot limit judicial inquiry when First Amendment rights are at stake."

Justice Stewart wrote a separate concurrence relying on the press clause of the Constitution. No one else on the Court referred to it.

So we had won. But how broad was the victory? At the least we knew that if any asserted state interests could justify a criminal law's punishing a newspaper for truthfully disclosing information it had lawfully gathered, the interests would have to be stronger than that in the *Landmark* case. How much stronger was unclear, as was the question of whether *any* state interest could ever justify criminal punishment for doing nothing more than telling the truth.

THE *DAILY MAIL* CASE

A year later I was back in the Supreme Court arguing in a case that, even more than the *Landmark Communications* case, would help to answer the question regarding the breadth of the court's ruling. This time the reportage concerned not a public official, but a minor who had engaged in criminal conduct.

In December 1977, in St. Albans, West Virginia, a town of fourteen thousand people thirteen miles outside of Charleston, Arthur Clinton Smith, age fourteen, set a bulletin board on fire at the Hayes Junior High School, for which he was brought before a juvenile court. As a result, Arthur's mother prepared to have him switch schools, though she did not follow through because her son felt that he had too many friends at Hayes.

Stuart Wayne Perrock was not one of them. It was Perrock, a key witness to the arson, who testified against Smith. The two became enemies following the fire and, as with many boys their age, their disputes played out in a series of fistfights. Smith told his parents that he wanted to "whip" Perrock.

On the morning of February 9, 1978, children filled the halls outside the school gymnasium as they prepared to enter their classroom for their 8:10 classes. While passing in the hall, Perrock and Smith exchanged words as they had many times before. Rather than fighting, Stuart took out a .22-caliber pistol and shot Arthur with three bullets to the chest. Seven eyewitnesses, including Stuart's brother, looked on in horror as Arthur died within four minutes of the shooting. Stuart immediately ran into the woods across from the school. As police helicopters, cars, and patrolmen searched for Stuart, they discovered a message scrawled into the snow: "Tell Smith I'm sorry." As classes were resuming at 11:00, Perrock was captured carrying the gun and a knife. He was returned to the school grounds by helicopter. The fourteen-year-old boy who had tried to apologize to his victim in the snow emerged from the helicopter handcuffed and surrounded by policemen. He was brought before the juvenile court in St. Albans, where, consistent with the requirements of law, all further proceedings against him were conducted in secret.

At 10:30 a.m., while Perrock was still attempting his escape in the woods, the *Charleston Daily Mail* was routinely monitoring the police band radio frequency. When it learned of the killing, reporters Mary Schnack and Chambers Williams were assigned to cover it. These journalists learned most of the details of the incident from eyewitnesses and the police. This information included the names of both students.

When the reporters returned to the office with their story, the staff and editors of the *Daily Mail* faced a difficult decision. A law existed in West Virginia that required, among other things, that newspapers obtain written permission from the court before printing the name of a juvenile in the custody of juvenile authorities. The purpose of the law was "to minimize the youngster's penetration into all negative labeling, institutional processes." "Adverse labeling," the state concluded, would only serve as a setback toward rehabilitation of the child. Violators were subject to up to six months in prison and a fine. In light of the law, the *Daily Mail* reported the story that afternoon without identifying the name of the suspect.

Later that day, a Charleston radio station, WCHS-AM, disclosed Perrock's name in the course of reporting the story. The following morning WCAW and WWAF, also in Charleston, mentioned Perrock's name on their early-morning broadcasts as well. Journalists on the *Daily Mail* heard these radio reports on their way to work.

The *Charleston Gazette* is a morning newspaper, and as such its first edition following the shooting was released the next morning. The *Gazette* also weighed the legal implications of identifying Perrock and decided to disobey the statute. Not only did the *Gazette* disclose his name in an

133

article and in the caption to a picture of him emerging from the helicopter, but a subsequent article written by Don Marsh, the editor of the *Gazette*, focused on the question of why the paper did so. He defended the decision to break the law by stating, "My own feeling is that the public interest in being informed of acts of violence in schools outweighs the undesirability of breaking a law, particularly a bad one." He described his views on the matter by writing that "the state juvenile statute is the kind of law that leaves juveniles almost immune from punishment in areas where youth crime is a serious problem." Marsh, who realized that he would face a legal challenge as a result of this decision, stated that the law was "unwise and possibly illegal," and that the *Gazette* "is willing to do whatever is necessary to have that belief tested as fully as courts allow."

By the time the staff of the *Daily Mail* met to discuss the afternoon paper, Perrock's name had been widely publicized in the *Gazette* and on at least three radio stations. At eight a.m. they phoned their counsel to ask for advice based on the recent developments. Since Stuart Perrock's name was by now readily available to the public, he concluded that it was senseless to continue to suppress it. The *Daily Mail* took the advice and printed Perrock's name in its February 10 edition. A few weeks later, indictments were returned against the corporate owners of the *Daily Mail* and the *Gazette*, as well as their publishers, editors, and the journalists who wrote the articles.

On June 27, 1978, the West Virginia Supreme Court of Appeals held the statute unconstitutional as an impermissible prior restraint on freedom of the press. The United States Supreme Court then agreed to hear the case, and it was at this time that I first became involved.

The West Virginia statute was similar to the one we had successfully challenged in the *Landmark Communications* case in Virginia in one critical way and dissimilar in another. Like the Virginia statute, the West Virginia one also criminalized the reportage of truthful speech of significant public interest. However, in this case, the speech did not concern charges of impropriety against a sitting judge, but criminal charges against a minor. In this case, moreover, the statute was not designed to protect the administration of justice, but the reputation of the child who had committed the criminal act.

There was another respect in which the West Virginia law differed from Virginia's. As the West Virginia court held, its statute had all the features of a prior restraint on speech, since it required judicial permission before publication was authorized. It was not a flat ban; it was, rather, a ban that could be lifted by a judge if he or she believed it was appropriate to do so.

On one level, this made the statute seem potentially less offensive than the one we had challenged in Virginia. On another, however, it made it more offensive still. Prior restraints on speech—limitations requiring the permission of some sort of state entity to speak—have been treated with particular severity by the courts. Viewed as similar in nature to licensing statutes, seventeenth-century English laws under which permission had to be sought from the Crown before certain topics could be addressed, prior restraints have always been viewed as limitations (in the words first written by Professor Bickel in our brief in the Pentagon Papers case and then adopted by the Supreme Court in the *Nebraska Press Association* case) that "fall on speech with a brutality and a finality all their own."

Dean Ringel and I quickly decided to focus on the twin arguments that the statute was a prior restraint on speech and that it was a punishment of truthful speech for including information that had been lawfully obtained and that related to matters of public interest. We had learned from the Supreme Court's ruling in the *Landmark Communications* case that only competing interests of the highest order could pass constitutional muster, and we therefore emphasized that the Supreme Court, in the 1974 case of *Davis v. Alaska*, had already addressed the question of how to balance the right of a juvenile's confidentiality against the Sixth Amendment rights of a defendant to confront his accusers. In that case, the Court had concluded that cross-examination of a witness who was a juvenile offender could include information about his being on probation, notwithstanding "whatever temporary embarrassments might result" to the witness or his family. If the prosecution insisted on using the juvenile to make its case, the Supreme Court had concluded, the defendant must be permitted "to probe into the influence of possible bias" in his testimony by referring to the witness's probation for juvenile offenses.

Oral argument took place on March 20, 1979. I tried to remember the lessons I had learned from the *Landmark Communications* case. There was no justification, I told myself, for being surprised by any question from the Court. I had spent months on the case, weeks in preparation for my argument. The members of the Court and their clerks had a hundred and fifty arguments to prepare for to my one. This time I was well aware of every other case that the Court had before it that could possibly bear on the *Daily Mail* matter.

Our client had won in the lower court, and so the first argument was by Cletus B. Hanley, a special assistant attorney general from West Virginia.

After Hanley finished his introduction, Justice Stewart quickly led him to concede that the statute at issue made no distinction between a situation in which what was published was "common knowledge" and one where it was not: the publication of both was criminal. Justice Blackmun then asked Hanley if he agreed—he did—that there was no claim in the case that the newspaper had obtained information illegally.

The statute, as written, applied only to newspapers and not to radio and television disclosure of a juvenile's name. When asked by Justice Blackmun why that was so, Hanley answered that the more modern means of communication were excluded because they were regulated by the federal government. Hanley then sought to distinguish the *Daily Mail* from the *Landmark* case by stating that the basis of the earlier ruling was the Court's view "that the judiciary does not need protection." This, he argued, was not true of minors, whose reputations did require protection. Justice White then asked Hanley a question on which I had not (to my frustration) focused— whether it is "against the law in your state for a police officer or judge to tell the press who committed the crime." When Hanley conceded that there was no such law, White observed that under the West Virginia law, "no matter how the press learned it, the statute would apply." Hanley agreed that that was true.

A few moments later Justice Blackmun returned to the issue of why West Virginia had not, if it cared so strongly about the reputations of juveniles, prohibited radio and television stations from broadcasting their names. Hanley responded inaccurately that there was a federal statute that made it illegal to print juveniles' names. When pressed by Justice Marshall on that point, he then conceded that while there were no federal limitations against publication, there existed federal power to do so. Justice Stewart wound up the questioning by asking when the West Virginia statute had been passed, and Hanley responded that while he was not sure, he thought that such a statute had been on the books for about thirty years.

I began my argument by pointing out that the statute had in fact been adopted in 1915 and that the present case was the first prosecution under it against any newspaper. Justice Stewart then observed that the statute's "limitation to the press" was fully explainable by the fact that it had been adopted "when there was no television and very little radio."

I turned next to the question of whether the statute was a prior restraint and quickly ran into hostile questioning from Justice Rehnquist. How, he asked me, could I argue that a prior restraint on publication of a name, subject to the juvenile court judge's approval, was worse than a statute that banned all references to a juvenile's name with no chance of an exception at all? I responded by emphasizing the difference between prior restraints and other statutes:

> If instead of a licensing statute, Mr. Justice Rehnquist, you had a flat ban on any kind of publication, I dare say it would likely be unconstitutional but it wouldn't be a prior

restraint. And the fact that the essence of this crime as alleged and the essence of this misdemeanor, which can lead to six-month jail sentences, here is not obtaining the permission of the court and printing without that permission in our view makes this a prior restraint—and in a far more classic sense than most of the prior restraint cases which this Court has had in recent years, far more than the Pentagon Papers case or the *Nebraska Press Association* case.

Justice Rehnquist seemed unpersuaded.

Q: And yet if the paper here had simply chosen to abide the statute and not seek permission and, say, were prohibited, as the editorial indicated they were, from publishing, it would have the same effect as the criminal statute and not be a prior restraint.

A: On the particular facts of this case, I think the paper would have been able to defend and indeed if a criminal case proceeds, would be able to defend on the grounds that permission wasn't needed. But the essence as I understand it—one of the things that is wrong with prior restraints, as I understand it, is that it establishes a censorial authority with a relationship to the censored entity which is one of the things that this Court has indicated it doesn't like, that it is particularly loath to accept in prior restraint statutes.

Now, I appreciate the fact that it is on its face anomalous to say that because there is this provision in the statute which says that you can go to a court and get permission, that that makes it a prior restraint, but in our view that is always what licensing statutes have. It is precisely that provision which brings into account the essential prior restraint relationship of the censored to the party who is doing the censoring, that you have to go and ask permission.

I thought my answer had been reasonably well articulated (although, in retrospect, I would now drop the sappy reference to what the Court "doesn't like"), but I was brought up short by the next question from Justice Stewart, who asked me if I would not agree that even in the absence of the provision for judicial authority to publish, the statute would be unconstitutional. I saw blinking yellow lights before me as I began to phrase my answer. CAUTION: If Justice Stewart, my ideological ally, was unpersuaded by (or thought others might be unpersuaded by) the argument, it was time to move on.

The prior-restraint argument had been our first because that had been the basis of the ruling in our client's favor in the West Virginia courts and because I thought it was the stronger of our two positions. With the warning implicit in Justice Stewart's question that I might not succeed with that tactic, I moved quickly to our other argument, rooted in the *Landmark Communications* case itself, that the statute should fall because of its imposition of criminal punishment with respect to truthful speech. Justice Rehnquist, however, chose not to let the prior-restraint issue pass, and so we returned to the fray:

Q: But you can read some of our cases indicating that a prior restraint is the most onerous of all prohibitions against publication, and I take it in your answer to my brother Stewart and my own question that that isn't necessarily the case.

A: Mr. Justice Rehnquist—

Q: It is most draconic.

A: —prior restraints by their nature are the most draconic restraints upon speech. That doesn't mean that a subsequent punishment statute in a particular case doesn't fall on speech with even greater brutality. Professor Chafee once wrote that if there were capital punishment for the advocacy of socialism, that that would have a pretty chilling effect. I would have no doubt that that would have more of a chilling effect on advocacy of socialism than this prior restraint statute would.

All I am saying is that you do have an established body of law about how to view prior restraints, it is our view that this is a prior restraint statute, and that that body of law ought to [provide] the overview with which you look at the statute.

Q: But prior restraint statutes aren't the most severe repressions of publication.

A: Prior restraint statutes, as this Court has indicated time and again, are to be viewed with particular harshness by this Court to see if there is an exception which allows the statute to stand, [and] this Court has indicated, as I understand all its prior restraint rulings, that prior restraints are presumptively unconstitutional, unlike other statutes, [and] that prior restraints bear a heavy burden, unlike certain other statutes.

Q: Why wouldn't a flat ban be even worse?

A: A flat ban may be even worse, just as a flat ban on publication of all literature by the King of England would have been worse than sending people to the censorial authority to get permission to print. Nonetheless, we have a body of law which says that prior restraints, because of the effects that they have, are particularly unconstitutional.

Chief Justice Burger came next with a question that I found ironic even as he asked it. We had placed figures in our brief demonstrating that the juvenile crime rate was increasing rapidly in the country and that it was therefore an especially newsworthy topic. The argument was a ruse, nothing less—an effort to appeal to some of the more conservative, less press-friendly members of the Court. Chief Justice Burger was himself one of the intended recipients of the message that the press serves a useful law-and-order function by publicizing crime and those who commit it. At the same time, however, we realized that whatever direction the juvenile crime rate was moving in, our legal arguments remained the same: By its nature the statute acted as a prior restraint that punished the truthful disclosure of lawfully obtained information of public interest. Chief Justice Burger now made me pay for our condescending effort to appeal to him:

Q: Mr. Abrams, I notice that you put—or at least you appear to put a good deal of weight on the fact that between 1960 and 1975, as we all know, there has been an enormous increase in juvenile crime and serious violent crime. Now, suppose the statistics were the other way, suppose it showed that juvenile crime was going down, would it make any difference to your constitutional point?

A: No, it would not, Mr. Chief Justice. I simply indicated that to indicate to you why the press might want to print that, for information of the Court, but that is not at the heart of our argument.

Q: It is really irrelevant, isn't it—

A: It is—

Q: —whether crime is going up or going down?

A: It is irrelevant as to the legal position of—

Q: It is a constitutional question.

A: Yes, sir. Yes, sir, it is.

Q: It is simply saying—

A: I suggested to you, since I thought you—

Q: It explains your interest, not—

A: —and that is the only reason that it is there.

Ugh.

Finally, I turned to the *Davis v. Alaska* case, which had held that the Sixth Amendment rights of a defendant accused by a juvenile effectively trumped the rights of the juvenile not to have his secret probation status revealed. I argued that if that was the case for the Sixth Amendment, the First Amendment should receive no less protection.

I then had another exchange with Justice Rehnquist about the fact that the statute applied only to newspapers, in which I argued that it simply could not achieve its end of aiding juvenile rehabilitation in light of its exclusion of radio, television, magazines, and even private conversations. Justice Rehnquist asked, in response, whether a newspaper might have particular impact since it could be read in a newspaper morgue ten years later, as distinguished from a radio or television program. I responded (in those pre-Lexis-Nexis, pre-Internet days) that while that was a potentially distinguishing factor with respect to newspapers, magazines also had indices, and that, in any event, West Virginia could not determine what out-of-state newspapers published and thus could not affect even all newspapers.

I wound up by returning to the facts of the case:

> This killing occurred in a community of 14,000 people. It occurred in a junior high school, the only junior high school in town. It occurred in front of at least seven eyewitnesses. Everybody in that community knows about this and everybody knew about it. [It is impossible] to think that a statute can pass constitutional muster where the interest that it is promoting is

that of protecting the right of the juvenile against the publicity for rehabilitation later on, when everybody in his community knows exactly what happened to him. . . .

Two more subjects were touched upon as I concluded. Justice Rehnquist referred to a case in Virginia in which the press had protested being excluded from a closed juvenile hearing. In response to his query as to whether my argument extended that far, I replied that we were making no argument with respect to any right of press access to closed juvenile hearings.

Then Justice Stewart asked if I viewed it as unconstitutional for a statute to make it a crime for a court aide or clerk to reveal information about sealed proceedings. I responded that, in my view, such a law would be constitutional. I sat down, far more content with my performance than I had been after the *Landmark Communications* argument. I had been prepared for just about every question and had, I thought, managed to steer clear of any particularly dangerous areas. I felt confident as we awaited the Court's ruling.

On June 26, 1979, the Court unanimously ruled in our favor. Chief Justice Burger's opinion did not turn on whether the statute was or was not a prior restraint, since even viewing it simply "as a penal sanction for publishing lawfully obtained, truthful information," the law required "the highest form of state interest to sustain its validity." A statute, he wrote, that sought "to punish the publication of truthful information seldom can satisfy constitutional standards." Relying heavily on the *Landmark Communications* case and two other recent rulings, the chief justice concluded that "if a newspaper lawfully obtains truthful information about a matter of public significance, then state officials may not constitutionally punish publication of the information, absent a need to further a state interest of the highest order." Here, he concluded, the interest in juvenile rehabilitation was simply not a strong enough mitigating factor, a proposition bolstered significantly by the Court's Sixth Amendment ruling in the *Davis v. Alaska* case.

Finally, the Chief Justice observed that the limitation of the scope of the statute to newspapers led inexorably to the conclusion that even if "the statute served a state interest of the highest order, it does not accomplish its stated purpose."

Justice Rehnquist wrote a separate concurring opinion, disagreeing with the Court's conclusion that a state statute punishing publication of the identity of a juvenile offender could not serve an interest of the "highest order," but agreeing that the statute must fall because of its scope being limited only to newspapers. "Since the statute largely fails to achieve its purpose," Justice Rehnquist wrote, it was "difficult to take very seriously" West Virginia's argument.

★　　★　　★

In two Supreme Court cases decided in the years afterward, the Court relied heavily on *Daily Mail* in striking down statutes that criminalized truthful disclosure of other information that had been lawfully obtained. In *Florida Star v. B.J.F.*, decided in 1989, a Florida newspaper had copied information from a police report that included the name of a woman who had been sexually assaulted. Under Florida law at the time, it was illegal to "print, publish or broadcast" the name of a victim of a sexual assault. Basing its opinion on the *Daily Mail* case, the Court, in an opinion written by Justice Marshall, reversed a civil judgment of $97,500 that had been awarded to the woman. As in the *Daily Mail* case, the Court concluded that the information published was both "truthful" and "lawfully obtained." The Court's opinion made clear that it was not holding "that truthful publication is automatically constitutionally protected" but only that the Florida statute at issue was "not narrowly tailored to a state interest of the highest order."

Justice Scalia wrote a separate opinion, joining the majority but only on the ground that the statute applied only to the press and not to society at large. Since the victim's friends and acquaintances remained free to speak at will about the very subject the press was barred from discussing, the statute did not protect an interest "of the highest order." Justices Byron White and Sandra

Day O'Connor disagreed with the opinion and would have sustained the Florida law.

Most recently, in 2001, the Supreme Court was faced with yet another case involving a statute that made criminal the publication of truthful information. In *Bartnicki v. Volper*, the statute in question was not a state law but a federal one, the wiretapping law, and the issue was whether the First Amendment barred punishing the press for accurately reporting the contents of a tape recording of an intercepted telephone conversation containing information of public significance. The defendants—two radio stations, their reporter, and the individual who furnished the tape recording— had played no direct or indirect role in the interception. The overheard conversation took place between two individuals who were deeply involved in negotiating a pact for a teachers' union in Wilkes-Barre, Pennsylvania. One of the speakers was the president of the local union, the other its chief negotiator. In the course of the telephone call, one said to the other, "If they're not going to move [their offer higher] we're going to have to go to their, their homes . . . to blow off their front porches, we'll have to do some work on some of those guys . . . " More of the same followed.

An unknown person intercepted and recorded the conversation and left it in the mailbox of the head of an association that opposed the union's proposals. He, in turn, gave it to a local radio station, which played it on the air. The lawsuit was subsequently brought by the two union officials under federal and state wiretapping laws that make it illegal to listen in on or to reveal such discussions. It raised anew the question of whether third parties—specifically the press—could be liable for disclosing truthful information that they had lawfully obtained.

The Supreme Court ruled that no liability could be imposed on the radio station or their employees. In an opinion of Justice John Paul Stevens, joined by Justices Sandra Day O'Connor, Anthony M. Kennedy, David H. Souter, Ruth Bader Ginsberg, and Stephen Breyer, the Court concluded (quoting from the *Daily Mail* case) that "state action to punish the publication of truthful information seldom can satisfy constitutional standards." Refusing, once again, to answer categorically the question of whether truthful publication may ever be punished consistent with the First Amendment, the Court concluded that the undoubted privacy interest in avoiding disclosure of telephone communications gave way "when balanced against the interest in publishing matters of public importance." In a separate concurring opinion, Justices Breyer and O'Connor appeared to limit their agreement with the opinion they had joined: the information revealed in the tapes of the telephone call was "of unusual public concern," and the speakers on the telephone were public figures with regard to the subject they had spoken about, the speakers' "privacy expectations were unusually low and the public interest in defeating these expectations is unusually high."

The Court's three most conservative justices—Chief Justice Rehnquist and Justices Antonin Scalia and Clarence Thomas—dissented, arguing that the Court's ruling "chilled the speech of the millions of Americans who rely upon electronic technology each day."

I played a small role in the case, together with my partner Landis Best, in submitting to the Court a friend-of-the-court brief for newspapers (including the *New York Times*, the *Washington Post*, and the *Los Angeles Times*), magazines (including *Time*, the *New Yorker*, and *Business Week*), and broadcasters (including ABC, CBS, NBC, and CNN) supporting the radio broadcasters before the Court. In the brief we focused primarily on the shared understanding of journalists "that they are entitled to seek information from those that have it and that they may print or broadcast the truthful and newsworthy information that they lawfully gather." Imposing liability, we argued, on "journalists and their organizations . . . for doing nothing more than accurately recounting wiretapped conversations made available to them, which they had no direct or indirect role in obtaining," should not be countenanced.

The Court agreed, but the closeness of the vote was ominous, as was the increasing number of justices who seemed willing to countenance the criminalization of truthful speech. The ruling in the *Landmark Communications* case had been unanimous in our favor; in *Daily Mail*, we had won Justice Rehnquist's vote only because the statute did not limit even more speech; in *Florida Star*, two justices dissented and a third (Scalia) apparently would have if the statute had been broader still; and in *Bartnicki*, there were three dissents, with the live possibility of two more votes against us in some case in the future.

And yet: we had won all the battles. So far.

CHAPTER 4

WAYNE NEWTON AND THE LAW

"Las Vegas today," Otto Friedrich wrote in 1986, "is what hell might be like if hell had been planned and built by New York gangsters." For much of the 1980s, I had just that view, as I spent months in that city preparing to defend and then defending NBC in a libel case brought against the network by the ultimate local icon, Wayne Newton.

It was always something of a shock to land there in Las Vegas's airport (named after Pat McCarran, a particularly repellent and reactionary senator), filled with screaming slot machines. Advertisements throughout the airport showed enormous pictures of Newton, microphone in hand, as he performed at the Aladdin Hotel. A taxi ride into the city required driving on Wayne Newton Boulevard. If a visitor was very lucky, his driver might tell him that his arrival date coincided with the celebration by the people of Las Vegas of Wayne Newton Day. And if one asked the driver what he thought of Wayne Newton (as I always did), the answer was invariably positive. Newton was good for tourism, one was told; he was good for taxi drivers, too, having entertained many of them for free at various points during his entertainment reign in Las Vegas.

Most important, Newton was the embodiment of Las Vegas, its ambassador to the world. Outsiders didn't understand Las Vegas, the natives told me. When the first federal judge assigned to the Newton case was impeached and convicted by the United States Senate after being criminally convicted for income tax evasion (he took money from litigants before him and, naturally enough, didn't report it), more than one local resident told me how unfairly the judge had been treated, how the rest of America, and particularly the media, just didn't get it. "Cashing a check here for forty thousand dollars in a casino," a Las Vegas newspaper publisher told me, "is like cashing one for forty dollars at an A&P anywhere else in the country." The judge, of course, had done just that.

NBC's decision to retain us to represent it and its journalists in Newton's Las Vegas had not been an easy one. The more insular a community is, the more advisable it usually is to have local counsel handle a trial, particularly when it pits a favorite son against a national entity such as NBC. But that presented its own problem. NBC had reported that after testifying falsely before the Nevada Gaming Commission, Newton had been granted a license to run the casino at the Aladdin Hotel, a property he was purchasing with a partner. In criticizing Newton, NBC was understood by many in Las

155

Vegas to be criticizing not only one of the city's leading citizens, but the Las Vegas way of life itself. NBC's difficulty in choosing counsel was that just about every lawyer in town seemed to have some connection with what Nevadans call the "gaming" industry—what much of the rest of the country calls "gambling." It was precisely because of that relationship that the NBC journalists who had prepared a twelve-minute piece about Newton entitled "Wayne Newton and the Law" were unwilling to entrust their own defense to any Las Vegas lawyer. NBC went along with their wishes, primarily because its expectation that *any* lawyer would lose against Newton in Las Vegas meant that the most important task of counsel was to ensure that the record was in the best possible shape for a subsequent appeal. And so off to the west to defend the case I went, together with my partner, Tom Kavaler, two associates, and a support staff of five.

BEGINNINGS

The events leading to the litigation had begun early in 1980. The FBI was then engaged in an investigation of a Connecticut mob leader named Frank Piccolo. Piccolo was a captain—a *caporegime*—in the Gambino organized crime family who ran their loan-sharking and gambling activities in Connecticut. In that capacity, he reported weekly in New York to Carlo Gambino, the boss of the family bearing his name, and delivered to him the state's rackets money. As part of its investigation, the FBI obtained judicial authorization to record telephone conversations of Piccolo over a sixty-day period.

Among the conversations overheard in the period from May 13 to July 12, 1980, were ones between Piccolo and his cousin Guido Penosi. Penosi was a leading narcotics dealer who was associated with both the Gambino and Lucchese organized crime families and who had (after his conviction for murder as a juvenile) twice been convicted of felonies. Wayne Newton and his projected purchase of the Aladdin Hotel and Casino in Las Vegas was the topic of some of the conversations of the two mob leaders; other conversations, the listening agents learned, contained references to discussions the mob leaders had themselves had or planned to have with Newton.

By 1980 Newton had achieved extraordinary national recognition as an entertainer. Acclaimed, if sometimes mocked, throughout the country, Newton's fame had reached unprecedented heights in Las Vegas, where he maintained his home and had performed in hotel showrooms since the early 1970s for sums that often exceeded $300,000 per week. Newton was routinely described as "the most successful performer in Vegas history" (*People*) and "the undisputed king of Las Vegas" (*Newsweek*). He was not only Las Vegas's king but its most admired citizen. The license plate on the Porsche he drove about town said "VEGAS 1" on it, and no one in Las Vegas would have begrudged him the title. It was no coincidence that President Reagan (on two occasions) and then-vice president George H. W. Bush (on two others) had visited with Newton at his Las Vegas home.

Newton had first met Penosi in the 1960s when Penosi had attended Newton's performances at the Copacabana Club in New York several times a week over a six-month period. They had spoken often, and Penosi had warned others at the club to "stay away from the kid" because he's "mine." During that time, Penosi and an individual who was fast becoming one of the nation's leading organized crime leaders, Carmine Tramunti, had given Newton an inscribed watch worth between $2,000 and $2,500. Tramunti had become the boss of the Lucchese organized crime family in 1967, a role he held through the early 1970s.

From their initial meetings at the Copacabana, the Newton-Penosi relationship grew closer. Newton's office calendar noted Penosi's birthday in large letters, and for a period of over twenty years Newton and Penosi met in New York, Florida (dining together both at Penosi's home and in a restaurant), and Las Vegas. On one occasion, Penosi visited Newton's Las Vegas home when Newton was out and spoke with his parents. On another, Penosi attended the wedding of Newton's brother in Las Vegas and also met privately with Newton on that occasion. In 1976 Newton flew to Los

Angeles in his private plane with his manager, conductor, drummer, guitarist, and banjo player to perform, without compensation, on a television pilot for Penosi's son. This was done as a favor to Penosi, who thanked Newton profusely and offered to provide help for him in the future.

In 1979 Penosi wanted to visit Las Vegas again but did not want to register (as the law required) as an ex-felon. Newton called the police, as a favor to Penosi, to advise them of the visit so as to avoid the need for any registration. Newton initially invited Penosi to stay at his home, but then arranged for him to stay as his guest at the Desert Inn Hotel, where Newton was performing. Penosi visited Newton's dressing room there as well as his home and brought a saddle as a present for Newton's daughter. According to Penosi, Newton invited him to a private party in his hotel suite, which Penosi attended.

In early 1980 Newton secretly took Penosi up on his long-standing offer of help. In 1979 Newton had invested in a Las Vegas tabloid called *Backstage* with a man named Ron Delpit, but after a number of months decided to end his financial involvement. When Delpit and an associate of his, Bob Adams, came to Newton's hotel suite to demand that Newton pay them money that they claimed he had promised to advance, Newton struck one of them and physically threw the two men out of his room. Several nights later, threats directed at both Newton and his daughter began to be made by telephone by an individual named Dapper, who was himself involved in organized crime. When the Las Vegas police were unable to stop the threats, Newton made a critical decision. Instead of contacting the FBI or any other police entity, he got in touch with his old friend, Guido Penosi.

Penosi, in turn, told Newton to call his "cousin Frank" and provided him with the Connecticut number of Frank Piccolo, who Newton called for help. Piccolo, however, needed further clearance from his mob family to proceed, and at a "sitdown" in the Bronx attended by members of the Genovese family, it was agreed that those threatening Newton should leave him alone. The threats stopped.

Penosi returned to Las Vegas in February 1980 after the threats against Newton had ended. He visited with Newton in his dressing room, where Newton thanked him for his help.

Around the same time, Mark Moreno, then Newton's longtime friend and business advisor, also began receiving threats. He went to Newton, who advised Moreno to call Penosi, who in turn directed him to Piccolo. After Moreno told Piccolo the story, Piccolo explained that since "we operate somewhat similar to a board of directors in a corporation, there is other people that I must speak to about this." Moreno saw himself, as he later put it, "being the center of discussion in a room filled with a lot of mob people."

A few days later Penosi asked Newton to speak

to Piccolo personally, and once again Newton phoned Piccolo to ask for his assistance. In this call Newton told Piccolo (as Penosi had suggested he do) that Moreno was "with" Newton and was part of Newton's team. Piccolo replied that that was all he needed to know.

Once again, Piccolo met with members of the Genovese family in the Bronx, where it was agreed that Penosi would personally pay $3,500 to have the threats against Moreno called off. The Moreno threats subsequently ceased.

Having done a major favor for Newton by causing the threats made against Newton and his daughter and against Moreno to cease, Piccolo then began to seek to "earn" from Newton by pressing Moreno to buy life insurance for Lola Falana, a friend of Newton's and a Las Vegas entertainer then being managed by Moreno, through an insurance agent introduced to Moreno by Piccolo. As Piccolo phrased it in a taped telephone call: "We'll earn it back with the guy. First of all, on the insurance guy, something should come back . . ."

Moreno tried to stall because of his fears that he was becoming entangled with Piccolo, whom he understood to be involved in organized crime. Moreno told Newton about the efforts to pressure him to purchase insurance and characterized it as "a quid pro quo, as a favor" for the help the organized crime figures had given to Newton and Moreno.

Newton's decision to turn to individuals highly placed in organized crime to assist him in dealing with the consequences of his financial—and physical—disagreement with Delpit and Adams ultimately led not only to the FBI's learning of his communications with the mob figures but also to NBC's doing so as well.

NBC's ROLE

In early July 1980 Brian Ross and Ira Silverman, two NBC journalists, became aware of the ongoing FBI investigation of Piccolo. Ross and Silverman were employed by NBC News as a reporter and a field producer, respectively, specializing in investigative reporting about organized crime. Each had received numerous journalistic awards for his previous work; Ross had been the recipient of the Peabody Award for his reporting on police corruption in Miami, the DuPont Award for his reporting on corruption in the Teamsters Union in Ohio, and an Emmy Award for his reporting on the Teamsters Union. Silverman had been the recipient of a number of awards for programs on police corruption in New York and an award from the city of New York for a program on New York fire companies; another program on which he worked, *The Billion Dollar Weapon*, had received an Emmy Award.

Ross and Silverman initially learned that Piccolo was being investigated and that wiretaps existed of telephone conversations between him, his cousin Penosi—who, the reporters learned, had been identified by almost every law-enforcement agency in Southern California as their number-one organized crime figure—and Moreno, Newton's associate. The conversations, the reporters were told, seemed to involve Newton and the Aladdin Hotel in Las Vegas. Shortly after receiving this information, Ross and Silverman established from clippings and wire stories that Newton was trying to purchase the Aladdin, which had been closed by Nevada gaming authorities after it was determined that organized crime figures had secretly controlled it. The fact that Newton had spoken with high-level mob figures and had been discussed by them with respect to his contemplated purchase of the Aladdin, the reporters learned, was a matter of intense interest to federal law-enforcement officials.

In the course of their research and investigation, Ross and Silverman traveled to Las Vegas, where they continually sought—and were denied permission—to speak with Newton. Silverman tried to call Newton for an interview about the Aladdin and Penosi but was told by Newton's secretary that Newton declined.

While the NBC journalists were pursuing their investigation, the Nevada gaming authorities were conducting one of their own in connection with Newton's application for a Nevada gaming license to own and operate the Aladdin. On a number of occasions in July and August 1980, Newton was interviewed by Nevada Gaming Board investigators. On one occasion, Newton answered under oath questions asked by several gaming board investigators, led by Fred Balmer, the senior of the four agents who were assigned to conduct the Newton case. It was his responsibility to coordinate the entire investigation, including both its financial and suitability aspects, and to ensure that an accurate accounting was completed and submitted to the board.

After repeatedly informing Newton that Penosi was involved in organized crime, Balmer then asked him to set forth "his entire relationship with Mr. Penosi." According to Balmer, Newton "was asked very specific questions, based on the information that we had, with regard to his contacts with Penosi, and in addition to that he was asked if there had been any additional contacts or is there any other financial or business or any other contact he had with relation to Mr. Penosi."

During the interview Newton mentioned that Penosi had come "about once a week maybe" to see him perform at the Copacabana Club in New York in the years 1963 and 1964; that during the past six months Newton had started receiving threatening telephone calls, at which point "either Guido called me or I called him and I don't remember which"; and that Newton believed the people threatening him were from Los Angeles, "so I might have called Guido to find out if he knew who they were."

During this same interview the following exchange took place:

> BALMER: Were you aware that Penosi had used his contacts with organized crime and had sent some individuals here to Las Vegas to handle this problem for you?
>
> NEWTON: No, I wasn't.
>
> BALMER: Were you aware that one of these individuals was an individual by the name of Frank Piccolo?
>
> NEWTON: No.
>
> BALMER: Have you ever heard of Frank Piccolo?
>
> NEWTON: No.

Somewhat later in the interview, Balmer said: "And we are also aware that after you did contact Mr. Penosi, he made contact with an individual who is from back East in the New England states, ah, Piccolo, who is heavily involved with organized crime also. He did come to the Las Vegas area and our information is he did take care of these individuals for you."

To which Newton responded: "Well, if it did happen, ah, I don't know who that is and I'm still getting threats as of last week."

By the end of Balmer's interviews of Newton— and despite the fact that he had given Newton what he called "a more than adequate opportunity during the interview with him to tell us anything that he knew about Mr. Penosi"—Balmer and his colleagues were unaware of any gifts from Penosi to Newton; any protection afforded Newton by Penosi when he performed at the Copacabana; the two men's dining together at a restaurant in Florida; Newton's doing a free TV pilot as a favor to Penosi, or Penosi thanking him for it; Penosi's offering to help Newton; Newton's sending a car to pick him up when he came to Las Vegas; Penosi's visiting Newton's house; any meeting between the two after the threats against Newton stopped; and Newton's speaking with Frank Piccolo or anybody else at Penosi's request in an effort to stop the threats.

Unaware of the Newton-Balmer interviews, Ross and Silverman continued to gather information on their own. They discovered that Newton had been in touch with Piccolo and that efforts of some sort had been made by Piccolo to sell insurance to Moreno. As part of their news-gathering efforts, Ross and Silverman went to Los Angeles, where they spent three or four days outside Penosi's apartment house in Beverly Hills. Ross, who attempted to interview Penosi, introduced himself and said: "I want to talk to you about your relationship with Wayne Newton." Penosi responded, "Who the fuck knows Wayne Newton?" and stalked away.

Upon returning to the East Coast Ross was told by a knowledgeable confidential source with whom he had worked before that police in New York, through either an undercover agent or a listening

166

device planted at the Ravenite Club, a well-known meeting place in New York City for members of the Gambino family, had learned that Piccolo had been asked by his associates in that family if he wanted to go in with them on a deal in Atlantic City, but Piccolo declined because, he explained, he had taken care of a problem for Wayne Newton and as a result was going to have some sort of interest in the Aladdin Hotel.

THE GAMING BOARD HEARING

Throughout this period of time, the two journalists contacted sources all over the country about Piccolo and Penosi, trying to fill in the details of what they had learned. On September 25, 1980, they attended a public hearing on Newton's application for a license to own and operate the Aladdin Hotel.

In his sworn public testimony before the gaming board, Newton stated that he first met Penosi when he was sixteen or seventeen years old and performing at the Copacabana in New York City. He acknowledged seeing Penosi in Florida at Penosi's home but testified unequivocally that Penosi had never visited him in his home. Newton summed up his relationship with Penosi by stating: "In the approximately twenty-one years from the time I met him, I might have seen this man four times. So, my relationship is just that of a fan."

After he had been advised by one member of the gaming board that Penosi was a purported member of the Gambino organized crime family, and asked if he was going to continue any relationship with him, Newton said: "On the basis of which I've known him, I don't think that there's been a relationship. The direct answer to your question obviously is no if he has those kind of connections."

Ross and Silverman were struck by two aspects of Newton's public testimony: first, the limited number of contacts Newton testified he had had with Penosi, and more particularly his failure to mention *any* of his recent 1980 contacts; and second, Newton's testimony that Moreno had nothing to do with the Aladdin and had no business relationship with Newton. They were also surprised that Newton was not even questioned about telephone calls they had learned he had made to the Clark County Sheriff's Office on behalf of Penosi when Penosi visited Las Vegas the previous year. When Ross and Silverman informed one of their law-enforcement sources about Newton's testimony regarding Penosi, their source said that Newton was not telling the whole story.

At the hearing the NBC journalists—who were aware that federal investigators had raised questions about the possible role of Penosi and Piccolo in Newton's purchase of the Aladdin—also heard representatives of the Valley Bank of Nevada testify that the bank was providing the financing for Newton to acquire his interest in the Aladdin.

On the basis of the sworn testimony provided to

it, the gaming board recommended that Newton and his partner (who previously had been denied a license because of *his* relationship with organized crime figures) be licensed. Members of the board had not been advised of, among other things, any of the following contacts between Newton and Penosi: Penosi's warning to individuals at the Copacabana to "stay away from the kid" or his reference to Newton as "mine"; Newton's receipt of the watch as a gift from Penosi; Newton's free performance, as a favor to Penosi, on the television pilot in Los Angeles; Penosi's thanks to Newton for his help on this program and his request that if Newton ever needed help, he should let him know; Newton's invitation to Penosi to stay at his house in Las Vegas; Newton's arrangement for Penosi to stay without paying at a hotel in Las Vegas; Penosi's gift of a saddle to Newton as a present for Newton's daughter; Newton's provision of a driver to bring Penosi to his home and Penosi's visit there; the marking of Penosi's birthday on Newton's office calendar; Penosi's assistance to Newton in stopping threats of harm received by Newton and his family; and Newton's belief that Penosi had saved his daughter's life.

Immediately after the conclusion of the gaming board hearing, Ross sought once again to interview Newton, walking next to him as Newton strode to his car. Ross pressed hard for information, and the entertainer responded angrily that he had last spoken with Penosi "maybe a year ago" and that

Penosi had made no phone calls to him. He also stated that he did not know anyone named Frank Piccolo.

At the car, Ross asked Newton about threats made to his family, inquiring whether Penosi had ever been in Las Vegas to provide protection for Newton or his children. Frank Fahrenkopf, Newton's long-time attorney, who had represented him in his successful effort to be licensed to own and operate the Aladdin, disparagingly replied, "Come on, that's silly." No other answer or explanation was offered by Fahrenkopf or Newton.

THE BROADCASTS

On October 6, 1980, *NBC Nightly News* broadcast a twelve-minute report entitled "Wayne Newton and the Law." Introduced by John Chancellor (who later told me that he had never heard of Newton), the program began with scenes of a stakeout of Penosi by investigators from the Los Angeles District Attorney's Office. Penosi was described by Brian Ross as "a New York hoodlum from the Gambino Mafia family, a man with a long criminal record, now believed to be the Gambino family's man on the West Coast, in the narcotics business and also in show business." The broadcast then noted that Penosi was a "key figure" in an ongoing federal grand jury investigation of the activities of the Gambino family in Las Vegas, an investigation that also involved

Wayne Newton. Newton's purchase of the Aladdin was noted: "A federal grand jury is now investigating the role of Guido Penosi and the mob in Newton's deal for the Aladdin." The broadcast went on to reveal that Newton had had financial problems, and continued: "Investigators say that last year, just before Newton announced he would buy the Aladdin, Newton called Guido Penosi for help with a problem. Investigators say whatever the problem was, it was important enough for Penosi to take it up with leaders of the Gambino family in New York. Police in New York say that this mob boss, Frank Piccolo, told associates he had taken care of Newton's problem and had become a hidden partner in the Aladdin hotel deal."

Newton himself was shown testifying before the gaming board on the subject of his relationship with Penosi: "On the basis of which I've known him, I don't think that there's been a relationship." The broadcast then stated that "federal authorities say Newton is not telling the whole story, and that Newton is expected to be one of the first witnesses in the grand jury investigation." The report concluded with scenes from Ross's attempted interview of Newton after the gaming board hearing and his attempted interview of Penosi, in which Penosi denied knowing Newton. Ross then indicated that "federal authorities say they know of at least eleven phone calls Penosi made to Newton's house in one two-month period" and asserted that these and other matters would be considered by a federal grand jury.

The segment was a sensation. Newton responded with a press conference the following day in which he called the broadcast "the most blatant display of national TV and media abuse I have ever witnessed." He said, "There is one thing and one thing only that is truth in what was shown last night. I do know Guido . . . I know him only, frankly, as a fan. The news stated that I had talked to him eleven times. I haven't talked to him eleven times in my entire life." When asked about Frank Piccolo, Newton said: "I don't know him, I've never even heard of him."

A month after the October 6 broadcast, Newton and Moreno testified before a federal grand jury in Connecticut. Newton was asked a number of questions about whether there was any relationship between his telephone calls to Penosi and Piccolo and his purchase of the Aladdin Hotel:

- "Did he [Penosi] ask anything from you?"
- "Did he discuss with you at that time the fact that he wanted to earn some money, or wanted you to do him a favor?"
- "Does he have any business interests with you or financial?"
- "Has he at any time?"
- "Were you ever approached by anybody, either connected with Mr. Penosi or

connected with this gentleman by the name of Frank, about their possibly assisting in the financing of the Aladdin?"

- "Are there any points sold for the Aladdin now that aren't a matter of record with the Gaming Commission?"
- "Do you feel now that you owe Guido Penosi a favor?"

Although Newton responded negatively to all of them, in the course of his testimony he did provide the grand jury with a great deal of information, much of which he had previously failed to reveal to the Nevada gaming authorities. Among other things, he described in detail to the grand jury—as he had not done to the Nevada gaming authorities less than three months before—his calls to Penosi's "cousin Frank." He also acknowledged that in February of 1980, after the threats against him had ceased, he had met with Penosi in his dressing room, and that he had told Penosi how appreciative he was that the threats had ended.

As for the efforts of the mob figures to pressure associates of Newton to purchase insurance—another topic Newton had failed to disclose to the Nevada authorities—Newton said that after the threats against Moreno had stopped, Moreno had told him that Frank had said that as "a favor for getting you off the hook" he wanted Moreno to take out an insurance policy on Lola Falana through a Connecticut insurance agent whose name was given to Moreno by Frank. Newton understood, he testified, that Frank had asked for the insurance policy "as a favor to him because of his intercession" and "that it was done as a quid pro quo, as a favor for him helping" Newton and Moreno.

On the evening of November 6, 1980, a portion of *NBC Nightly News* narrated by Ross recounted Newton's appearance that day before the Connecticut grand jury investigating Piccolo. The broadcast began by identifying Piccolo and then reported on Newton's one-hour session with the grand jury and his comment upon leaving the courthouse that he could not talk about the investigation but was cooperating with the authorities. The broadcast stated that "federal authorities want to know why Frank Piccolo became involved in solving problems Newton was having last year with a business deal, and whether Piccolo had anything to do with the Aladdin Hotel deal." It continued: "Newton has admitted he asked for help from an old friend who was close to Piccolo, but Newton says he had no idea his friend was part of one of this country's most powerful Mafia families." The broadcast concluded with the statement that Moreno had also testified before the grand jury that day and that federal authorities wanted to question Lola Falana, "who federal authorities think may be a victim of a scheme to defraud her involving Frank Piccolo and her manager . . . Mark Moreno."

Seven months later, on June 12, 1981, Piccolo

and Penosi were indicted by a federal grand jury in Connecticut for attempted extortion of Newton, Falana, and Moreno. The indictment was also the subject of a report that evening on the *NBC Nightly News*. Based on the indictment itself and a press release pertaining to it released by the U.S. Attorney's Office in Connecticut, Ross reported the charge that "the mob tried to move in on Newton and Falana last year, when Newton asked two Mafia figures to use their power and influence in the underworld to call off threats and demands made against Newton by other mobsters from New York." He reported as well the government's charge that after Piccolo took care of threats against Newton and Moreno, "in return, Piccolo wanted a piece of the earnings of Newton and Falana and the proceeds of an insurance policy on Miss Falana." The piece continued with the statement that Newton, before the gaming board, had said he had no relationship with Penosi and that he had told NBC News he did not know Piccolo, "but today's indictment indicates that Newton told a much different story to the federal grand jury." The report concluded: "Authorities say Wayne Newton became a victim of the mob scheme, and that Newton will be a key government witness against the two Mafia figures he once went to for help."

Penosi was tried in Connecticut in March 1982, but the jury was unable to reach a verdict. He was retried in May 1982 and acquitted, having argued to the jury that it was Piccolo and not he who had sought to extort money from Newton. Piccolo was in no position to deny the charge: he had been shot to death at a telephone booth on a street in Bridgeport, Connecticut, on September 19, 1981.

LITIGATION

Newton filed his libel action against NBC on April 10, 1981. While the lawsuit cited all three broadcasts that concerned him, the first was at the heart of the case. Newton took issue with a number of statements that had been made, but his central claim was that the piece had falsely implied that he was secretly acting on behalf of organized crime at the Aladdin. The broadcast, Newton argued, had conveyed the message that mob figures had become hidden partners at the hotel. NBC argued that the report was true, and that while its journalists had deliberately refrained from accusing Newton of acting on the mob's behalf, everything in the broadcast about Newton's relationships and contacts with organized crime figures was verifiable, as was NBC's charge that he had testified falsely before the Nevada Gaming Board.

Discovery in the case—pretrial depositions, motions, and the like—was brutal. Ross gave pretrial testimony for sixteen days, Silverman for fifteen, and Newton for twenty-one. Much of it was unpleasant, often vituperative. Newton's lawyer,

176

Morton Galane, screamed at NBC witnesses; we screamed back at him. He routinely accused us of lying, often fabricating events as he did so, making impossible even the most basic civil relationship between counsel. From falsely charging me with "signaling" Ross about how to answer questions, to verbally abusing the most inconsequential witnesses as they testified, Galane made each aspect of the proceedings a trial of its own. I have never taken part in a case in which I disliked opposing counsel more or thought he had misbehaved more often. When Ira Silverman, furious at Galane's tactics during Silverman's deposition, stalked out of the room in which his testimony was being taken, I felt like going with him.

Midway in the case, Galane was—incredibly—nominated by President Ronald Reagan for a federal judgeship, and we seriously considered advising the Department of Justice of what we believed was his lack of proper judicial temperament for the position. Ultimately we stayed silent, concluding that anything we said would likely be perceived as the disgruntled complaints of opposing counsel. When the *Wall Street Journal* published an article revealing that Galane had given local journalists "gifts" of hundreds of dollars each to ensure, as he put it, "fairness" in their coverage of him, the nomination was withdrawn. We were again left with an opponent we despised in a community that was his home—and, far more important, Newton's domain as well.

While I hated every minute of every deposition, there were some unforgettable moments as we prepared for trial. That summer I brought my fifteen-year-old daughter, Ronnie, with me to Las Vegas during her vacation. After we checked in at Caesar's Palace Hotel, we went to our room and found ourselves in a palatial space covered by a thick red carpet, in which stood a single round bed under a large mirror. When I went downstairs to ask to change rooms, explaining that I was with my daughter, the quickly raised eyebrows of the receptionist reminded me that I was not the first older man to check in with his daughter.

There were memorable work-related moments, too. One was when we received an expert report prepared on Newton's behalf by Richard Wirthlin, President Reagan's pollster, that was designed to show that NBC's broadcast had led many viewers to associate Newton with organized crime. Based upon telephone interviews with one thousand adults residing in the United States, the report focused on what people liked most about Newton (his singing, it turned out) and least about him (also his singing). The problem—and unexpected benefit for us—was that the same study showed that more people viewed Newton critically because of his *mustache* (4 percent) than because of any supposed connection with organized crime (1 percent).

Then there was the deposition my partner, Tom Kavaler, took of Guido Penosi, who arrived at the deposition open-shirted, adorned with large gold jewelry and dressed—I know of no other way to say it—like someone involved in organized crime. Tom questioned Penosi about his relationship with Newton and received detailed responses. When Tom asked Penosi, as he sometimes was obliged to, if he had engaged in one criminal act or another, Penosi would respond, "I take the Fifth" (pronounced "Fiff"), and Tom, at every break, would carefully assure Penosi that he was just doing his job. Penosi seemed amused, and so were we.

Later, during Penosi's trial in Connecticut, an NBC cameraman was called to testify about Ross's efforts to engage Penosi in a conversation about Newton. When asked how Penosi had responded to Ross, the cameraman responded in a low voice that Penosi had said that "we should fuck off." At this point, it appeared that the judge had dozed off for a second. Now he focused on the witness and asked the question. "He said to do what?" The cameraman turned to face the judge and responded loudly, "Fuck off."

For all these moments of levity, preparation for the trial was intense and all-consuming. When both sides were finished with their pretrial work, we moved for summary judgment, a ruling from the court that there were no material issues of fact that needed be decided by a jury and that the legal issue of what NBC had said was true or otherwise legally privileged must be decided in our favor.

The judge, an elderly California federal jurist named Myron D. Crocker, who had been assigned to the case after the criminal conviction of our previous judge, concluded that we had "made a substantial and persuasive showing" that each of the statements made in the three challenged broadcasts was either true or otherwise legally protected. Notwithstanding that showing, Judge Crocker denied the motion on the ground that the jury could still find that the broadcasts left a false impression that the mob had financed Newton's acquisition or interest in the Aladdin and that he held a hidden interest in the hotel for the mob. At the same time, Crocker denied our motion for a change of venue out of Las Vegas. There was no reason to believe, he concluded, that a Las Vegas jury could not provide a fair trial to NBC. As I read that order, I could not help wondering if the trial would begin on Wayne Newton Day and if I would then look the judge in the eye and wish him a happy one.

TRIAL

The trial itself was interminable, lasting thirty-six days spread over a period of two months from its commencement on October 16 until its conclusion on December 17, 1986. Until its conclusion, though, almost everything went as well as or even better than we had hoped. Ross and Silverman were steadfast in the defense of their broadcasts. In the face of repeated verbal assaults by Galane, both stayed cool and offered powerful defenses of their conduct. Perhaps even more important, Fred Balmer, the chief investigator of the Nevada Gaming Board, turned out to be a consistently helpful witness, making plain his disdain for Newton's sometimes false and more often misleading answers to the questions Balmer had asked him when he conducted his investigation. When Balmer testified that in his view, Newton had been licensed to run the Aladdin only because the process had been "juiced," there were audible gasps in the courtroom, followed by large page-one headlines in both local newspapers the next day.

Newton's own testimony was the centerpiece of the trial. He testified for four days on direct examination by Galane about his rags-to-riches rise to stardom. He cried when he spoke of his fears for his daughter's life. He stared contemptuously at Ross and Silverman as he described how he felt when he was accused (he said) of being a front for organized crime—and then cried again. Newton had never been viewed as much of an actor, but his performance in court, genuine or not, was powerful and (I feared) potentially persuasive to a Las Vegas jury.

How to cross-examine Newton was a topic that Tom Kavaler and I, together with our associates Dev Chatillon and Ira Dembrow, spent weeks discussing. To come on too strong could make the jury even angrier at NBC and more sympathetic to Newton; to come across too weakly risked whatever chance we had before the jury as well as possibly imperiling our chances on appeal. We decided that I would be polite but firm, risking, if necessary, the animosity of the jury for the potential benefits of bringing Newton down in its estimation, and, at the least, establishing a strong record for an appeal. After an hour and a half or so of introductory cross-examination of Newton, I took a break and received a disturbing preliminary verdict: both Ross and Silverman, Tom told me, thought I had been too weak in my examination, too unwilling to beard the lion in his den.

I returned to court determined to be firmer. Newton had consistently minimized his long-term relationship with Penosi. He had been asked by one gaming board member if Penosi had ever visited him in his home and denied such a visit had ever taken place. "No, sir," he had said. I plunged in quickly on this topic.

> Q: Mr. Newton, that was not true, was it?
> A: No, sir, not in the context in which you are stating it. It was true in the context in which I interpreted the question.
> Q: Mr. Penosi had come to your home, had he not?
> A: I sent a car for him, yes, sir.
> Q: Mr. Penosi talked with you at your home?
> A: I assumed we talked, yes, sir.

Q: He stayed at your home for twenty, twenty-five, thirty minutes, I think you said?

A: Approximately fifteen, thirty minutes, somewhere in there.

Q: He went away from your home in the car that you had provided him.

A: I didn't provide him a car. I provided him a ride. I believe I had someone pick him up and take him back.

Q: You believe you told the whole story [the broadcast had attributed to federal officials the view that Newton had not told "the whole story" in his testimony] when you responded to the question has he ever visited you in your home and you said, "No, sir"?

A: In the context in which I understand the question, yes, sir.

There had been other unmistakable falsehoods in Newton's testimony to the gaming board in which he understated his contacts with Penosi. "In the approximately twenty-one years from the time he met" Penosi, Newton had testified, he "might have seen this man four times." But the "four times" (later redefined at the trial by Newton as "four occasions") turned out, on cross-examination, to be scores of times. The first supposed "occasion" was the entire period in the 1960s in which Newton had actually seen Penosi regularly, sometimes

183

nightly, in New York; the second encompassed a number of meetings and dinners in Florida; the third involved Penosi's attendance in Las Vegas at the wedding of Newton's brother; and the fourth involved various meetings with Penosi, again in Las Vegas, in 1979. Newton's computations also totally overlooked his 1976 meeting with Penosi in Los Angeles and their 1980 meeting in Las Vegas, let alone all telephone communications between them.

A third Newton falsehood to the gaming board related to his relationship with Moreno, whose own relationship with a mob figure was a source of concern to members of the board. In response to a specific and narrow question by a member of the board asking whether Moreno was "a representative of [his] in any way, shape, or form," Newton replied that they had "no association whatsoever." In fact, cross-examination of Newton and Moreno revealed that by the time of the gaming board hearing, Moreno had, on behalf of Newton: checked out one proposal to purchase the Aladdin Hotel and prepared a backup deal for another; arranged and attended meetings on Newton's behalf relating to the purchase of the Aladdin; sought potential partners for Newton; reviewed the management contract of Newton's co-licensee at the Aladdin; drafted Newton's contract to become executive director of entertainment at the Aladdin; and generally advised and worked for Newton on a round-the-clock basis from May through August of 1980.

Our effort, of course, was not simply to show that Newton had repeatedly testified falsely but that he had failed, as the broadcast had said, to tell "the whole story" of his relationship with Penosi. As a result, I drilled deeply into Newton's views about organized crime, a subject he clearly sought to avoid.

Newton had been told unambiguously by chief gaming investigator Balmer that Penosi had been involved in organized crime. I took the next step with him.

> Q: Did you believe Mr. Balmer that Mr. Penosi was involved in organized crime?
> A: I had no reason to consider it either way, Mr. Abrams.
> Q: Is it a matter of indifference to you?
> A: Relatively so, yes.

Newton had called Piccolo after being told to do so by Penosi. Balmer, in questioning Newton for the gaming board, pressed the point and so, as a result, did I:

> Q: When Mr. Balmer said to you, Mr. Newton, that after you did contact Mr. Penosi he made contact with an individual who was back east in the New England states, did you tell him that in fact you had called someone in the New England states—

A: No, sir, I didn't.

Q: —at the request of Mr. Penosi?

A: No, sir, I didn't. I didn't know where I called.

Q: You dialed an area code, Mr. Newton?

A: Yes, sir.

Q: You had no idea what part of the country the area code was in?

A: No, sir.

Q: And when Mr. Balmer said to you Mr. Penosi made contact with an individual who was from back east in the New England states, "Piccolo" he called him, who was heavily involved in organized crime, why didn't you tell him that you had made two telephone calls at Mr. Penosi's explicit request to someone else to help solve your problem?

A: It didn't occur to me, Mr. Abrams.

Newton had constantly downplayed his relationship with Penosi. But why had he called him in the first place?

Q: Now, before you called Guido Penosi, did you even think of contacting any other body of law enforcement other than [Las Vegas] Metro, which had already told you what you've testified to?

A: No, sir.

Q: Did you even consider calling the FBI?
A: It wouldn't have helped.
Q: You know that, Mr. Newton?
A: Yes, sir.
Q: You knew that then?
A: No, sir.

When Newton left the hearing room where he testified before the gaming commission and Ross had sought to interview him, the following exchange had occurred:

ROSS: When was the last time you talked with [Penosi]?
NEWTON: Maybe a year ago. Thank you.
ROSS: He hasn't made phone calls to you?
NEWTON : No.

Both of these answers were false. Newton had spoken with Penosi on a number of occasions earlier in 1980, Penosi having called him on some of them. On cross-examination, I played for Newton and the jury a videotape of his exchange with Ross, and we then went to the mat:

Q: Was that true, Mr. Newton?
A: No, it wasn't. But I didn't realize that I was under oath to Mr. Wimp [Brian Ross] over there.

I paused. Standard cross-examination guidance is

not to ask any question to which one does not know the answer. But Newton was so filled with bile at Ross and his colleagues that I decided a few more jabs could do us no harm.

> Q: Mr. Newton, you don't tell the truth when you're not under oath?
> A: It depends on who's asking, Mr. Abrams.
> Q: How do you decide when to tell the truth?
> A: I decide to tell the truth when it's important enough and the person asking me has some validity and should be concerned with what I say, and how I say it.

After further questioning about whether Ross had, as Newton testified, behaved in a "Gestapo-like manner," I played a portion of the tape again and followed with additional questions:

> Q: The words that were just said—please correct me if I'm wrong—[were], "He hasn't made phone calls to you?" Answer: "No." That wasn't true either, was it?
> A: My attorney had tapped me on the back and said, "No comments; just keep walking."
> Q: Is that what you said? "No comment?"

A: My attorney had tapped me on the back and said to me . . . "No comment."

Q: I'd like you to listen to my question. My question is, did you tell the truth when Brian Ross said, "He hasn't made phone calls to you," and you said, "No"?

A: I wasn't even necessarily talking to him, Mr. Abrams.

Q: Were you talking to him?

A: No, I wasn't.

There was more, much more of the same, and by the time the trial had ended we felt we had a fair chance to win. The Las Vegas odds on the trial (Las Vegas bets on *everything*) had shifted enormously and were now three to two in our favor, as Balmer's testimony and then Newton's had seemed to go well for us. As the betting favorite, we felt hopeful enough of a victory that we obtained bodyguard protection for ourselves and our colleagues. We had not been threatened but felt anxious enough that a bit of extra protection could do no harm.

But as the days passed (it took the jury a full four days to decide), we became more and more depressed. When the jury sent a note asking how to compute interest on an award, noting simultaneously that no one should draw any conclusions about how they would rule from their query, we drew the right conclusion and became still more depressed.

Finally, the jury returned. They seemed in a happy mood; I was not. We not only lost the trial but did so in astronomical amounts. The jury awarded Newton $7.9 million for loss of past income and $1,146,750 for loss of future income; $5 million for damages to his reputation; and $225,000 for physical and mental suffering. In addition, the jury found that one or more of the NBC journalists "harbored ill will or hatred toward [Newton] and intended to injure him" and threw on another $5 million in punitive damages. To the total sum of $19,271,750 awarded by the jury, prejudgment interest of $3,485,523.80 was added, and a total judgment of $22,757,273.80 was entered.

Judge Crocker was stunned by the amount. When the jury announced that it had reached a verdict, Crocker had turned to me privately and whispered that the total would be no more than $100,000. Instead we found ourselves facing what was then the largest jury verdict against the press in American history. We quickly filed papers before the judge, asking him to overturn the verdict or, at the least, order a new trial. As regards the large sums awarded by the jury, Judge Crocker ruled in our favor, striking the jury verdict of over $9 million for Newton's claims of lost past and future income as being unsupported by the evidence, and concluding that the jury's award of $5 million for damage to Newton's reputation "shocks the conscience of the court because the broadcasts did not tarnish his outstanding reputation." Nonetheless, Judge Crocker upheld the jury's verdict that NBC was liable and upheld its pain-and-suffering award of $225,000 as well as its punitive damage award of $5 million. He gave Newton a choice: Either he had to file what is called a remitittur (a sort of waiver) of all sums except $5,225,000, or there would be a new trial in federal court in *California* on all issues. While Judge Crocker had finally come around to the view that we could not get a fair trial in Nevada, he had still left Newton with an enormous judgment, one that Galane immediately characterized as "higher than any libel award ever affirmed by an appellate court in the history of this nation by five times." Unwilling to risk a new trial outside Nevada, Newton agreed to accept the $5 million plus.

THE APPEAL

But that did not mean he would receive it.

We took the next legal steps open to us by turning to the United States Court of Appeals for the Ninth Circuit, the court that hears appeals from western states, including Nevada. On April 13, 1990, I rose to argue before a three-judge panel in Pasadena, California, comprising Chief Judge Alfred T. Goodwin, Judge Dorothy W. Nelson, and Judge William A. Norris. The panel, chosen at random, was about as close to a dream

191

team as I could have wished for. Judge Goodwin, a Republican appointed by President Nixon, had been a journalist in his youth and was a highly respected jurist with a reputation for being open-minded. He would later write the opinion determining that the reciting of the Pledge of Allegiance with the words "under God" in it in public schools was unconstitutional, a ruling later reversed by the Supreme Court. Judge Nelson, appointed by President Carter, was the former dean of the UCLA Law School and a forthright protector of constitutional rights, including, specifically, First Amendment rights. Judge Norris had clerked for Justice William O. Douglas, one of the most liberal and First Amendment-protecting judges in the Supreme Court's history, and had himself written many rulings strongly supportive of free speech.

I began by discussing Las Vegas and the risks of permitting a local jury to punish the national media for attacking a prominent and powerful local figure. Galane himself had observed that Newton was "beloved" and "worshipped" in Las Vegas and that he had commenced his litigation not only for himself but "for Las Vegas as well." In these circumstances, I argued, there was particular need for the closest judicial scrutiny to ensure that First Amendment rights were not compromised.

Judge Norris, who asked almost all the questions posed by the court to both Galane and myself, then asked me a lengthy series of questions regarding the scope of review of the jury verdict in the case—i.e., the degree to which an appellate court could second-guess what the jury had done. I argued that since the case involved enormous potential punishment of NBC for engaging in speech, the court should engage in the closest sort of review, not affirming the jury verdict unless it was itself of the view that we should lose. Judge Norris responded that the law did not provide the court of appeals with quite that much authority, but that the review by the court would certainly be far more rigorous than was normal.

Judge Norris then asked me a number of questions about the degree of deference that should be given to the jury's decision as to the credibility of witnesses, noting that the Supreme Court had been highly deferential to such determinations. I responded that there were no facts on the appeal that depended on overturning credibility determinations, since we were not asking the court to "believe" any NBC testimony where it conflicted with that of Newton. After a number of exchanges with me, Judge Norris summarized the entire series of questions and the answers I had given by stating that in the First Amendment area, perhaps the approach that should be taken was to give less deference to a jury's determination of credibility and more to other evidence so as to guard against local jury bias and to ensure the protection of First Amendment rights. I agreed.

I concluded my argument with a few comments

about the dangers posed by the case. There was no serious claim, I said, that particular statements in the broadcast were untrue, only that the overall impression it presented was false. This was a dangerous notion in any case, I maintained. Our brief had argued against judicial recognition of the very concept of libel suits by public figures based on the "impression" left by a publication. But if ever that concept was recognized, I argued, it should not be in a case such as this. For here, I said, any "impression" that Newton was holding some form of hidden interest in the Aladdin Hotel came from Newton's own false statements. It was only because Newton had lied to the Nevada Gaming Board and to the NBC journalists themselves that Ross and Silverman had become so suspicious of his conduct and went on to investigate the possibility that organized crime figures were in some way involved with the Aladdin. How, in that context, I asked, could NBC be held liable because its use of words such as "Newton," "Las Vegas," "mob," "lying," and "grand jury investigation" could be said to have left some sort of incriminating impression? Unless Newton had proved that the journalists had meant to leave a false impression, I said, there could be no liability.

As I was about to sit down, Judge Nelson asked me to comment about our change-of-venue motion. It was a good opening, allowing me to refer once again to Wayne Newton Boulevard, Wayne Newton Day, and other manifestations of

Newton's intimate association with the Las Vegas community.

Now it was Galane's turn. The fact that my colleagues and I were personally offended by his tactics had not made him a weak opponent. For the trial, he had mastered an enormous amount of facts and prior testimony and had presented his case clearly and powerfully to the jury.

Now it was his moment to set forth the facts upon which a judgment against NBC could be sustained, and from beginning to end he failed the test. Galane's brief had berated NBC's behavior but had contained little in the way of factual support for the proposition that Ross and Silverman knew or suspected that what they were saying was not true. Galane had argued briefly in his written submissions that they had contradicted themselves in their trial testimony as compared with what they had said in their pretrial depositions, and he began his oral argument by referring to that discrepancy. Judge Norris immediately interrupted to observe that that had been set forth in a footnote to Galane's brief. Was there any other evidence he was relying on, Judge Norris asked, other than these "self-claimed contradictions"?

Galane responded that the "self-demonstrating nature of the videotape" showed that NBC had accused Newton of fronting for the mob when he sought to be licensed to run the Aladdin Hotel. Judge Norris disagreed, saying sharply, "I've reviewed that." When Galane responded that the inferences to be drawn from the videotape were clear, Judge Norris disagreed, asking Galane for "any other evidence you would cite to provide independent support" for the claim that NBC had prepared the program with "actual malice"— knowledge of its falsity or serious doubts as to its truth. Galane responded hesitantly, and Judge Norris quickly interrupted to ask him if the most offensive inference from the broadcast was that the mob had obtained a piece of action in the Aladdin Hotel because of favors they had done for Newton. Galane responded that the broadcast had been structured around the issue of monetary assistance, noting that it had referred to the "financial problems of Newton" that had been solved by the mob. Now Judge Norris interrupted angrily, correcting Galane by stating that the broadcast had not said that at all. " 'Whatever the problem was,'" Judge Norris quoted the broadcast as saying, the mob had solved it. Galane responded that an average viewer would necessarily conclude that the problem was a financial one.

Galane then argued that on the broadcast the reporters had ignored and omitted confirmed evidence about threats to Newton and his daughter. Judge Norris responded by asking what Newton's attorney Frank Fahrenkopf had said at Newton's car when asked by Ross about threats. Galane twice replied that the question Ross had asked was misleading, and after twice being rebuked by Judge Norris for not responding finally acknowledged that Fahrenkopf had said, "Don't be silly."

Judge Norris then posed a hypothetical question.

"Assume that the reporters have reason to believe the following. A public figure is making telephone calls to an identifiable member of the Mafia, those calls are being made at a time when the public figure was negotiating for the purchase of a major Las Vegas hotel, federal authorities were investigating the connection between the public figure and the Mafia figure and were concerned about possible mob involvement in casinos in Las Vegas, and there was evidence that the known mob figure had stated that he had or was going to have a piece of the action and that federal authorities had raised a series of questions, but no answers. Is this report protected by the First Amendment?"

Galane acknowledged that it was.

Judge Norris took the next step. If the impression left by the broadcast "was that a series of questions were raised about mob figures and the hotel casino, you're not challenging that, are you?" When Galane started to answer, Norris interjected, "Do you believe the facts here go beyond that?" and then "What's so different about this case?" Galane remained silent for a second, and when Judge Norris again asked what in the record supported Newton's argument that the NBC reporters had purposely left a false impression about him, Galane referred to a twelve-page section of his brief in which he had discussed the factors on which he was relying to establish actual malice. Judge Norris quickly dismissed that explanation, saying that Galane's brief had been of little help to him because it did not specifically enumerate and identify any particular basis for concluding that the NBC journalists had meant to leave a false impression.

The argument ended soon afterward. We felt confident, very confident, about the result, and this time we were correct. On August 30, 1990, the court rendered its unanimous opinion reversing in all respects the judgment that Newton had won and ordering that judgment be entered in favor of NBC. Written by Judge Norris, the opinion concluded that Newton had failed to demonstrate actual malice on the part of NBC or its journalists.

Judge Norris made it plain that the court was concerned about the fairness of the trial of NBC in Las Vegas before a local jury enthralled by a "hometown hero." Newton was, he wrote, a "revered figure in Las Vegas," which celebrated Wayne Newton Day and had renamed the boulevard outside the airport in his honor. "We recognize," he wrote, "that the risk of unbridled favoritism of local juries generally informs a decision about venue rather than standard of review. However, in a case involving core First Amendment values, we cannot ignore the risk that a jury's credibility determinations may also subvert those values."

Newton was concededly a public figure, Judge Norris wrote, although Newton himself had earlier "strongly contested" that status (and had been sanctioned by Judge Crocker for pressing this utterly implausible legal position and ordered to pay $55,000 to NBC to cover its expenses with respect to the issue). Now it was uncontested. Newton could therefore prevail only if he demonstrated that NBC had realized that its broadcast was false or "subjectively entertained serious doubt as to the truth" of what it had said. In this case, Judge Norris wrote, Newton had failed to meet his burden.

The facts in the case, Judge Norris wrote, were hardly in dispute. Quoting at length from Newton's testimony before the gaming board and his later testimony at trial acknowledging in substance the false and misleading character of what he had said, the court identified one falsehood after another in Newton's testimony. He had, Judge Norris wrote, "testified falsely that Penosi had never visited him at his home." He had "also testified falsely before the gaming board that Mark Moreno was only a friend, that Moreno had no business or contractual position with him, and that Moreno was not his manager," when Moreno's clear testimony was to the contrary. He had "falsely stated" to Ross that he had last spoken with Penosi "maybe a year ago" and that Penosi had made no phone calls to him. "In fact," Norris wrote, Newton "did not tell the whole story to the Nevada State Gaming authorities."

In the end, Norris wrote, "almost all of the facts reported by NBC in the October 6, 1980 broadcast are uncontroverted. Newton went to Penosi with a problem and Penosi called Piccolo who helped solve the problem. Piccolo and Penosi later discussed 'earning off' Newton and possibly 'earning off' his ownership of the Aladdin Hotel. Piccolo and Penosi were investigated and indicted by a federal grand jury, which heard the testimony of Wayne Newton. All these facts are beyond dispute."

Judge Norris turned, in conclusion, to Newton's argument that the inclusion in the broadcast of a reference to his "financial problems" suggested "that NBC tried to bolster the idea that Piccolo had a hidden share of the Aladdin and so knowingly attempted to defame Newton." It was unacceptable, Judge Norris wrote, to make a finding of actual malice based on the *truthful* statement in the broadcast that authorities had indicated that Newton had financial problems. They had said precisely that, Norris pointed out, and they had spoken accurately. Prior to purchasing the Aladdin, Newton was $75,000 a month short in meeting his then-current obligations. With his new obligations undertaken in running the Aladdin Hotel, Newton would owe another $85,000 a month. Beyond that, Norris wrote, it was "undisputed that a disagreement over an amount not less than $20,000" had led to a fight between Newton and at least one low-level member of an organized crime family that, in turn, had precipitated the threats to Newton and his daughter and led Newton to go to Penosi for help. In circumstances such as these, NBC could not be held liable for leaving any supposed false impression. Only if NBC had meant to leave such an impression could the network be held liable, and there was no basis to conclude that in this case.

With this ruling, the case was all but over. Galane sought reargument from the court of appeals, and on April 5, 1991, the court denied the motion. Not long afterward we received a check from Newton for $135,000 in court costs, a small fraction of the millions of dollars in legal fees paid by NBC but still very satisfying. A few months later, the Supreme Court declined to hear the case.

By the time it came to an end, the case had lasted for twelve years. Notwithstanding the scorching language of the Court of Appeals, Newton admirers in Las Vegas falsely continue to treat the case as a "history-making win" for him and to misattribute to the appeals court the view that NBC's report, rather than Newton's testimony before Nevada gaming authorities, was inaccurate. Newton's later reflection on the case was right about one thing: "the trial," he observed, "set a precedent that is referred to even now after the turn of a century."

CHAPTER 5

THE HEROIN TRAIL

Late in 1971 the publisher and senior editors of *Newsday*, a Long Island daily newspaper, met to discuss an ambitious concept for a series of articles. A growing number of young men and women who lived on Long Island had been dying from overdoses of heroin. Could *Newsday*, publisher William Atwood asked, do a series of articles tracing the flow of heroin from the poppy fields of Turkey to the veins of Long Island kids? Robert W. Greene, the Pulitzer Prize-winning chief of the paper's investigative team, was asked to make an assessment of whether it should undertake such an effort. Greene traveled throughout the United States and France, interviewing present and former officials who had been active in seeking to stem the flow of heroin. He ultimately concluded that *Newsday* could and therefore should examine the issue in depth, and the paper's senior executives agreed. *Newsday* journalists began to work on the single most daunting and expensive series in the institution's history, a series that would lead to a libel action that would stretch over thirteen years and ultimately involve critical testimony of the most startling surprise witness I have ever seen.

Early in 1972 a team of *Newsday*'s investigative reporters began a lengthy investigation into the primary routes of heroin trafficking from Asia and Europe to Long Island. For six months Greene and reporters Les Payne and Knut Royce traveled throughout Turkey and Europe, interviewing government and underworld sources about the heroin trade. Three more *Newsday* journalists were assigned to study the flow of heroin into and throughout the United States.

Newsday published the result of the team's efforts in February and March of 1973 as a series of thirty-two articles entitled *The Heroin Trail*. The series was acclaimed as an extraordinary in-depth account of drug trafficking. A year later *Newsday* was awarded the Pulitzer Prize Gold Medal for public service for the series.

In 1974, the New American Library also re-published, in slightly modified form, the *Newsday* articles as a paper-bound book. In the book, as in the *Newsday* series, over three hundred individuals in the United States, Turkey, and Europe were listed and described as heroin traffickers. Over fifty of them were from Turkey. One of them, Mahmut Karaduman, was described as follows:

The owner of the Karavan nightclub in Istanbul's Galatasaray Square, middle-aged Douman [Karaduman] divides his time

204

between Istanbul, where his brother handles base shipments, and villas in Switzerland and Lebanon. He specializes in smuggling by the Black Sea route. His lieutenant, a Turk named Gabi Kaiat, lives in Bucharest and handles transshipments on the Romanian end.

Of all the individuals identified in the original *Newsday* series and in its book version, the only complaint received concerning *The Heroin Trail* came in the form of a lawsuit filed by Karaduman.

Karaduman himself, a resident of Istanbul, had first learned of the *Newsday* articles in the spring of 1974 when they were reported on in the Turkish press. He learned of the book that October when his daughter and son-in-law telephoned him from their home in Geneva, Switzerland, to tell him that a friend had happened upon a copy in a Washington, D.C. bookstore and had sent it to them. Almost a year later Karaduman started a lawsuit, claiming he had been libeled.

For years, the case languished in the New York courts. Karaduman's original claim based on the references to him in the *Newsday* series was dismissed as having been filed too late. (Under New York law, libel actions must be filed within a year of publication of the articles leading to the suit, a rule that is followed rigorously.) Years later, in 1980, the New York State Court of Appeals, the state's highest court, concluded that while all claims against *Newsday* for what it had published in its newspaper and against the book's publisher had been properly dismissed as untimely, the case against *Newsday* itself could proceed with respect to claims arising from the publication of the book; all other claims were barred.

For years afterward the case moved glacially, until finally, in June and July 1986, the trial began before a New York jury. After twenty-four days of testimony, including eleven days of testimony translated from Turkish, a mistrial was declared when two of the six jurors told Justice Kenneth L. Shorter that they could no longer continue to serve. Karaduman had not even completed the presentation of his case when it was dismissed; *Newsday* had not called a single witness. It was the stuff of Dickens: A colossal amount of time and money had been wasted with no result other than an order to begin all over again.

About a month later I received a call from Leonard Horowitz, an attorney with Times-Mirror Inc., the parent company of *Newsday*, asking if I would agree to represent it in the retrial. When we met, I told him that I would be pleased to do so, but that I was committed to try the Wayne Newton case for NBC in the fall of 1986 and thus could not turn my full attention to the Karaduman matter until it was concluded. Horowitz told me that that should not be a problem, since the Karaduman retrial would not likely begin until the spring of 1987.

Shortly after our Las Vegas debacle in the Newton case (and years before our ultimate victory in the court of appeals), Horowitz and I lunched again. His question to me this time was more pointed: Was I so dispirited by the disastrous result of the Newton trial that I had any qualms about proceeding to represent *Newsday* in its trial? I assured him that I was confident of a reversal of the Newton decision and that, more to the point, my desire and ability to represent his client were unimpaired. Of course, I meant every word of what I told him. What I thought and did not say, however, was that I had *better* win against Karaduman. Newton might have bested us before a Las Vegas jury; in this case we were home in New York defending a local newspaper against a Turkish businessman it had accused of having trafficked in drugs. There could be no excuses for losing.

PRETRIAL

Although the five weeks of trial in 1986 that had ended so inconclusively may have frustrated the parties involved, for us, newly retained to re-present *Newsday*, the transcript of the aborted trial was a godsend. Dean Ringel and I pored over its pages, seeking to master our opponents' strategy as we formulated our own.

The *Newsday* journalists who worked on the series had told the first jury a powerful story. Greene, Payne, and Royce had spent three months in Turkey and another three months traveling throughout Europe in their effort to compile information about heroin traffickers, often placing themselves in grave personal peril as they consorted with drug dealers and other criminals. The enormous commitment of time and effort by *Newsday* included continual checking and rechecking of what the journalists had been told. Based on information provided them from underworld sources who were themselves smugglers of heroin and a "chemist" who processed heroin, the journalists were able to compile a list of Turkish heroin traffickers. They had been introduced, they said, to the smugglers and the "chemist" by Galip Labernas, the former top narcotics officer in Turkey. Every name on their list, they had testified, had been cross-checked with Labernas and two other high-ranking Turkish officials, who had signed off on the accuracy of the information regarding every person on the list.

In the course of their reporting, the *Newsday* journalists took notes on what they were being told. At the end of each day, they typed their notes, retaining copies of the typed versions so as to help them recall what they had learned. The journalists were well-spoken, dedicated, and obviously knowledgeable. Having read their truncated but revealing testimony in the 1986 trial and then having met them, I expected them to fare well with any jury.

We faced two major problems, however. The first

was that the journalists were totally dependent on their sources. No one from *Newsday* had actually *seen* any drug transaction involving any of the named narcotics traffickers. The basis—the entire basis—of what they had written about Karaduman and the other drug-linked figures was what they had been provided by individuals in a position to know, and the confirmation of the accuracy of that information provided by other individuals in a position to know. In fact, Greene and his colleagues were explicit that but for the confirmation of the names on the list by the three high-ranking Turkish officials, they would not have submitted the list for publication.

In legal terms, then, the journalists were relying on hearsay: unsworn-to information provided by third parties. Of course, much of the best journalism is nothing but hearsay, a recapitulation of what people tell journalists about what they have seen and heard. Journalists use hearsay the way the rest of us do in our daily lives. We learn from it, repeat it, and if we trust it, rely upon it. At trial, however, hearsay is not admissible as proof of the *truth* about anything. We could not, therefore, demonstrate the truth of the assertions made about Karaduman in the book simply because reputable sources had said precisely what *Newsday* had attributed to them.

Yet even if we could not prove truth, as lawyers define it, I thought our chances of winning the case were good. Under New York law, journalists may not be found to have libeled even a private party with respect to matters of public concern (the charge that someone is a heroin trafficker is certainly that) unless they have been grossly irresponsible in their journalistic work. So long as they believed the journalists about the steps they had taken to verify their information, the jury should not find them to have acted irresponsibly at all.

But there was a critical, potentially disastrous problem with our defense. If, as we argued, *Newsday*'s journalism, as reflected in the book, was far from being irresponsible, it was because the newspaper had accurately reported what its sources had told it. But in the 1986 trial, Karaduman had put at issue the truth of the journalists' testimony as to just that.

Bob Greene had testified that Omar Aypun, the chief of the homicide squad in Istanbul and former head of Narcotics in Istanbul, had told him that each of the individuals (including Karaduman) on the list compiled by the journalists was engaged in drug trafficking. But Aypun, in a 1984 deposition, had stated that he was never involved with narcotics, that he did not recall speaking with any of the American journalists, and that he "never identified Mahmut Karaduman as a person dealing with narcotics . . . to anyone," including the journalists.

Similarly, Les Payne had testified that he had interviewed Orhan Erbug, the head of the entire Turkish police, who likewise had confirmed that

Karaduman as well as the entire list of others identified by *Newsday* were traffickers in heroin. Leon Segan, Karaduman's attorney, argued in response that Erbug had denied that he ever knew Karaduman at all, let alone confirmed his status as a drug trafficker.

Finally, the single most important Turkish source—Galip Labernas, the former top police narcotics officer in Turkey, whom the journalists had testified was their prime confirming source— had testified that their testimony that he had confirmed that Karaduman was involved with drugs was false. Karaduman's name had not been mentioned to him by the journalists, he insisted, and if it had been, he would have told the journalists that Karaduman was not involved with drugs at all. In the first trial, Labernas had acknowledged that forty-seven of fifty-three individuals listed by *Newsday* as having been in the Turkish narcotics trade were indeed so involved. Labernas had also testified that he had no recollection as to five others. The single remaining name, Karaduman, he had testified, was not only erroneous but had never even been discussed with him.

This testimony, if repeated at the trial that loomed before us, would not by any means necessarily doom our cause. It did mean, however, that the credibility of the three American journalists would be central to the case's resolution. If the jury believed they had done what they said (and their notes reflected), there should be no finding of gross irresponsibility. But if the jury believed the Turkish police officers, difficult days lay ahead.

The direct conflict in testimony also led us in a different direction. Was it absolutely clear, we asked ourselves, that we could not prove that Karaduman had participated in drug transactions? The journalists, of course, could not testify to any such activity on the basis of their personal knowledge. That was our hearsay problem. But was it conceivable that we could come up with an eyewitness who could be of help? I called Jules Kroll, the CEO of Kroll Associates, the nation's most acclaimed investigative firm, to ask him if he could inquire, through the extensive range of former law enforcement officials employed by him, whether Karaduman was known to be a drug trafficker in Istanbul. Jules promised to get back to me.

TRIAL

In our opening statements, both Segan and I played to what we viewed as our strengths. I focused on the care *Newsday* had taken in preparing the articles, he on what he argued was their lack of truth. I talked about the dangers the three American journalists had endured, he about the stature of Labernas. I said not a word about the accuracy of the book's references to Karaduman; he was all but silent about the extraordinary commitment

Newsday had made to prepare the articles or the good faith of the journalists in doing so.

For a time, the trial proceeded in predictable fashion. Karaduman testified effectively. Tall, soft-spoken, and well-dressed, a distinguished-looking man of sixty-five, he testified in Turkish with an English translator. He told the inspiring story of his life, a story of a self-made man who had gone to work as a small boy to help his impoverished family survive, whose schooling was prematurely ended because of the need to support them, and who had, by hard work and dedicated effort, built a successful import-export business. It had begun in the scrap metal field and later expanded to include meat, olives, and cement. It did not include drugs.

Virtually everything the book had claimed about him was untrue, he said, and everything of consequence was certainly false. Not only were specific facts asserted by *Newsday* about him incorrect (he owned no villas in Switzerland, for example, but simply stayed with his daughter and son-in-law in their attractive home there), but the core of its presentation was untrue. He did not own the Karavan Club (his brother did), and he rarely frequented it. In fact, he went there (it was downstairs from his office) only at lunchtime. Karaduman told the jury that he consumed no liquor, smoked no cigarettes, and absolutely, without equivocation, had never consumed drugs or ever taken part in any drug transaction. He had never been a drug smuggler and had never been involved with narcotics in any way.

When he was told about the book by his daughter and her husband, he said, he immediately retained Segan to commence a libel action against *Newsday*. Unlike a newspaper, Karaduman testified, a book "will be present in all libraries and it will never be lost." He was crushed, he said, when his grandson saw the book.

Karaduman had testified that he did not own the Karavan Club, and I quickly turned in my cross-examination to that subject. Segan had stated in his pretrial deposition of Bob Greene that Karaduman had owned the building in which the Karavan Club was located. Was that true? Karaduman denied that he had ever owned the building.

As for the club itself, Karaduman's testimony remained unambiguous. Occasionally, he went there during the day; his children played there sometimes; but it was only open for business at night, from 11:00 p.m. to 3:00 or 4:00 a.m., and Karaduman never went there at those times. "Never," he said, "not even once."

I had received some information that would later be of significance in the case and asked Karaduman about it. Had he ever had drinks at the Karavan Club with American Drug Enforcement Administration representatives? Suddenly, he seemed less sure of himself. "I don't remember," he said. Had he ever taken business associates of his there?

Again, the same response: "I don't remember." A bit later, I returned to the same subject and his answers were more definitive. He had never spoken to any American police or drug agents—ever. "Why would I?" he asked. "Why would it concern me?"

Our three key journalistic witnesses were each called to the stand by Segan, a common tactic of plaintiffs' lawyers in libel cases. I thought each was persuasive in his depiction of the exhaustive efforts the three had made to ascertain the truth both in and out of Turkey about its leading heroin dealers. They had initially spoken with American law enforcement sources, they testified, who put them in touch with Turkish police (in particular Labernas), who in turn introduced them to a heroin "chemist" and drug smugglers who identified for them the leading Turkish drug dealers. They had then confirmed what they had been told with the three Turkish police officials.

Greene, Payne, and Royce testified at length about their investigation, particularly the three months they had spent in Turkey. When necessary to refresh their recollections, they consulted their typed notes of what they had been told and by whom. When confronted with the fact that each of their three most critical Turkish sources had testified in one proceeding or another that they had not provided the confirmation about Karaduman that the journalists claimed, they responded coolly and (so I thought) persuasively that the Turks had testified falsely.

The most critical witness called to the stand by Segan was Galip Labernas. Although all three of the Turkish officials the American journalists had testified they relied upon had denied the accuracy of their testimony, only Labernas had come to New York. That made his testimony especially important: if he was lying, so, probably, were they; if he was telling the truth, little else would matter.

Labernas, who had worked closely with American drug enforcement officials for many years, testified to a number of meetings he had had with the American journalists. They initially had told him, he claimed, that they had come to Turkey to write a series about hunting and fishing, and he had assisted them in making appointments to do so. In their first meeting they had said nothing at all about drugs.

He had then, he said, received a letter from an American drug-fighting colleague of his, asking him to assist Greene, Payne, and Royce with regard to inquiries they were making about narcotics trafficking in Turkey. Royce had then told him that while they had come to write about tourism, hunting, and the like, now that they were there they thought they would write about narcotics as well. After the journalists made a trip to Afyon, a city in southern Turkey, they met with Labernas again and asked him to review certain names they had acquired and to tell them whether they were indeed involved in narcotics. Greene read the names to him, Labernas testified, and

Labernas had commented on each one. Some had already been convicted of smuggling; others were suspected of it; still others were not smugglers at all. A few names were unknown to Labernas. Karaduman's name, he said, was never even discussed. It had not been raised by the Americans, and Labernas consequently had not responded to any question about him.

As for the alleged drug trafficking, Labernas's testimony was unequivocal:

Q: Mr. Labernas, as far as you're concerned today, have you ever found from your information from the very day that you ever started as being a narcotics investigator up to the present time, whatever knowledge you required, have you ever found Mr. Mahmut Karaduman ever involved in narcotics dealings?

A: No.

As I began my cross-examination of Labernas, I had two aims. Since his testimony had unambiguously accused the three American journalists of lying, it was imperative to strike at Labernas's own credibility. Since he had confirmed that the journalists had asked him about each of the other individuals listed in the book as drug smugglers, it was also critical to extract from him confirmation that it was correct about them. That, at the least, should help to combat any suggestion that the journalists had simply conjured up the list published in the book.

I started with an affidavit that Labernas had prepared and reviewed in 1978, which stated that on one of the occasions he met with the *Newsday* journalists they had passed to him a "written list with some names recorded and asked him some information." Labernas had denied in his direct examination that he had been given a list at all, claiming that the names had been read to him by Greene. The difference was potentially significant, since Karaduman's name was on the list the journalists had produced in court, a list they had testified they had shown him. When I confronted Labernas with his affidavit affirming that he had been passed a list, he again denied it, claiming that the translation from Turkish to English might have been incorrect. When I read to him from another statement prepared by him that stated "they showed a list of names in a notebook," Labernas insisted again that nothing had been shown to him, but only read to him. After a flurry of objections from Segan, I asked Labernas again if he had understood that he had said that the journalists had shown him a *list* of names in a notebook. Again, Labernas asserted that he had seen no list. I then read to him from his pretrial deposition, in which he had said once again that he had seen a "list" given to him by the American journalists. Again Labernas claimed that the translation must have been at fault.

The jury seemed interested in Labernas's testimony but was otherwise inscrutable. It was, I thought, a reasonably effective beginning in suggesting that the witness was malleable regarding the truth, but it was impossible to assess its impact on the jury.

Before turning to the substantive issue of just what Labernas claimed to have said to the journalists, I confronted him with other inconsistencies in his prior statements. One line in an affidavit he had signed had said that he had been introduced to Greene's wife at one of the meetings in Turkey. He acknowledged that Greene's wife had not been there. Another had said that the journalists had given him a letter from his former American colleague during his second meeting with the journalists. He conceded that they had given it to him at a later date.

There was more of the same in other areas, useful contradictions all, but by no means breathtaking ones. A jury might be persuaded that he was backing and filling. Then again, it might conclude that there had been some translation problem or that the errors had been inconsequential.

Labernas did state, as he had at the first trial, that he had confirmed for the Americans forty-seven of the fifty-three names identified in the book as drug smugglers. This was a potentially useful admission, since it would permit me to ask the jury later why the journalists would have deliberately included Karaduman's name when it was unknown in this country and when they had so many others they could cite.

There was no minimizing the importance, however, of those areas in which Labernas and the three Americans disagreed. Had Labernas, as Greene had testified, introduced the American journalists to the Turkish underworld "chemist" named Ozpetek? It was Ozpetek, Greene had testified, who had furnished many of the names on the list of Turkish drug dealers they had compiled, a list that included Karaduman. According to Labernas, however, Ozpetek was in jail in 1972 and thus could not have been introduced to the Americans then. More important, Labernas flatly denied that he had ever introduced Ozpetek to them.

I pressed Labernas about Ozpetek's whereabouts in 1972.

> Q: Did you say a moment ago that he was in jail in 1972?
> A: I believe so. I believe so because I believe he was in jail in relationship to a murder and I believe when there was a general pardon, he may have gotten out at that time. They had killed one of his rich friends' father for money.
> Q: I just want to know was it your testimony that Mr. Ozpetek was in jail in 1972?
> A: That is how I know it.

After that bit of confusion, I tried to clarify things.

Q: I want to read to you from your testimony last year, July 11th, 1986, page 2066, line 11:

> *Question*: Is that the fact that you saw him, Mr. Ozpetek, sometime in 1978, 1979 and not 20 years ago?
>
> *Answer*: Maybe I may have seen him. He was not in jail in 1972. If he's out, if he came out, I may have seen him.

A: If I have given such testimony, that was my belief. I believe that he was in jail in 1972.

Q: When did you start believing that?

A: When I was working, he had committed a murder and he was in jail. I retired in '72, so he must be in jail then at that time.

Q: Did you ever mention Mr. Ozpetek's name to Mr. Greene?

A: I don't remember.

Was I making progress? If the jury thought that Labernas was improvising by the moment, absolutely. If the jury believed there were continuing translation problems, maybe not.

Then there was the Turkish drug smuggler the journalists had testified Labernas had introduced them to, a man named Hadaya. Like Ozpetek, they said, Hadaya had provided the names of Turkish drug traffickers (including Karaduman's), which they later confirmed with Labernas himself.

Labernas had testified earlier that he had not introduced Hadaya or anyone else he believed to be a drug smuggler to Greene. Greene and his colleagues had said the opposite. Now, once again, Labernas flatly denied the accuracy of the testimony of the journalists.

> Q: My question is, you know, do you not, that Mr. Greene has testified that you introduced another man as a chemist?
> A: Yes, in his testimony he said so.
> Q: And your testimony is that you did not introduce anyone as a smuggler, is that correct?
> A: I didn't introduce any smugglers.
> Q: My question is, did you say to Mr. Greene that you were introducing him to a smuggler?
> A: No, I didn't.

I could not tell, when Labernas sat down after three days of questioning by Segan and me, how he had been perceived by the jury. They looked at him intently but gave no indication as to whether or not they found him a credible witness.

When Segan ended the presentation of his case, he had presented more than sufficient evidence to warrant a jury's ruling in his favor—if, that is, they had believed his witnesses and disbelieved mine. Karaduman had staunchly denied being involved in drugs in any way. The three Turkish law enforcement officials (and most particularly Labernas) had put at issue the central prong of our defense: that the journalists had been told, by multiple Turkish sources in a position to know the truth, that Karaduman was in fact a drug trafficker. For our part, the three journalists had each been called to the stand by Segan and had each testified powerfully and in great detail about all the steps they had taken to ensure that the names they had printed were correct. The critical step, they all testified, was the confirmation by the three Turkish officials. All acknowledged that if they had not received that confirmation, they would not have used the names that they had collected (Karaduman's included) in the book. It was as clear and as muddled as that.

Everything, then, rested on the credibility of our witnesses. But by this point we had in reserve a new witness, a spectacular, Perry Mason-like surprise witness, who would change the nature of the trial.

THE SURPRISE

Although I had not said a word about the truth of the book's allegations regarding Karaduman in my opening statement, I was hoping that Jules Kroll would come up with something with which we could move our focus from simply detailing the care the journalists had taken to the issue that every juror wants most to hear about: was the story true?

Two weeks into the trial, Kroll telephoned me. Colleagues of his, he said, who had worked for the DEA had located a witness who was prepared to testify that he had been involved in a drug deal with Karaduman in Istanbul. I was stunned. I asked him if he was certain, thinking that while nothing could win the case more clearly for us than if the jury believed that Karaduman had been involved with drug trafficking, nothing could doom it more definitively than putting on an unpersuasive witness.

It was one thing for us to argue that because *Newsday* had been sufficiently careful in its journalistic work, we should prevail; it was quite another to argue that Karaduman was in fact a trafficker in drugs. Once we argued that, we opened *Newsday* up to substantial punitive damages if the jury rejected the arguments. But it would have been malpractice not to argue that point if we believed we had a good chance of proving it.

At my request, Kroll had the prospective witness and individuals for whom he had worked as an undercover agent flown to New York so that I could meet with them. The witness was about five feet tall, well over 250 pounds, and unprepossessing. He spoke some English but was far more comfortable in Arabic, his native tongue.

Perspiration rolling down his face, he told me his story.

His name was Faraculah Arras. He now lived in Los Angeles, where he worked as a tailor. When he had lived in Istanbul in the early 1970s, he had acted as an undercover drug dealer for the Bureau of Narcotics and Dangerous Drugs (BNDD), the American drug enforcement agency that was the predecessor to the DEA. But before that, in 1966, he had met Karaduman at the Hilton Hotel in Istanbul and had purchased forty-two kilos of morphine base from him, for which he paid 210,000 Turkish liras. He had then carried the drugs by car to France.

The story was perfect. But was it too good to be true? Did I, and would a jury, believe it? I cross-examined Arras for hours, and he answered all my questions persuasively. He paused occasionally but gave every indication of trying to remember events of fifteen years before, not fabricating them. Sweat continuously poured down his face as he spoke, but that seemed more likely a function of his weight than of nervousness brought about by any attempts at falsification. I asked his former BNDD handlers if they believed him. They did. I asked more questions designed to trap him. He passed every test I set.

In New York practice, unlike that in federal court, there is no requirement that witnesses be identified in advance. Surprises are commonplace in jury trials, and Arras's testimony was as surprising as anything I could have conjured up in *Newsday*'s defense. But just before he was to appear in court, one of his handlers gave me distressing news: Arras would not testify if he had to reveal his American home address. He was afraid of retribution if he did so.

This was a potentially insurmountable barrier. It was one thing not to disclose to my opponent that Arras would testify; it was quite another to refuse even to provide his address when he did testify, thus potentially preventing Segan from checking out the bona fides of his very existence.

Speaking to him though a translator, Dean Ringel and I had begged Arras to reconsider. Suppose, we said, we tried to persuade New York State Supreme Court Justice Arthur Blyn that the address should not be made public. Would he agree that we could provide the address to Judge Blyn and Mr. Segan in private, allow the judge to hear all of his testimony, and then decide whether to keep the address secret? Otherwise, we told him, he probably would not be permitted to testify. We left the room so Arras could consider our none-too-satisfying offer. A few minutes later word came back to us that he would testify on that basis.

I asked Judge Blyn for a meeting before we began to put our case on. From the start he had seemed unsympathetic to our side, telling me once privately during Karaduman's testimony that he thought *Newsday*'s behavior was a classic example of McCarthyism. We should settle the case, he urged, since we would lose it if we did not. This was not unusual advice from a settlement-oriented judge. What was more disturbing was the strong sense I got from Judge Blyn that he thought we *deserved* to lose the case. Now he and Segan seemed transfixed by what I had to say to them.

Our first witness, I announced, would testify to certain criminal conduct he had engaged in together with Karaduman.

Judge Blyn was literally speechless. "I'm sorry?" he said.

"Certain criminal conduct," I repeated, "that he had engaged in together with Mr. Karaduman." But the witness was afraid to provide his address, I explained, as he was concerned about being harmed if he testified. Would the court agree that the address could be kept secret? Judge Blyn replied that he was aware of such requests being made in criminal cases but not civil ones, and that he would therefore have to consider the question.

Segan responded skillfully. The issue was not limited to the address of the witness, he said. We should be obliged to specify before his testimony what he would say. I responded that no lawyer had been obliged to provide such information before any other witness testified and that there was no basis for requiring it here.

Judge Blyn agreed to that proposition; no offer of proof would be required. But, he said, he needed time to consider whether the witness's address had to be provided. Segan pressed on, seeking advance notice as to the nature of the testimony. Certain types of criminal conduct would be irrelevant to the case, he said, although narcotics would not be. I decided to take the bait, hoping it would help me with Blyn. "I represent," I said, "that it has to do with narcotics." Again, Blyn and Segan stared at me. Was I really going to produce a witness who would provide direct evidence that Karaduman had engaged in drug trafficking?

Segan tried another tack. Let us take a break for a few hours, he said, to think about it. This was the last thing I wanted. I wanted no time for thinking at all. I wanted the fearful Arras on and off the stand as quickly as possible. I wanted him out of the courthouse, out of New York, and back at his Los Angeles tailor shop. Give me ten minutes, I asked the judge, to speak with Arras once more. I left the room and, speaking through the Arabic translator, begged Arras to testify without conditions. If he did, I said, we could finish his testimony that day and he could leave quickly and return to Los Angeles. If not, I said, the testimony would begin late, and possibly extend through the following day. Why not start now and get it over with?

Arras finally agreed. He took the stand, a translator beside him, and provided his address to the court reporter.

I started my examination bluntly, to alert the jury

to the importance of what they were about to hear. "Have you ever met Mahmut Karaduman?" I asked. "In 1966," Arras answered. Every juror snapped to attention.

I then briefly took him through his life story, beginning with his birth in Mirdin, Turkey, through his work as a tailor in Istanbul and then his move to Beirut, Lebanon, where he resided from 1956 to 1970. He testified that he had made frequent trips between Beirut and Istanbul in that time period. I then moved to the core of the matter, trying to ask the briefest of questions requiring the shortest, clearest answers. Where did you meet Mr. Karaduman? I asked. "With my Lebanese friends, at the Hilton Hotel," he responded. Judge Blyn intervened immediately, asking which Hilton Hotel. "In Istanbul," Arras replied.

When I asked what they had talked about, Segan shouted an objection, which was sustained by Judge Blyn. Just testify, the judge instructed, to what Karaduman had said, not what his Lebanese friends had said.

BLYN: Mr. Arras, I want to know what Mr. Karaduman—you speak Turkish, correct?

ARRAS: Yes.

BLYN: Mr. Karaduman speaks Turkish, is that correct?

ARRAS: Of course.

BLYN [*yelling*]: You needed no interpreter for a conversation between yourself and Mr. Karaduman, is that correct? . . . So I want to know, Mr. Arras, just what Mr. Karaduman said to you, not what the other Lebanese said.

ARRAS: He met with me. I was going to transport the morphine base to France as the driver, and I did.

When the words "morphine base" were finally spoken, I let my breath out a bit. The story would be told, I knew, whatever objections were interposed. Blyn might be angry, Segan would be furious, but the story would be told. And so it was.

ABRAMS: What did Mr. Karaduman say to you?

ARRAS: We agreed, he gave me—

BLYN [*with greater irritation*]: Look, Mr. Arras. What did Mr. Karaduman say with his mouth to you, his words?

ARRAS [*triumphantly*]: He said through his mouth that "I can give you as much goods every week as you request."

ABRAMS: Did he say what kind of goods he was talking about?

ARRAS: Morphine base.

Now we were rushing downhill, picking up speed as we went. What was said, I asked Arras, about the morphine base? Karaduman, he responded, had told him, "My first dealings are always in cash. Afterwards I will give you credit." I decided to gild the lily a bit: "Is that what Mr. Karaduman said?" I asked. "From his own mouth," Arras responded, looking up at Judge Blyn as he spoke.

We turned to price. What was said about that? "Five thousand Turkish lira," he responded. "Five thousand lira for what?" I asked. "For a kilo," he said. Now we were really working in tandem. "Who said that?" I asked. "Mahmut," was the answer.

Arras then described how he and Karaduman went to Arras's room, where Karaduman had said he would take the cash and deliver the morphine base. "Was the cash in the room?" I asked. Yes, said Arras, 210,000 Turkish lira, which he gave to Karaduman. The cash was counted, Arras said, in ten-thousand-lira amounts, and he had handed it to Karaduman. "You personally handed it to Mahmut?" I asked. Looking up once again at Judge Blyn, Arras responded, "I gave it with my own hand to him."

Arras then described how two men came upstairs with a bag. Karaduman, he said, "counted the money, by the ten thousands."

By this point Judge Blyn himself was hooked. "What happened then?" he asked, posing the question every eager listener has always asked of every great storyteller. The money was taken away by Karaduman's compatriots, Arras said, and Karaduman left the room. Arras himself then returned to Beirut and began a four-day drive, with the kilos of morphine base in the car's trunk, to Marseilles, France, where they were removed and distributed to French recipients.

He had, Arras testified, seen Karaduman once more. In 1970, he had come across him by chance in a hotel restaurant in Munich. Karaduman had said to him, "You haven't been around for a while, where have you been?" When Arras said that he had quit working with the Lebanese, Karaduman had replied, "Now we are doing white." That meant heroin, Arras explained. To my surprise, there was no objection to Arras's explanation of Karaduman's use of the word "white"; even Segan seemed momentarily transfixed as Arras continued his recollection of the Munich meeting. Karaduman had said, "The goods were bulky, but now with the small volume you can make really good money." After that encounter, Arras said, he had never seen Karaduman again.

I concluded Arras's direct testimony by completing his recounting of his involvement with drugs. He had worked for three years, from 1969 through 1971, for the BNDD, on an undercover basis. He had never been convicted of a crime. The only narcotics deal he had ever done before working for the American authorities was with Karaduman. Now he was a tailor again.

I showed him a picture of Karaduman (who had briefly returned to Istanbul and was not present in court). Yes, Arras responded, that was Mahmut.

I sat down. By this point, Arras was not the only one drenched in perspiration.

Segan was now faced with a lawyer's worst nightmare. He had been counsel for over a dozen years to a man who had brought a libel suit claiming he had been falsely identified as having trafficked in heroin. Never in that time period had *Newsday* offered any argument (or evidence) directly showing that Karaduman was in fact a heroin trafficker. Now, before a jury, a live witness had testified that he had done a drug deal with Karaduman and had been offered another.

Segan made a brave effort to deal with the totally unexpected situation with which he was faced. He challenged Arras's recollection of Karaduman's appearance; he challenged Arras's description of how he had been contacted only two weeks before, twelve years after the case began; he suggested that Arras's former superiors in the BNDD had told him what to say. But every such thrust Arras parried effectively and persuasively.

In the courtroom during the trial sat Steve Swenson, a former BNDD agent who had accompanied Arras to New York. I had told Segan and Judge Blyn that Swenson would not be a witness, but Arras had no idea of who would testify about what after he completed his testimony. Segan tried to make headway with this:

Q: I will ask a simple question. Since you met [Swenson] for the first time in

seventeen years, did you say hello to
him?

A: Of course.

Q: And he said hello to you?

A: Yes.

Q: Tell me, where did you meet him?

A: At the Los Angeles airport.

Q: Mr. Swenson brought you here?

A: No. I had my ticket.

Q: You mean you met him and you came
together on a plane?

A: Yes.

Q: And when you got off the plane, did
you both go to Mr. Abrams' office?

A: No. We went to the hotel.

Q: Two different rooms?

A: Of course.

Q: And then you both, after the hotel, went
to Mr. Abrams' office?

A: Yes.

Q: And while you were talking with Mr.
Abrams, was Mr. Swenson present?

A: No.

It was worth the try, but it simply didn't crack
Arras. Referring again to Swenson, Segan asked
if Arras had met him prior to the time two weeks
earlier when Arras had been contacted about
testifying. "No, no, never," Arras responded.
Segan proceeded:

Q: And he was in Mr. Abrams' office when you were there; is that right?

A: He was also at the same hotel with us. He was at the same hotel with us.

Q: What hotel was that?

A: Plaza.

Q: Okay. So that Mr. Abrams' office made arrangements for you to be at the Plaza, Mr. Swenson to be at the Plaza and the other gentleman from San Francisco at the Plaza; is that right?

A: I don't know who rented their rooms, but I know that my room was arranged by Mr. Abrams' office.

Q: All right. And all three of you, you do know, stayed at the Plaza?

A: Yes.

Q: All right. Do you meet anybody else from—at Mr. Abrams' office that would be involved in this case?

A: I didn't understand.

Q: I could understand that. You're a witness in this case; is that right?

A: Yes.

Q: And you met Mr. Swenson, and we know he's not going to be a witness, but you met him at Mr. Abrams' office; is that right?

A: He told me, "Tell the truth, whatever you have seen."

I could not suppress a smile and did not try to.

Segan did get the jury to laugh a bit when Arras tried to blame his former wife for his engaging in a drug deal in the first place. "I was hoodwinked" into participating, Arras claimed, by his wife's repeated demand for more material goods. "Hoodwinked by your wife?" Segan asked. Yes, said Arras.

But on every substantive issue Arras remained firm. By 1970—the year, Arras had testified, he had met Karaduman in Munich—Arras was already working for BNDD. Did he tell the American authorities about his contact? Segan asked. Yes, replied Arras. Did the Americans send him to do a buy from Karaduman? At that point, Arras responded, he was a marked man, and shortly afterward the Americans sent him to the United States under an assumed identity to protect him.

What about Arras's memory? He had testified with precision about events that had occurred nineteen years ago. Was the testimony suspiciously specific? Segan pressed on.

> Q: And we're now talking about 1968 to 1987, so we are talking about nineteen years ago, isn't that so?
> A: Yes.
> Q: Okay. And you remembered that it was 5,000 Turkish liras a kilo, right?
> A: Yes.

Q: And you remembered that 5,000 was the amount, the price, and the total price was 210,000, right?

A: Yes.

Q: Okay. And if you divide that into 210 you get 42 kilos, right?

A: Yes.

Q: Okay. Tell me while you were sitting in Mr. Abrams' office, did any of the so-called—these drug agents help you calculate those kilos?

A: No.

Arras had testified that at the meeting with Karaduman at the Hilton Hotel, Karaduman had, for future identification purposes, torn four Turkish ten-lira notes in half, keeping four halves for himself and giving the others to Arras. Segan pressed on about that topic.

Q: Did they suggest to you this business about the tearing of the dollar to match one number against another? Did somebody suggest that to you?

A: I was the one who told them.

Q: I see. And was it a dollar? You said it was ten dollars?

A: Turkish liras.

Segan did all he could to discredit Arras or at least throw doubt on the accuracy of his recollections. I have always thought he conducted himself admirably when he found himself, without notice, confronted with a witness from lawyer hell. But by the end of the cross-examination Arras had held up well to all that Segan could offer. He had even drawn a few friendly smiles from the jury when Segan tried to link Arras's role as a tailor to that of drug smuggler. Segan had established that among Arras's customers in Beirut for whom he had made suits were narcotics dealers who would come to his shop with guns in their back pockets. When Segan asked if Arras had sewn morphine base into the suits, Arras looked at him as if he were mad: morphine base was heavy, and the notion that it would be sewn into suits was ludicrous. "No," he answered. Segan continued, asking if there was "no such thing as sewing morphine base into clothing." Again Arras looked at Segan disbelievingly. "How is it so?" he asked. "The reason I'm asking the question," Segan responded, "is because you are the tailor and the expert, maybe you can tell us." "It's possible," Arras replied dismissively, "that it can be in a car, but it's not possible that it can be in a suit."

After Segan completed his cross-examination of Arras, I called to the witness box three former BNDD officials, who vouched in turn for Arras's reliability and verified his testimony that he had been an undercover agent for the BNDD.

One of them went further. He had been in the Karavan Club, he testified, with a Turkish narcotics policeman a number of times. On five to ten of those occasions, Karaduman had been there, had offered to buy drinks for them, and had provided them with nuts and dried fruits. This testimony was of obvious significance, since Karaduman had testified that he had never even been in the club in the evening, let alone spoken with any American narcotics officials.

I then called each of the three journalists back to the stand to remind the jury of the extraordinary efforts they had made to find the truth.

Arras's testimony necessarily led both Segan and myself to change the focus of our summations from what we had told the jury in our opening statements. Segan had to cope with Arras; I had to decide how much to rely upon him. I really had no choice. Having called Arras to the stand, I could scarcely minimize his testimony—and, I thought, I had no reason to do so, either.

I began my summation by paying tribute to Segan for trying a beautiful case. (A compliment never harms the complimenter.) I then moved right to the new core of our own case. Segan had claimed, I said, that this was a lawsuit about a book that represented, in effect, that Karaduman was involved in drug trafficking. "He was," I said. "He shouldn't have brought this suit."

Segan had argued in his opening to the jury that *Newsday* never imagined that Karaduman would "come across the ocean, that this man would fight for his good name, that this man would persevere in this case all those years." I turned that formulation on its head, arguing that Karaduman "never imagined, it could not have occurred to him, that what would happen in this courtroom" is that we would put before the jury "someone that was there, present and personally involved with Mr. Karaduman in a criminal act involving narcotics."

Karaduman must have thought, I said, that with Labernas's testimony on his side as well as that of the other two Turkish police officials, *Newsday* would be left at trial without any direct support that Karaduman had indeed been involved with drug trafficking. But now, I said, we had offered testimony of the highest level of specificity that Karaduman had taken part in precisely the illegal conduct that *Newsday* had reported.

I turned next to Labernas's testimony and put it to the jury to decide whether *Newsday*'s journalists or he had been telling the truth. There was "no way to reconcile" the testimony, I said. Someone was lying, and it was up to the jury to decide who it was.

Was the book's reference to Karaduman true? I returned to Arras's testimony, pointing out that its accuracy had been bolstered by the testimony of his former BNDD chief, that Arras had been an informant for three years for American drug authorities in Europe, and that he was paid based upon the judgment of his superiors as to his honesty and reliability. Beyond that, I said, we had offered credible and persuasive testimony from another BNDD agent that he had seen Karaduman on five to ten evenings in the Karavan Club. Whom should you believe, I asked rhetorically, Karaduman or this high-ranking American official whose job was preventing the flow of drugs from Turkey to the United States?

Again and again I emphasized the scope of the differences in testimony. "Please bear in mind," I said, "how many people who have testified here you would have to find were lying, who I called to the stand, in order for you to rule in this case in favor of Mr. Karaduman." There were the three reporters; there was Arras; there were the three DEA agents. Were all of them lying? If not, how could Karaduman win?

I reviewed the testimony of each of the three journalists, emphasizing the specificity of their recollections and the internal consistency of what they had said. I contrasted that with the bobbing and weaving of Labernas. "You remember," I said, "all the translation stuff," the denial that he had ever been given a list of Turkish drug traffickers by the journalists. "He says 'bad translation'," I concluded; "I say 'bad liar.'"

Segan began his summation by seeking to deal immediately with one of his primary problems. "Where did the journalists get Karaduman's name from," if not from the Turkish sources they claimed to have relied upon? His answer: "I wasn't there. I wasn't there in 1972." And more broadly, it did not matter. What did matter was Arras and what our reliance on him said about our case.

Do you realize that for twelve years we have struggled to bring this case before you? For twelve years we have wanted to present Mr. Karaduman on the stand in front of this jury. For twelve years we have waited for this moment to come before you.

And what does the defense do, but trot in a person, if he is in fact a human being or person, who was spoken to two weeks ago, folks, two weeks ago. You know when he testified, April 30th. That meant around the 15th of April, two weeks after we were into this trial, they found this witness.

Do you know what that meant, folks? Do you know what that meant? Before Mr. Arras, they had nobody to establish any suggestion that Mr. Karaduman was involved in narcotics. Oh. Oh.

As for the journalists, Segan disclaimed any argument that they had "willfully" acted wrongfully in their reporting. They had had a "grab bag of names" and had acted wholly irresponsibly in picking out Karaduman's name and publishing it. The reporters had lied in Turkey about why they were there and should not be believed here. The four American BNDD people we had called to testify, Segan correctly observed, had not said that Karaduman had engaged in drug trafficking. "You didn't hear a word" from them to that effect, Segan told the jury, but only from Arras.

What sort of journalists were these, he said, that "never, never tried to contact Karaduman?" They had testified that they had gone to the office building in which he worked. They had said that they went to the Karavan Club but that it was closed. But if they "had gone to the third floor, they would have found Mr. Karaduman," and if they had even looked in the directory in the building, they would have seen his name.

Labernas was the key witness in the case, Segan maintained. He had testified for twenty-one days, including his pretrial depositions and his testimony at the first trial. He was an honest and honorable man, and there had not been a single serious inconsistency in any part of his testimony. "Mr. Labernas said something very simple. He said, 'I want to tell you something. They never even mentioned Karaduman's name to me at all. And I'll tell you something else. If they mentioned Karaduman's name to me, I would have said just that. You got the wrong person. I will tell you that what I know about him, he is not somebody involved in this area.'" Labernas was "the greatest narcotics cop, the most knowledgeable man that Turkey has ever had" dealing with drugs, Segan reminded the jury. He was well worthy of belief, especially when contrasted with the reporters, who had been so slipshod in their research and had taken so little care in their writing.

At its core, Segan said, *Newsday*'s case was utterly lacking in substance. No BNDD or DEA files had been produced supporting a word of Arras's story. If the accusation against Karaduman was true, why were there no written records supporting it? "Let me tell you," Segan said, "nobody, nobody in this trial who is credible has established the fact that Mr. Karaduman was ever involved in drug trafficking." If the jury accepted Arras's testimony, he acknowledged, "we walk home. That's the end of it." But Arras should not be believed, this "witness who came in two weeks ago, who came in, who was spoken to two weeks before he arrived on the scene." There was not, Segan maintained, "one piece of bona fide evidence to tie Mr. Karaduman" to drug trafficking.

At two p.m. on May 11, 1987, the jurors returned from lunch to hear Judge Blyn's charge. He asked them to respond to three questions. The first was whether the references to Karaduman in the book "concerning his involvement in illegal drug trafficking" were "substantially false." If they answered that question affirmatively, they then would address the second question: whether *Newsday*, acting through its reporters, had acted "in a grossly irresponsible manner." Finally, if their answer to question 2 was yes, they were instructed to answer an additional question of what damages, if any, they chose to award to Karaduman.

A few hours after the jury had retired to deliberate, they asked to have "Mr. Labernas's testimony read where Mr. Abrams read to him the names from the list and he confirmed them." That request (which sounded favorable to our case) was accommodated later in the afternoon. About an hour later, the jury sent an additional note stating that they wished "to finish deliberating in the morning because we are having difficulty answering No. 1 on the sheet at this time."

Court was adjourned for the day, and the jury went home. I was confident, I kept telling myself. I was right to be confident. The journalists had been persuasive, Arras had been persuasive, and, I believed, I had been persuasive.

The jury returned the next morning and shortly after lunch told the court attendant that they had reached a verdict. They returned to the courtroom to announce their verdict. The answer to the first question was yes: Karaduman had proven substantial falsity in the book. I couldn't, wouldn't, believe it. Had they really believed Karaduman and not Arras, Labernas and not the *Newsday* journalists? This was not the Newton case, I told myself; this was not Las Vegas. But then the jury answered the second question. No: the reporting had not been grossly irresponsible. So, in the end, we had won, if somewhat unsatisfactorily, since the jury had found substantial falsity in the reporting. But we had a victory, and I tried to make myself believe that that was good enough.

AFTERMATH

After the verdict a number of the jurors crowded around me. They wanted to talk to me, and I most certainly wanted to talk to them. In New York courts, unlike those in some other states, such post-verdict discussions are permitted, and I was eager to learn what testimony they had ultimately relied upon to reach their verdict. I invited them all to join me for lunch a week later at Windows on the World, the beautiful restaurant then atop the World Trade Center.

Four jurors showed up, all of them women, all black.* I learned a lot that day. They all told me that they were sure that Karaduman had been involved with drugs. They had believed Arras, but a number of them already had come to that view of Karaduman as they observed his own testimony. "We could tell," one of them told me, "that you were worried that we would believe Karaduman. But we know drug dealers in Harlem, and we knew he was one."

What was it about Karaduman that led to their reaching that conclusion? We could tell as soon as

* The other two jurors, one a hispanic male, the other a black woman, were unable to attend.

246

we saw him, one juror said. And there was something else. "How would you feel," one of them asked me, "if you were about to take the subway uptown to Harlem and you saw him get into his limousine at the end of each day? And he's asking us to give him twenty million dollars?"

If all that was true, I asked, how could they rule against us on the first issue they decided? How could they say that Karaduman had proved that the references to him were false? They had disagreed on that issue, one of them explained. And after all, another said, you did fail to prove that every word in the book was true. The book had said that the smuggling was done on the "Black Sea route," and I had not mentioned a word about the Black Sea. As for Arras, he had talked about driving all the way from Beirut to Marseilles. Where was the Black Sea in that?

I was floored. Judge Blyn had instructed the jury that the issue was whether Karaduman had proved that the book was *substantially false* about him. But if they believed that Karaduman had been involved in drug trafficking, then the book was substantially true, whatever the reference to the Black Sea. How, consistent with the jury charge, could we have lost on the truth issue?

The answer was unavoidable: The jurors had not understood the charge or, if they had, had paid little attention to it. They had decided that we should win and made certain that we had. The particular route they had chosen to award the victory to us may have deviated from what the law required, but it did embody what the jury wanted to do or wrongly understood it was supposed to do.

There was a final comment made to me at that lunch that I have never forgotten. As we were having coffee and were walking about the private room I had reserved to see the magnificent views below, one of the jurors came up to me. "You know," she said, "we could have given twenty million dollars of *Newsday*'s money to Mr. Karaduman." "Yes," I said, "I know you could have, but you did what you thought was right, and that's why the jury system is so great." "Yes," she responded, eyeing me more probingly, "but we *could* have given twenty million." I looked at her. I repeated that I understood that, and that was why I and all the people at *Newsday* were so grateful for the efforts of the jury and their dedication to their task. She looked at me as if I were an ass. "What I mean—" she began to say, but by then I had moved quickly away from her.

I did not want to hear a word more. Suppose, I thought, she followed up that statement by asking for something. I cut the conversation off without hearing a word more. I had to return to my office, I said, as I fled out the door. I never learned what her next line would have been.

CHAPTER 6

McCARTHYISM AND LIBEL

When Senator Joseph R. McCarthy first approached a podium in Wheeling, West Virginia, on February 9, 1950, to claim that he had in his hand a list of 205 "men in the State Department who have been named as members of the Communist Party and members of a spy ring," all of whom "were known to the secretary of state as being members of the Communist Party," no one could have predicted the full impact of his charges. His claims were, of course, all untrue. McCarthy had no list; the number 205 was bogus and would change repeatedly through the years; and his accusation that Secretary of State Dean Acheson "knew" that there were any Communists in the State Department was a lie. Nonetheless, from that day forward, McCarthy's representations of massive Communist infiltration into the federal government, of knowing complicity of Democratic administrations ("twenty years of treason"), and of grave and immediate peril to the public distorted and darkened the national landscape. By the time the scourge of McCarthyism had subsided four years later, after the Army-McCarthy hearings of 1954 and the censure of McCarthy by the Senate, the wounded and sometimes destroyed victims included present and former government officials, teachers, authors, and artists, and, not least, the reputation of the United States as an open, tolerant democracy.

The impact of McCarthyism stretched far from West Virginia, but when Helen Whitney, a prize-winning ABC producer and writer, decided in 1982 to return to the McCarthy days to survey the damage inflicted, she devoted almost half of the one-hour program that resulted, *American Inquisition*, to the impact of McCarthyism on another small West Virginia town. The segment focused on the plight of Luella Mundel, the chairman of the art department of Fairmont State College in Fairmont, West Virginia. As described by the narrator of the program as the segment began, in 1951 Mundel "was not a political activist, but had tastes, convictions about art, about religion, unfamiliar to these streets. And at a local American Legion seminar about subversives, she angrily stood to challenge what was being preached there. Her contract was dropped by the college. A state education official accused her of being a poor security risk. She then sued for slander, but in the trial that followed in Fairmont's courtroom, it was Luella Mundel and her right to speak freely, to be different, that wound up being tried."

After a brief sequence quoting part of her savage

cross-examination at one of the two slander trials commenced by her (the first had ended in a mistrial), the documentary brought Luella Mundel back to the Fairmont courtroom:

LUELLA MUNDEL [*voice-over*]: I can't remember much about Fairmont. I remember the courtroom. Bad vibes.

HELEN WHITNEY: Coming back here today wasn't easy, was it?

LUELLA MUNDEL: No, it's very unpleasant. It's an ordeal. My name is Luella Mundel, and I was in this courtroom about thirty years ago. I had been accused of being a security risk and an atheist by the president of the school board, and as a result I lost my job. And so I decided to sue the president of the school board for slander. I didn't realize that the person who brought the suit would be the one who was on trial.

There then followed a series of recollections by historian William Manchester about Fairmont in 1951; by Madeleine Hand, wife of the Fairmont college president at the time, about Mundel's special vulnerability at the time "because she had different ideas than the people in the community" and "did not hesitate to express her views"; from George Hand, the former college president, about his decision to hire Mundel; by Mrs. Hand about how Senator McCarthy's speech in Wheeling had "set the stage for much that happened, all that happened later," and how that speech had "terrified people"; and about how the American Legion had then scheduled "antisubversive" meetings in Fairmont. Those meetings were conducted by a group of speakers who often appeared together at such "Americanism" meetings. Some were former members of the Communist Party; others claimed to be expert in the conduct of the Party. All of them portrayed a nation at enormous imminent risk of virtually uncontrolled Communist infiltration. The broadcast continued with a group of individuals who lived in Fairmont in the early 1950s, who recalled the tone of the Americanism seminars held there and how those meetings "got people fired up to where they're just stomping" and asking, " 'Where are these guys that we're mad at?' "

Next to appear was Victor Lasky, a right-wing journalist who had reported on the trial and conviction of Alger Hiss and who later would become well known as a writer of harsh criticism of Democratic political leaders, including President John F. Kennedy, Senator Robert Kennedy, and former labor secretary and United Nations ambassador Arthur Goldberg. Lasky's was one of three distinct recollections set forth in the program concerning what had occurred at the American Legion meeting in Fairmont on March 31, 1951. "Well, I gave my usual talk about the danger of

Communist infiltration," Lasky said. "I also took the approach that we could not get hysterical about this problem, that while there are witches, we should not engage in witch hunts. But I conceded there were witches." Mundel then appeared on screen, followed, in turn, by Lasky.

MUNDEL: When I got there I thought some of the remarks were asinine. For instance, some speaker referred to the *New York Times* as a pink sheet. I thought that was absurd and I think I said so. There were a number of other comments that were made that I think I challenged.

LASKY: All I know is that an hysterical woman got up and began to assail me or—and the rest of the speakers. And I had to respond to try to calm her down. If anything I was a calming influence. Believe me, she was hysterical.

Newton Michael, an elderly former American Legionnaire who had also attended the 1951 meeting, then shared his recollection: "As I recall, Mr. Lasky called her a Communist. This seemed to agitate her very much, and she called him a Nazi. And with that he became very, to me, very angry, and she became angry also."

Next, a number of people offered their own recollections of the mood in Fairmont in March

253

1951 and the events that had occurred there. Manchester then summed up what had occurred to Luella Mundel: "What did Luella Mundel mean to these people of Fairmont? Well, they weren't quite sure about her religion—she didn't go to church, and Fairmont people did. And so it was assumed that she was an atheist. And that was bad. She painted surrealistic pictures—that was strange. And she spoke casually about sex, and that was wicked. She was a threat to Fairmont as it existed then." After a commercial break he continued: "Tagged as a Red, she couldn't find a job anywhere. She was running out of money. And in desperation she filed suit for slander against the woman who had called her a security risk, and that woman was to be represented by Bible-thumping, flamboyant United States Senator Mansfield Neely of West Virginia."

The slander trial commenced by Luella Mundel against "the woman who had called her a security risk," the former chairman of the Fairmont school system, Thelma Loudin, was then recalled by a number of people who were involved in it. Senator Neely had conducted a blistering and often cruel cross-examination of Mundel. He had read each of the Ten Commandments to her and asked if she agreed with them. He had mocked her artistic views, denigrated her free-thinking and essentially atheist religious beliefs, and taunted her about her views about sex. It had been a disaster for Mundel, a humiliation that led her to run in tears from the courthouse, to abandon the litigation, and ultimately to attempt suicide.

"I have no feeling one way or the other," said Lasky, reappearing on camera after a discussion of Mundel's subsequent difficulty in finding a job. "I feel sorry for her very much. I mean, I didn't have nothing to do with it. I didn't ask her to come to the meeting. I didn't ask her to shoot off her mouth. I have no idea why she was there. She was there with a claque and she rather enjoyed being Joan of Arc. I don't—I didn't set the fire to Joan of Arc."

When the program was broadcast, Lasky was furious. He complained bitterly to ABC, claiming that he had unjustly and inaccurately been accused of having called Mundel a Communist and thus being responsible for her dismissal, her lawsuit, and her attempted suicide. ABC responded by broadcasting a correction that acknowledged, with regret, its lack of fairness to Lasky and that contained a statement that he had made in his original interview: "I did not label her a Communist. I never did. And I don't think she would have told you that I did, or did she? I never labeled her anything. I can't believe I would have labeled anyone, 'cause I've never labeled anybody unless they were Communist."

Not satisfied with the network's apology, Lasky commenced a libel action against ABC.

I was friendly with Helen Whitney, who had conceived of the McCarthyism documentary and written, directed, and produced it. I had known her husband, Benno C. Schmidt, Jr., for many years, and we had taught together at Columbia Law School, when he had served as dean, and then at Yale Law School, after his appointment as president of Yale. The Schmidts asked ABC to retain me to represent the network in the litigation (Helen was not separately named as a defendant), and when it did, I quickly began the task of analyzing the relevant facts.

ABC's DEFENSE

From my very first review of the case, two defenses seemed particularly attractive. The first related to the very nature of defamation.

Libel law requires a plaintiff to meet four tests. One is to show that the offending piece was "of and concerning" him. A person cannot sue because a program has libeled another. A second is to prove that what was said was a false statement of fact. Mere opinions cannot be libelous, only factual untruths. A third is to demonstrate that the language used was defamatory—that is, that it subjected the person who claimed to be a victim of libel to "hatred, ridicule, obloquy," or the like. Not every false statement constitutes defamation, only ones that by their nature harm a reputation. The fourth is to show that what was published is not "privileged," given a sort of a free pass by the First Amendment or some appropriate body of state law.

In this case, I thought, we had a reasonable chance of persuading our judge (or, if necessary, our jury) that the broadcast had not in fact defamed Lasky. The broadcast, after all, had made plain that it was not Lasky who had called Mundel a security risk, but Thelma Loudin, the state education official. It was Loudin whom Mundel had sued, and it was that litigation that had led her to dash from the courtroom and, ultimately, to attempt suicide. Perhaps, I thought, we could incorporate those facts into an argument that the broadcast had been essentially neutral about Lasky: Newton Michael had accused him, Lasky had denied the accusation, and ABC's narrator had said nothing at all about Lasky's culpability for events that had occurred thirty-five years before in a meeting in which emotional charges and epithets had been hurled to and fro throughout a turbulent day.

The second approach would be far more pointed at Lasky. The claim that Lasky *had* been responsible for Mundel's travails was certainly open to us. Newton Michael had said as much by recalling that Lasky had called Mundel a Communist. So had Mundel, in a pre-broadcast interview with Helen Whitney, in which the following exchange occurred:

257

MUNDEL: One of the things I said to Victor Lasky was, "If I'm a Communist, you're a Nazi."

WHITNEY: How clear is your recollection of that? Does it stand out?

MUNDEL: Yes, I remember that very clearly.

WHITNEY: Was it a high point in that meeting? You do remember it?

MUNDEL: Yes, I sure do.

WHITNEY: What was it that caused you to say that?

MUNDEL: Although I don't remember exactly what Mr. Lasky said, it was quite evident from my reply that it was a response to his allegation that I was either a Communist or a security risk or something of this sort.

WHITNEY: So you're pretty clear that you wouldn't have said that unless he called you a Communist?

MUNDEL: Well, I'm sure. It wouldn't have been an appropriate response otherwise.

Yet there were obvious problems with that defense from the start. For one thing, given that ABC had already apologized for the supposed unfairness of the broadcast, how successful could we be in defending it?

Factual issues were involved as well. No transcript was available of what had occurred at the Americanism seminar in Fairmont, or of either of

Mundel's two trials. Newspaper coverage of both trials existed, but none contained any reference to Lasky's having made a direct charge that Mundel was a Communist. There was, as well, a letter to Lasky from Harold D. Jones, the librarian at Fairmont State College, where Mundel had taught, dated November 14, 1951, which had recalled the exchange between Mundel and Lasky the previous April:

> Dr. Mundel asked you whether you believed an audience such as you were addressing could be expected to detect Communists on the basis of the information which they received at the seminar? It was further suggested that a careless grouping of liberals and Communists in the minds of some persons might result in a threat to civil liberties of non-Communists. You, in turn, asked Dr. Mundel what civil liberties have you lost? And later you stated in reply to a remark or question made by Dr. Mundel, "I know you are not a Communist."

If Jones had more or less contemporaneously recalled what had occurred at the meeting in these terms, how well would we do in arguing, three decades later, precisely the opposite—that far from saying "I know you are not a Communist" to Mundel, Lasky had said that she *was* a Communist?

At the start of the case, then, there seemed to be two people who remembered an exchange in which the Communist/Nazi epithets were exchanged—Michael and Mundel—and two who maintained that it had not occurred—Jones and Lasky. Under American libel law, Lasky had to persuade the jury that what ABC had said was false. It would therefore have to determine whose recollection was correct and who, if anyone, was lying.

We tried first to avoid being heard by a jury at all. The argument that ABC had not defamed Lasky could be viewed as one of pure law and thus capable of being resolved by a judge alone. Seeking to do so, we began our defense of ABC by moving to dismiss the case on the ground that the broadcast itself was not defamatory and that regardless of what facts Lasky presented in court, no reasonable jury could conclude that it was. After a lengthy argument before federal judge Mary Johnson Lowe in the United States District Court for the Southern District of New York, sitting in Manhattan, Judge Lowe concluded that although Lasky's characterization of his role in the program might be "strained," she could not definitively rule in our favor as to what the broadcast conveyed. That must be left to a jury.

TRIAL

By the time the trial began in late January 1988

before a different federal judge, John M. Walker Jr., both sides had far more knowledge about how the prospective witnesses would testify. Depositions had been taken of Helen Whitney and the other ABC personnel involved with preparing the broadcast and of each of the four individuals (Lasky, Mundel, Michael, and Jones) who might be called upon to describe the Americanism seminar and Lasky's role in it. Based on that testimony, my associate John Sanders and I had made a critical decision about how to present our version of what had occurred in Fairmont so many years before: We would *not*, we decided, produce either Mundel or Michael.

The problem with using Mundel as a witness was well characterized by Whitney in her testimony at the trial. When she was filmed, Whitney said, "she was in obvious distress"; her answers tended to be monosyllabic; she often seemed near tears recalling what had occurred.

In the clear-eyed and hard-hearted world of trial lawyers, those characteristics might seem useful ones for an advocate of the position that Lasky bore responsibility for the harm that had befallen Mundel. But in her pretrial deposition, in which she was questioned under oath by Lasky's attorneys, Mundel's recollection of much of what had occurred at the seminar thirty-seven years before had been limited. She clearly recalled Lasky's accusing her of being a Communist or a fellow traveler, but remembered far less about other things that had been said to or by her.

More important, her story was more sympathetic than she herself was. Her anger at Lasky too often took the form of sarcasm; her distress at having been dismissed by a foolish and frightened school board could too easily be taken as contempt for the people who had so mistreated her. Her attitudes may have been justified; but to a lay jury they might also come across as being unattractive. We decided that in portraying Luella Mundel as a victim of Lasky and his colleagues, we would fare better with an absent victim.

As for Michael, his problem was age (he was eighty-two when the trial began) and the quality of his memories. He recalled the Lasky-Mundel exchange just as he had described it in the broadcast. But he was reluctant to come to New York to testify, had suffered an injury to his head in a fall not long after the broadcast, and had done about as well in his deposition as we thought he would likely do if he testified. Our concern was not that he could not express his recollections well; rather, it was that once exposed to him personally, a jury might doubt his ability to remember what he had seen so long before and thus question Whitney's decision to include him in the broadcast in the first place.

To proceed without live testimony from either of the two individuals known to ABC who recalled Lasky referring to Mundel as a Communist or the like therefore seemed a prudent litigation deci-sion. But doing so made even more critical our cross-examinations of Jones and Lasky.

Whitney made a powerful presentation to the jury. She emphasized that Lasky was by no means the central focus of the broadcast, which had instead dealt far more broadly with the evils of McCarthyism by depicting the plight of Mundel, an outsider in her community, after she had been confronted with McCarthyist charges. Lasky, she testified, had "played a role in what happened" to Mundel, but "her troubles had a more complicated origin" rooted in what the broadcast had charac-terized as "her statements" and "convictions about art and about religion" that were "unfamiliar" to her neighbors. Lasky had been treated fairly, she testified, and, indeed, could have been treated far worse if she had set out to do so. She could have included harsh and unattractive statements he had made, which did not appear in the broadcast, in juxtaposition to the fragility of Mundel. She could have contrasted Lasky's insensitivity about the consequences to Mundel of losing her job ("I mean, what's the big deal? A lot of people lost jobs") against its actual crippling impact. She could, in short, have loaded the program against Lasky, but she had not done so.

Helen, I thought, had impressed the jury with her evident skill, dedication, and idealism. The one thing she could not provide, however, was validation that Lasky had ever accused Mundel of being a Communist. She had not been there in 1951; neither had anyone else from ABC. That issue would ultimately be determined by the jury's decision about what the four witnesses of the event had to say.

As the trial began Harold Jones was called as a witness by Lasky's attorneys. Jones had been the head librarian and chairman of the library department at Fairmont State College from 1947 to 1952 and had been present at the American Legion meeting in 1951. He had, he said, "coaxed a colleague" of his "to attend the seminar with him," and he had sat next to her during the seminar. That colleague was Luella Mundel. The critical testimony that Lasky's lawyers wanted from Jones he quickly gave them:

Q: Did Ms. Mundel question Mr. Lasky?
A: Yes, she did.
Q: Did Mr. Lasky call Dr. Mundel a Communist?
A: No, he didn't.
Q: Did Mr. Lasky imply that Dr. Mundel was a Communist?
A: No, I think not.

Lasky's counsel, Kathleen McGuan, then handed Jones the letter that he had written to Lasky from Fairmont on November 14, 1951. At McGuan's request, he read into the record the portion of the letter that had quoted Lasky as telling Mundel "I know you are not a Communist."

I had interviewed Jones at my office the weekend before the trial began and was aware of the totality of his recollection of the American Legion meeting. It was far better for us than Lasky could have imagined. As I began my cross-examination, I asked Jones first if he recalled Mundel's responding to a comment of Lasky's by saying, "If I am a Communist, you are a Fascist." He agreed. He had made precise notes of Mundel's remarks. "To put it exactly," he stated, Mundel had said, " 'You must be a Fascist. If I am a Communist, you must be a Fascist.' " This validation of the central recollection of Mundel and Michael by a witness called by Lasky stunned the courtroom. I proceeded:

Q: Are you very clear in your recollection about that?
A: Yes.

Unable to specify precisely what Lasky had said to provoke such a response by Mundel, Jones proceeded to explain why he had written the letter to Lasky in the first place. Lasky, he recalled, had said to Mundel in the midst of their overheated exchange, "What civil liberties have you lost?" Jones's letter was written to let Lasky know that as a result of the meeting and Lasky's words at the meeting, Mundel had indeed "lost a great many civil liberties," and had sustained "serious consequences" when, six weeks after the Americanism seminar, she had been accused by Thelma Loudin of being a security risk. As a result of that, Jones testified, Mundel had been fired.

I returned again to the critical question of what Lasky had said.

Q: What were Mr. Lasky's words which led you to say that his words had had serious consequences?

A: Oh, it wasn't any special words. It was the entire—his entire speech and those of his colleagues on the platform. I didn't attribute this to any particular—

Judge Walker then intervened with a question of his own: "How did they contribute to the misfortunes of Ms. Mundel?" Jones responded eagerly. "Oh, well," he said, "they created an atmosphere of anxiety in this community, and I think they created perhaps a desire on the parts of some patriotic West Virginians to find a Communist or a poor security risk or something."

I concluded with a series of questions based on what Jones had told me in my office. Lasky, he testified, had behaved at the meeting in a loud, aggressive, and polemical fashion. I wound up by giving Jones the chance to use a phrase he had articulated in my office. Lasky "may not have set fire to Joan of Arc," he had told me, "but he did provide kindling." I told Jones I would ask him a question in court to which that could be the answer. His response came out better in my office than in the courtroom, but it was still marvelous.

Q: You recall in that broadcast the observation, the statement by Mr. Lasky that he had not set fire to Joan of Arc?

A: Yes.

Q: How would you put it?

A: Well, I would say Mr. Lasky and his fellow speakers probably, probably—I couldn't prove it—provided some kindling for the injuries that were done, subsequently done to Dr. Mundel. Saying that he held the match, no.

Q: What do you mean by kindling? I'm a city boy.

A: Of course, they were referring to Joan of Arc, and by kindling you mean small pieces of wood that catch fire easily.

Q: Thank you, Mr. Jones.

There was no redirect examination.

Taken as a whole, Jones's testimony was enormously helpful. Confident as he was that Lasky had not used the word "Communist" with direct reference to Mundel, his recollection that Lasky had said *something* that led her to respond by saying "If I am a Communist, you must be a Fascist" undid much of the harm of his specific recollection about what Lasky had *not* said. More broadly,

Jones's testimony about the general character of Lasky's statements, his evident sympathy for Mundel and—most important—his placing of blame upon Lasky for much of what would later happen to Mundel, was a boon of inestimable value to us.

The centerpiece of the trial, as we always knew it would be, was Lasky's own appearance on the witness stand, which took place on Friday, January 29. A short, energetic man of seventy who leaned forward in his chair throughout his testimony, Lasky came ready to impress a New York City jury with his roots in the city. He had attended, he testified on direct examination, elementary school, junior high school, high school, and Brooklyn College in New York. He had worked as a journalist for many years, starting in 1941 as the New York correspondent of the *Chicago Sun*. He had served in the Army from June 1942 until 1946, and then returned to the *Sun*, where he covered veterans' affairs and, ever more intently, Communist activities. When he returned to New York City in 1947, he was hired by the *New York World-Telegram* to report on a variety of subjects.

Two years after his return, he testified, he was assigned to work with another journalist at the *World-Telegram*, Fred Wolfman, on stories relating to communism. Lasky's reporting on the Alger Hiss case in the early 1950s, he said, "sort of gave me a national reputation." In 1953, he testified, he was coauthor of a documentary film called

The Hoaxters, which focused on the menace posed by communism to the United States. Lasky emphasized his moderation and caution in the picture. "We made it emphatic," he said, "that you cannot get hysterical about this problem. The worst thing in the world is for people to start calling each other names, Communists, Fascists," and the like.

Lasky then described his continuing writing career for a variety of magazines, including *Reader's Digest,* the *Saturday Evening Post,* and others. His testimony then turned to a book he wrote in 1955 with Ralph DeToledano on the Hiss case, entitled *Seeds of Treason.* It was, he said, highly praised by the *New York Times* and the *Herald Tribune.*

His next book, he said, was titled *JFK: The Man and the Myth.* It was a "monumental seller" from the time of its publication in August 1963 until President Kennedy's death in November. At that time, Lasky testified, he had asked his publisher to cease publication. Kennedy's death, he said, "was a terrible blow to us." He and his wife went to Key Biscayne, Florida, he testified, where he received a call from his agent telling him that the orders were still pouring in. That, Lasky emphasized, was "not what I had hoped for. I had known President Kennedy. It was a shock to me. I had liked President Kennedy. It was a terrible blow to the country as well as me."

Lasky continued to cite his other publications,

including *The Ugly Russian;* its successor, *Robert F. Kennedy: The Myth and the Man,* which was aborted almost at the time of publication by Kennedy's assassination in 1968; and a book attacking former Secretary of Labor Arthur Goldberg. By the end of the day, Lasky had portrayed himself as a serious journalist, a person of high and well-deserved reputation.

When the trial resumed on Monday morning, February 1, Lasky began his testimony about his appearance at the Americanism seminar in Fairmont in 1951. He had been a speaker, he recalled, at American Legion meetings on five or six occasions during the early 1950s. Invited by the Americanism Commission of the American Legion, he appeared in the Fairmont Hotel ballroom with a number of other speakers, whose qualifications he described, explaining that many of them had been involved with the Communist Party at some point in their lives. Among those speakers were Rabbi Benjamin Schultz, who was, Lasky testified, "one of the world's leading authorities" on antireligious activities in the Soviet Union, and Paul Crouch, a former Communist whom Lasky praised as an expert.

Lasky himself had spoken after lunch and given his "usual speech about Soviet espionage in America, particularly dwelling on the Alger Hiss case." After the speech, he testified, Luella Mundel, who appeared "very agitated" and "terribly upset," was one of the individuals who questioned him from the audience. The critical questions were finally asked:

Q: Did you call Dr. Mundel a Communist?
A: No. N-O, exclamation point period, no.
Q: Did you call her a Red?
A: No. N-O, exclamation point period.
Q: Did you imply it?
A: No, sir.
Q: Did Dr. Mundel say anything to you that made you angry?
A: She never made me angry. I've seen— I've had bigger arguments in my time with my wife.
Q: Mr. Lasky, have you ever personally labeled any person a Communist?
A: Never. Unless they were a Communist. I called Joe Stalin a Communist.
Q: But did you ever conduct an investigation of anybody that led to them being labeled a Communist?
A: Absolutely not.
Q: Or a member of the Communist Party?
A: No, sir.

According to Lasky, Mundel appeared "distraught," and he tried to calm her down. Their exchange had lasted between a minute and a minute and a half.

Lasky's lawyer, Jarris Leonard, then turned to Newton Michael's recollection that Lasky had called Mundel a Communist. There were many inaccuracies in Michael's testimony, Lasky said, in addition to that core falsehood. Michael had insinuated, he said, that Lasky was the only speaker, when there were seven or eight in all; Michael had said that Lasky had spoken in the morning, when he was not even present at the time; Michael had insisted that Lasky had participated in a small session during a noontime break to talk informally about some of the things he had said. None of this was true, Lasky said angrily: "That was the spirit world!"

Lasky's "spirit world" exclamation alerted me. It was voiced with such fury at Michael that members of the jury looked as if they had been slapped. The tone, the discordant music of the answer, plainly disturbed Lasky's counsel. Leonard carefully phrased his next question this way:

> Q: My question, please listen to my question, did you participate in such little sessions, during a break or noon hour?
> A: No, sir, I was having my lunch.

Lasky then proceeded to describe his negotiations with ABC for a correction, their willingness to run one, and his disappointment that the correction that had been run had never, in so many words, actually apologized to him: *it* merely had said that ABC's broadcast had been "unfair" and had included a direct quotation from Lasky denying that he had ever called Mundel a Communist.

In speaking with Helen Whitney over the preceding weekend, I had mentioned to her that his claim about seeking to stop all publication of his book attacking President Kennedy seemed contrary to what the *New York Times* had reported his publisher had actually done. Publication had in fact been shut down, but then resumed a week or two later. It was a small point but potentially useful in challenging Lasky's credibility. I also told her that I thought I would spend some time questioning Lasky about his relationship with President Kennedy. Given his sustained attack on Kennedy in his book, I said, it could not have been good. Perhaps I could score some points about this before a New York City jury likely to remember Kennedy with regard and a deep sense of loss. While none of this had anything directly to do with what had happened in Fairmont in 1951, it seemed to me that Lasky's penchant for exaggeration in this area might provide another fruitful basis for an inquiry.

Helen responded that she was friendly with Kennedy's sister Jean Kennedy Smith. Would it be useful if she attended the session? "Absolutely," I said, thinking that Lasky looking directly at the president's sister when I asked him about his supposed friendship with Kennedy might unnerve him as he testified.

I began my cross-examination immediately

with the Kennedy matter. From the start, our interaction was hostile.

> Q: You referred to the fact that you had written a book called *JFK: The Man and the Myth*?
> A: Yes, sir.
> Q: You described how you had known President Kennedy, how you liked President Kennedy; you said what a terrible blow [his death] was to you?
> A: Yes, sir.
> Q: And you said that you asked Macmillan to stop publication of the book from the time of the president's death; is that correct?
> A: That's right.
> Q: You didn't tell the jury, did you, that the book started to be sent around the country again two weeks later; isn't that the case? You didn't stop publication, you stopped for two weeks, isn't that right?

Lasky was shaken. Instead of answering directly, he said, "You want me to tell you what happened?" When I responded, "I want you to answer," and Lasky angrily started to denounce the question, Judge Walker interjected with an instruction to him: "Just answer the question." I started again.

Q: Isn't it true, Mr. Lasky, that there was a period of only two weeks in which the Kennedy book was not shipped?
A: I have no idea. I had nothing to do with it.

I then read at laborious length from a *New York Times* article from 1963 confirming that Lasky's publisher had indeed resumed shipments of his book, and asked:

Q: My question is, does that refresh your recollection?
A: Doesn't refresh my recollection at all.
Q: That a two-week moratorium at all—
A: May I tell you what happened? I was away—

Again Judge Walker interjected, telling Lasky that if he did not answer my questions, we could "be here for years." He directed him to respond to my questions and only to my questions.

By this point, Lasky had moved beyond irritation to overt anger. I moved to the side to be sure that Lasky saw Jean Kennedy Smith and confronted him directly:

Q: You weren't trying to suggest to the jury, were you, under oath, that you, Victor Lasky, were some sort of friend of President Kennedy?

A: I was no real enemy of his. We were political adversaries in a sense. I have a lot of political adversary friends who are friends.

Q: Was President Kennedy a friend of yours?

A: No, not particularly. I knew him slightly.

I then turned to testimony Lasky had given about the book he had written about Arthur Goldberg, in which he had said that he had "wound up in front of a Senate committee about it." I pursued him again:

Q: Would it be a bit more accurate to say that you wound up in front of the Senate committee because Governor Nelson Rockefeller paid the money for you to write the book, and that the book was used by Governor Rockefeller in his campaign for governor against Justice Goldberg? Isn't that what the investigation was about?

A: I had no idea when I wrote the book that the money came from Governor Rockefeller, period.

Q: Didn't Governor Rockefeller—

Once again, Judge Walker was obliged to intervene. The question, he told Lasky, was whether when he testified, the issue had been whether Rockefeller had paid for him to write the book. Lasky's voice was lower as he responded.

> A: It was one of the issues in the confirmation hearings of Nelson Rockefeller for vice president, yes.
> Q: You didn't tell the jury, did you, that Governor Rockefeller apologized for the book, did you?
> A: I wasn't asked.
> Q: Did Governor Rockefeller apologize for your book?
> A: I have no recollection. He probably did.
> Q: Is it your best recollection that the governor apologized?
> A: I have some vague recollection. I know I didn't apologize.
> Q: Is it your best recollection that the governor apologized?
> A: I have a vague recollection that he apologized. For what I don't know.

Lasky moved uncomfortably in his chair as he awaited the next question. He was learning, I thought, the truth of Luella Mundel's observation about her own slander suit: "I didn't realize," she had said on the broadcast, "that the person who brought the suit would be the one who was on trial."

I turned to the broadcast. Lasky acknowledged under questioning that when he had brought the case, he had thought that it was only

Newton Michael who had told ABC that he recalled Lasky having called Mundel a Communist, a security risk, or the like. Now, he agreed, he understood that Luella Mundel had said much the same thing. Was he testifying, I asked, that Mundel had lied in her recollections? He stated that he didn't know "whether she was lying, but she is an elderly woman, and I have suspicions." Was he testifying, I asked, that Newton Michael was lying in what he said to ABC? Once again the temperature rose.

A: You know, somebody doesn't have to be a liar.

Q: No, I want you to try to answer. I want to focus first on whether you are testifying that he was lying.

A: I don't know what he lied about. What was it precisely that you want to know? The two or three remarks which made no sense which contradicted each other about whether I called her a Communist or insinuated she was a Communist?

Q: Mr. Lasky—

A: That's hogwash.

Q: Mr. Lasky, you have seen, have you not, in this courtroom, as the jury saw it, the interview of Newton Michael in which he said that his recollection was that you had called Luella Mundel a Communist, and that she had responded?

A: But he also said other things.

278

WALKER: No, he asked you a question. Mr. Abrams, wait a minute. Mr. Lasky, wait a minute. Mr. Abrams hasn't asked a question yet. If you will wait, let him ask the question, then you can answer. Mr. Abrams, do you have a question pending?

Q: Yes. My question is, you sat here and you saw together with the jury the passage of the interview with Mr. Michael in which he said, in substance, maybe I am not quoting exactly now . . . "Lasky called her a Communist and she called him a Nazi and they both got very angry"?

A: Yes, I remember that. That's why I started the suit.

Q: That is why you started the suit. And my question here now is simply whether you are saying that Mr. Michael was lying, and by that I mean deliberately saying something that was untrue.

A: I don't think he was lying.

I then turned to the testimony of Harold Jones. His testimony had obviously disconcerted Lasky. Why not use cross-examination to punish Lasky about Jones in a manner that could not possibly hurt us? I began slowly.

Q: You heard Mr. Jones testify in court, right?

279

A: Yes.

Q: And you had in fact talked to Mr. Jones, did you not?

A: I brought him here.

Q: You brought him here?

A: Yes.

Q: You visited at his house once; is that right?

A: No, I had lunch with him several times.

Q: You brought him here to testify?

A: Yes.

Q: You recall, do you not, that one part of Mr. Jones's testimony was that Ms. Mundel, in response to something you had said, said, "If I am a Communist, then you must be a Nazi." Did you hear him say that?

A: I heard him say it.

Lasky then testified, without being asked, that he had never been told any of these things by Jones in his lunch with him. It was an invitation I could not refuse.

Q: You were surprised at his testimony?

A: Yes, I was surprised to hear that you had talked to him.

Q: Mr. Lasky, do you believe that you are the only one who is allowed to talk to witnesses?

A: No.

Q: Are you saying Mr. Jones was lying to this jury?

A: I don't believe he was lying.

Q: In his testimony?

A: That was his best memory.

Q: You heard Mr. Jones testify that you behaved at that meeting in Fairmont in a loud and aggressive and polemical fashion? That's what he said. Do you remember that?

A: Yes, sir.

Q: Are you testifying that Mr. Jones was lying when he said that here in court to this jury?

A: No, I am not.

Q: And you heard Mr. Jones testify that you were not a calming influence at the meeting?

A: That was his opinion.

Q: And you aren't testifying that it was anything more than, what, a wrong opinion?

A: It's not my memory at all. As God is my witness, that is not my memory at all.

I returned to the Jones letter. Jones had sought help from Lasky to aid Luella Mundel. Asked if he had ever written back to Jones, he said that he had not. Asked if he had ever telephoned Jones, he said again that he had not. Asked if he had ever written to Luella Mundel, he responded that she had never written to him nor he to her.

I turned to the cleanup question:

Q: We have now had at least three people who recall for this jury an exchange between you and Luella Mundel in which their recollection was that one of the things that was said was that Luella Mundel said to you, "If I am a Communist, then you are a Nazi." Mr. Jones recalled that, Mr. Michael recalled that, Ms. Mundel recalled that. My question to you is this: Do you disbelieve them, Mr. Lasky?

A: As I said in my interview with Ms. Whitney, the tape, people have different recollections after thirty-two years. The fact is, and this is the important fact you don't seem to want to get out, that Mr. Jones told you right here, I said that I never called her a Communist. I had never called her a Communist. You heard it. What else do you want to know?

Q: I want to know all about the meeting, and that is what I want to explore.

A: Nobody knows anything about the meeting, including your own people. I asked them repeatedly, what happened at the meeting. They said they don't know, you tell me. It was just another meeting to me. I have gone through a hundred of these—a hundred of these arguments. I told you I had bigger arguments with my wife and still do.

Q: I know, Mr. Lasky.

A: What are you making a big deal out of something of an argument?

Judge Walker intervened again, admonishing Lasky to answer my questions. Now I asked a tougher one.

Q: What happened to Luella Mundel is a big deal, isn't it?

A: She lost her job. I have lost a job. I didn't go on national television to cry about it.

Members of the jury winced. I paused to let the cruelty of Lasky's remark sink in and then proceeded.

Q: The question I was pursuing a moment ago, Mr. Lasky, was this: We have had three witnesses live or by deposition who were at the meeting, and you were at the meeting.

A: I was.

Q: So far, that's what the jury has heard, four people; right?

A: Yes.

Q: They have heard Mr. Michael's recollection, they have heard Ms. Mundel's recollection. They both recalled, as they testified, that you said something to the effect which they understood at least, something to the effect that she was a Communist or fellow traveler, something like that; and that she responded by saying, "If I am a Communist, then you're a Nazi."

Mr. Jones's recollection was that you did not say she was a Communist but that at some point she responded to you by saying, "If I am a Communist, you are a Nazi."

My question focuses on the second half of it, Mr. Lasky: Having heard these three people who were there, do you have any reason to think that they are shading the truth, lying in some way in their recollection of what she said to you?

A: You want me to tell you the truth?

Q: Only the truth.

A: Yes.

Q: First about Mr. Jones. What is Mr. Jones's reason?

A: I am not accusing Mr. Jones of anything.

As for Michael and Mundel, Lasky responded in an increasingly agitated way that he "wouldn't send somebody to the chair" on the basis of testimony such as Michael's, and that he suspected that Mundel had lied:

Q: Lied in court under oath to a jury?
A: I suspect she lied. The whole thing is a lie. The whole thing was a frame and a fixup. There is not one note before the broadcast that I called her a Communist coming from Ms. Mundel. It was all after the broadcast, Mr. Abrams, after the broadcast. It's funny, and you will send somebody to the chair with that kind of evidence? Come on.
Q: Are you testifying that Luella Mundel lied when she said that her recollection was of the—
A: She had a faulty recollection.
Q: She had a faulty recollection.
A: OK.

I decided that we had had enough with respect to Lasky's exchange with Mundel. Taking a broader look at the Fairmont meeting, I turned to the nature of the other speakers. Rabbi Schultz had been praised by Lasky. Was he aware, I asked, that the New York Board of Rabbis had condemned Schultz "for using the smear technique of the scandalmonger"? Was he aware that Rabbi Stephen Wise, a leading rabbi in New York City, had said of Schultz that he was "probably a profiteering Communist baiter, unworthy to be even a member, not to say a rabbi, of a Jewish congregation"? As the jury stared at him, Lasky responded angrily, defending Schultz and saying that his critics simply disagreed with him politically.

I moved on to Paul Crouch, another speaker at the meeting.

> Q: Could you tell us again about Mr. Crouch?
>
> A: Mr. Crouch had been an underground member of the Communist Party. He was very active in Hawaii and Panama, and as it states here, he had testified at the trials of Harry Bridges and [William] Remington. I didn't know too much about him.
>
> Q: Did you ever know, Mr. Lasky, that Mr. Crouch's testimony had been stricken from the record on the grounds that he had committed perjury, and that the United States did not defend against the charge that Mr. Crouch had committed perjury in his testimony about who was and was not in the Communist Party?
>
> A: What the hell has that got to do with me?
>
> WALKER: It's just a question.
>
> A: No, I didn't know anything about it.

WALKER: All right.

A: And I didn't even invite the man to the meeting. I hardly knew him. So what does it have to do with me?

Q: Mr. Lasky, I am asking you because you were describing these people.

A: Yes, and I described them the best I could.

I turned next to the correction run by ABC in which the network had acknowledged that it had been "unfair" to Lasky and that it "regretted the omission" of a passage of Lasky's interview in which he had flatly denied ever calling Mundel a Communist. At his deposition, he had stated that if ABC had not only acknowledged that it believed it had been unfair to Lasky but also apologized to him, he would have been satisfied; he had said, "It would have gone a long way to satisfy me, yes." Lasky affirmed that that statement was accurate and that it still reflected his views.

I had saved for last something Lasky had said that I had found particularly offensive. I had recently read the autobiography of Edward G. Robinson, the renowned tough-guy movie actor, who had himself been accused of Communist ties. Lasky had testified that he had helped Robinson, but the actor's moving and evocative memoir told a different story, which captured the essence of the evils of McCarthyism. As Robinson described it,

Lasky had "helped" him by drafting an obsequious and demeaning twenty-six-page confession for him in which Robinson basically confessed to being a dupe of the Communists. I asked Lasky if that was the supposed "help" he had provided. It was, he explained, "part of the help." I pursued him.

Q: So you drafted that? Am I right?

A: Yes.

Q: And it said, in effect, "I was a dupe, I was stupid, I was foolish," things like that?

A: That's what he had told me in private.

Q: Had he told you in private that that's what he wanted to do?

A: No. I told him what I was going to do, among other things. The three- or four-track program which I had in mind for him to do. That was—that's just one part of a series of things that I thought he had to do to clear his name.

Q: Didn't you tell Mr. Robinson that one of the things he had to do to clear his name was to make that confession?

A: I said—it was a suggestion that he read the article I wrote for him, which I did for nothing, by the way, and look at it, and I think it would go a long way in clearing up any misunderstandings about his background.

This was in direct conflict with what Robinson had himself written in his autobiography. I picked up a copy of the book and proceeded with my questioning. As I read from it, I could feel the jury recoiling from Lasky.

Q: I am going to read to you from Mr. Robinson's autobiography, page 255, in which he said the following:

Let me give you a small idea of what happened. Victor Lasky, a newspaper man, publicist, and ardent antagonist of Communism, a role he shared with George Sokolsky and Victor Reisel, both newspaper men with large followings, came to me and chided me about my folly for having sent this check to the Trumbo family. And clucked even more over my intensive affiliation with Communist front organizations.

He was particularly miserable about my association with the American Committee for the Protection of Foreign Born, which he assured me was a Communist-dominated front. Thus implying that its active members including Reinhold Niebuhr, Dorothy Thompson and William Allen White were either Communists or dupes.

Dupes. Yes, that was the word. All I had to do to clear myself of all these charges new and old was to admit publicly and in print that I was a dupe. [H]e, Victor Lasky, would write it all out for me and secure its publication in some nice conservative journal like, I suppose, *American Legion Magazine.*

He prepared 26 pages of my dupedom. I only had to read one page to feel the urge to throw up.

I told Mr. Lasky politely and firmly that I wished no part of his attempt to set the world straight. The piece he fashioned made me out a fool who out of brainlessness and an overzealous consideration for mankind had been blindly led into organizations that wished to destroy America.

Does that refresh your recollection, Mr. Lasky?

A: Absolutely not. It's absolutely untruthful. I never went to him. He came to me through my—our mutual agent, Mr. Hebert.

Q: Is it true, Mr. Lasky, that you offered to write everything out for Mr. Robinson, and secure its publication in some journal like the *American Legion Magazine?* Is that true?

A: I never mentioned the *American Legion Magazine.* I thought his was a piece for the *Saturday Evening Post,* how he was duped into working for Communist front organizations.

Q: Did Mr. Robinson tell the truth when he wrote that he told you politely and firmly that he wanted no part—

A: He never told me. He never said that to me, as God is my witness.

A number of jurors turned their heads away from Lasky. It seemed a good sign.

SUMMATION

On February 8 at 10:00 a.m. the summations of counsel began. Leonard spoke first on Lasky's behalf, beginning with a list of what the case was *not* about. It was not about the loyalty-oath program imposed by President Truman in 1947, which had been mentioned in passing in ABC's telecast; it was not about Senator McCarthy; it was not about the many Emmy Awards won by Helen Whitney in the past; and "most importantly, ladies and gentlemen, this case is not about political philosophy."

I thought it was a creditable, if defensive, start. Just as NBC's only chance to prevail over Wayne Newton in Las Vegas had been to somehow try to avoid seeming to try Las Vegas itself (we had failed), Lasky had to avoid being judged by a generally liberal, pro-Kennedy, anti-McCarthy New York City jury based on "political philosophy."

Leonard turned to the program. It had, he said, almost been true. Close to the time it was due to be completed, ABC had a story that "was simple, direct, compelling, and true." This is what ABC had developed:

A schoolteacher, an art teacher by the name of Luella Mundel at a small college in West Virginia in the early 1950s, stood up at an American Legion seminar on Americanism, and she challenged the speakers. That was absolutely true. But Luella was an outsider. She was different; she didn't go to church, and that wasn't good in Fairmont. She painted surrealistic pictures. But most of all she was part of a group of outsiders that had been brought in by Dr. George Hand, the then-president of the college, who himself was an outsider.

He was an outsider and he brought some of these people in. Now the local member of the state college board was not happy with George Hand. She was trying to find a way to embarrass him and to undercut him and get rid of him and all of the outsiders that he brought with him.

So when she heard about Luella Mundel's activity at that American Legion meeting, standing up, challenging those speakers, at the school board meeting that summer where contracts were being renewed and raises were being considered, she zapped Luella Mundel. And when she was asked why she zapped her, she said because she's an atheist and she's a poor security risk.

That was ABC's initial and real story, Leonard argued. But the story lacked a villain. ABC could have told the story in a way that was accurate and fair. It could have used Victor Lasky to "add credibility to the story," to "set the stage for what happened."

But needing a villain, Leonard argued, Helen Whitney had irresponsibly used the Newton Michael charge against Lasky, and "Michael fingered him just as certain as Brutus put the dagger cleanly and clearly into Julius Caesar." Michael was unreliable, Leonard maintained; his testimony was inherently inconsistent. He was the Fairmont equivalent of "the town talker or the neighborhood talker. You ask him a question, he's got an answer, and if you will stand there and listen long enough, he will just keep talking. And if you ask him a question about somebody who isn't around anymore, he'll really tell you some stories."

Whitney, said Leonard, knew well that Michael could not be trusted. He quoted a question I had asked Helen during my direct examination—"Why did you include Newton Michael's statement in the program?"—and her answer, that

Michael had a "very clear memory." In fact, said Leonard, Michael was "all over the lot," and Whitney knew it.

As for Mundel, Leonard continued, Whitney's own testimony proved that she had not trusted her. I had asked Whitney why she had not asked Mundel in so many words whether Lasky had called her a Communist. Leonard read her answer loudly:

Well, I didn't do it for the reason I didn't, you know, ask Mr. Lasky. I knew what she'd said the night before but I wanted it fresh. I started out, you know, it's true she mentioned the exchange about the *New York Times* and I went back to that. And it didn't seem like a firm recollection at that point and I went away from it.

That was the critical testimony, Leonard said.

Ladies and gentlemen of the jury, Helen Whitney was under oath, she was telling the truth, and the truth of the matter was that she herself did not believe the Newton Michael statement. She couldn't have believed it. Because she knew that the statement was incredible on the day she filmed Newton Michael in Fairmont, West Virginia, in March of 1983.

Again and again Leonard returned to the same theme: Lasky had been unjustly blamed for the ruination of Mundel. He concluded:

Ladies and gentlemen of the jury, I contend that they created the villain in Victor Lasky. In creating him they defamed him, they ridiculed him, they held him up to contempt. We contend they did that by publishing and issuing to a lot of people who watched that program that night all over this country and statements and the program, taking it in its entirety, the important link that Lasky was between Mundel, the Legion meeting, the firing, he was that linchpin. That statement and that program was untrue.

I began my response by answering the argument that the thrust of the program had changed because of some sort of problems in its preparation. "Until today," I said, "I had thought that I had some idea why this case was filed, why it's here, why you are here. I thought, based on watching Mr. Lasky testify and listening to him, that it was political or personal reasons which led him to be very angry. I didn't know until today that it was based on fantasy, as well as anger."

The fantasy, I said, was that the program had changed. I read from early summaries, written before a frame was filmed, that were consistent with what ABC had finally shown its audience. I quoted from Helen's testimony about what Mundel had told her the night before the filming; that "she remembered her exchange with Victor Lasky and she remembered feeling accused, and in the ballpark of being Communist, fellow traveler, following the Communist line or something that made her respond. And she was very clear about this, 'If I am a Communist, you're a Nazi,' or 'Fascist' or something like that."

I then returned to the core of the case. There was no doubt of some facts. Lasky and Mundel

were at a meeting together. They argued. Mr. Lasky said something. I am going to come back later to what he probably said or didn't say. But there's no argument here, except for Mr. Lasky, about one thing and that is what she said in response. In response to something he said, she said, "If I'm a Communist, you're a Nazi." Everybody remembers it that way, everybody except Mr. Lasky. Mr. Jones, who is here in court today, the second row on the right, Mr. Lasky said he brought him to court, he took him to lunch a few times— that Mr. Jones. Mr. Jones was as clear as a person could be in court in recalling those words being spoken by Luella Mundel, in response to something Victor Lasky said.

Newton Michael remembered it just that

way. Luella Mundel remembered it with great clarity just that way.

What sort of man, I asked, was Lasky?

You saw—you saw the real Victor Lasky here. You saw it in front of you. You saw it when I asked him, wasn't it a big deal that Luella Mundel was fired? And you remember his answer. Mr. Lasky responded, "She lost her job. I lost a job. I didn't go on national TV and cry about it." The Victor Lasky on that program was presented very fairly, very moderately; it was a different, kinder, softer Victor Lasky than you saw before you.

"I have to say some harsh things about Mr. Lasky today," I told the jury, "and I regret it. Mr. Lasky referred to my clients as 'these arrogant lying bastards.' Mr. Lasky referred to this broadcast as 'a piece of crap.' I'm sorry to use that language and I don't mean to shock you, but that's that way it is. You heard it once and you can survive it from me."

I paused, letting the ugly words lie in the air, and returned to another theme. The program, I argued, had not really blamed Lasky at all. He was portrayed as the person Luella Mundel had argued with, not the one who had fired her. I asked the jury to consider a question.

Imagine you are back in your homes. Never seen this before. Someone calls you up. Someone says to you, "Did you see the ABC documentary on McCarthyism?" You say yes. He says, "Did you hear there is going to be a libel suit about it?"

Am I wrong that you would say, "Who's going to sue?"

And am I wrong that if the answer was "Victor Lasky is going to sue," you'd say, "About what?"

The jury, I argued, should dispose of the case by concluding that ABC had not defamed Lasky at all. But if they concluded that Lasky had been held up to ridicule, I said, they should rule that the charges against Lasky were *true*.

What did we know about the truth of what had happened thirty-one years ago?

Well, we know there was a meeting in Fairmont, West Virginia, at a time in which people were frightened, very frightened and easily agitated and easily led, about the spread of Communism.

We know that speakers would come to those towns and talk to them about Americanism, and you saw this on the broadcast, in a way which left the audiences excited, apprehensive, looking, looking around.

And Victor Lasky spoke at that meeting on March 31, 1951. He came with other people. He spoke after other people. You remember that from my cross-examination of Mr. Lasky. Those were people Mr. Lasky was very proud to be associated with, experts he said, experts in Communism: Rabbi Schultz, remember all about that; Paul Crouch; former Communists, people that were experts.

You remember the exchange Mr. Lasky and I had about Rabbi Schultz and Paul Crouch, both of whom he described in such glowing terms when he started to talk.

And then I started to quote to Mr. Lasky from his own article in which people had described—serious, responsible people had described—Rabbi Schultz as a person whose activities were irresponsible and improper if not reprehensible; the person who used the smear technique of the scandal-monger; the person described by Rabbi Wise as probably a profiteering Communist baiter unworthy even to be a member, not to say a rabbi, of a Jewish congregation.

Mr. Lasky finally cried out at me, "I didn't invite them. I didn't ask them to come." These were the people he went with and there were speeches about Communists threatening people, Communism threatening the people in Fairmont, and we know, we know in this courtroom that there was an argument between Mr. Lasky and Luella Mundel; and we know that voices were raised, and we know that things were said; and as I said to you earlier, one thing we can be sure of is that in response to something Mr. Lasky said, the response was, "If I am a Communist, you must be a Nazi," and everyone, everyone except Mr. Lasky, remembers that as clearly as possible.

How should the jury decide whom to believe? I turned to Lasky and addressed the jury slowly.

I have to say that the Victor Lasky you saw in court was, and this is the softest word I can use, a careless man, careless with facts, careless with truth, and careless about people. I don't mean that because he can't remember everything in his deposition. That is hard. But I mean it because of the contradictions that you saw and the answers that you saw right in front of you with a Victor Lasky that started out suggesting to you what a buddy he was with President Kennedy, and wound up after just two or three questions saying that he wasn't a friend at all, knew him only slightly.

The Victor Lasky that described to you how, when he wrote his book on Arthur

Goldberg, he quote "wound up" in front of a Senate committee, and didn't bother to tell you that he wound up in front of a Senate committee because Governor Rockefeller had paid for this book this "journalist" wrote when Governor Rockefeller was running against Arthur Goldberg, and that Governor Rockefeller apologized for that.

You remember the passage about Edward G. Robinson. Mr. Lasky got up in front of you, praised himself to the sky. He took care of Edward G. Robinson. I read to him from Mr. Robinson's autobiography; he said it's absolutely untrue, "absolutely untruthful," what I read to him.

How can you tell whom to believe? I asked. Look and decide what sort of man Lasky was. The jury had seen him clearly enough, seen that he was a reckless man. I concluded this way:

You have been told and rightly told that reputation is at stake in this case, and so it is. And I just want to ask you to preserve the reputations of people who deserve to have reputations in this courtroom. Those are the people who have done this broadcast, that did their best, that flew around the country, that did research, that prepared a serious, sober, beautiful documentary.

And I ask you to give them back their reputations brought about by this frivolous lawsuit.

THE JURY

Judge Walker's charge to the six-person jury began shortly after ten a.m. on February 8. He asked its members to decide each of three questions and to report back after they had unanimously agreed on them. The first was whether the broadcast "considered as a whole" was defamatory of Lasky. After the jurors decided on their answer to that question, Walker told them, they should send a note to the court stating that they had done so.

The second question, which the jury would reach only if they had concluded that Lasky had been defamed, was whether the broadcast had been substantially false. Walker made plain that if Lasky had used language such as "Communist," "fellow traveler," or "security risk" with respect to Mundel, the broadcast could not be found substantially false. If Lasky had not used such language, however, the jury was obliged to make a finding of substantial falsity.

The final question put to the jury would be answered by it only if we had lost on the first two. Lasky, a well-known writer on matters of national concern, had been determined to be a public figure and was therefore obliged to prove that ABC had broadcast its documentary with actual knowledge of its falsity or with reckless disregard of whether it was true. The third question was whether ABC had done so.

Shortly after the jury left the courtroom to consider the case, they asked to see once again the portion of the broadcast relating to Mundel. They watched it carefully as it was replayed for them.

We heard nothing more from the jurors until 3:20 p.m., when they sent a note saying that they had reached a verdict on question one—whether the broadcast had defamed Lasky. At the same time they asked to review the Jones letter regarding Lasky "for our continued deliberations."

As the jury filed back into court I tried to conjure up some optimistic scenario but could not do so. If we had won on the defamation issue, why would the jury need to see the Jones letter again? If we had won, what confusion in the jury's mind would lead it to conclude that "further deliberations" lay ahead of it? And if we had lost, we were totally dependent upon the jury's believing that Lasky had called Mundel a Communist. As I tried to force myself to conjure up an optimistic scenario, my hopes were dashed.

When Judge Walker asked the foreman of the jury if the jury had agreed upon its verdict to question one, the answer was, "Yes, we have, Your Honor." When he asked for their decision, the answer came quickly: "Yes"—Lasky had been defamed.

As Walker instructed the jury to return to the jury room to consider question two—falsity—my spirits dived. I thought again of Las Vegas and my wrongly self-induced optimism that we had a good chance of winning the Newton case. This jury, I thought, was friendly to us, had believed our witnesses, seemed appalled at Lasky's behavior. Had I misled myself once again? More broadly, I had thought the argument that the program had not defamed Lasky was a strong one. I had devoted a great deal of my argument to that issue. The jury had rejected my argument—had rejected, I could not help thinking, me. The jury had understood the broadcast to have been far from the neutral portrayal of Lasky that I had claimed. It had, they had determined, accused him of calling Mundel a Communist. But was the defamation true or not?

Twenty-five minutes later the jury sent a new note. They had reached a verdict on the second question, whether Lasky had proved that the broadcast was false.

"What is your verdict?" Judge Walker asked. The foreman paused and replied, "The verdict is no."

For a half-second my mind blurred. Was I sure that a "no" answer was the one we wanted?

Yes, absolutely. "No" meant "Yes, the broadcast was true." "No" meant that the jury thought that Lasky was responsible for Mundel's woes, that he had called her a Communist, that the broadcast was vindicated. "No" meant that we had won.

I squeezed Helen Whitney's hand and looked around the filled courtroom as cheers and applause filled the air. I thought of Luella Mundel and Edward G. Robinson. I turned to look at Lasky's table. His face lay on the table before him, covered by his hands. He did not move for a long time.

CHAPTER 7

THE BROOKLYN MUSEUM CASE

When recent college graduates were polled late in 2002 about whom they wished to emulate most in the world, their first two choices were their mothers and their fathers. The third was Rudolph Giuliani.

The masterful leader of New York City at the time of the horrors of September 11, 2001, the Giuliani of those days was commanding yet empathic, plain-spoken yet eloquent. When *Time* chose him as its Person of the Year, it praised him for being "tender without being trite, for not sleeping and not quitting and not shrinking from the pain all around him." Giuliani was Mayor of the World, *Time*'s profile concluded, a view consistent with that of Queen Elizabeth, who knighted him only a few months later.

I knew a different Giuliani. Two years earlier, in the course of defending the Brooklyn Museum against the mayor's efforts to punish it for presenting an art exhibition he claimed was "sick," I found myself confronted with an authoritarian Giuliani, a bullying Giuliani, a Giuliani deeply contemptuous of the First Amendment.

None of this came as a surprise to New Yorkers familiar with the mayor's prior conduct. While he had served the city well in many respects, particularly in overseeing a police department that significantly reduced the amount of crime in the city, in other areas, such as communicating with the city's immense minority population, he seemed tone deaf. And when it came to the First Amendment, a constitutional rule rooted in the idea that the freedom to criticize government and government officials is central to a free society, he was a constant problem, a frequent opponent, an enemy.

When members of the New York Police Department, the Human Resources Administration, and the Administration for Children's Services had each sought to say things publicly of which the Giuliani administration disapproved, they were forbidden to do so by the city government. In three separate lawsuits commenced in federal court, the Giuliani administration was blocked from preventing or punishing the speech. When dissident groups—organizers of a Million Youth March in Harlem, supporters of legalizing marijuana, taxi drivers protesting city policies, protesters against alleged police brutality—sought to criticize the administration in parades or demonstrations, they were likewise forbidden to do so; it took four separate litigations in federal court to protect the rights of these would-be dissenters. When activist organizations such as

Housing Works Inc., a group that provided housing and other services for homeless and formerly homeless persons with HIV and AIDS, and Families First, a community center that provided counseling services, criticized the Giuliani administration, only judicial intervention saved the former from being defunded and the latter from being evicted from city housing.

In all, over thirty-five separate successful lawsuits were brought against the city under Giuliani's stewardship arising out of his insistence on doing the one thing that the First Amendment most clearly forbids: using the power of government to restrict or punish speech critical of government itself. While the city garnered a few victories in court (rulings, for example, that let stand the city's zoning laws designed to limit the spread of various "adult" facilities), in the overwhelming majority of cases it lost, but only after forcing those who wished to (and were entitled to) speak out to seek judicial remedies.

The same was true in other First Amendment-related areas. The Giuliani administration took a starkly restrictive view of the city's freedom of information law, thus requiring people who wanted information about the workings of city government to retain counsel and go to court to challenge the city's refusal to make public what was supposed to be public information. When journalists sought to cover public events such as parades or demonstrations on the street, they were often placed in pens, away from the newsworthy action, and frequently barred from sites where members of the public were free to walk.

So often was it necessary for the courts to step in to restrain the Giuliani administration from violating the First Amendment that Professor Amy Adler of New York University Law School observed that "it seems as if I could teach a First Amendment course just on Mayor Giuliani." The Court of Appeals for the Second Circuit, the federal appeals court for New York, Vermont, and Connecticut, offered a similar observation based upon its own unhappy experience with the mayor. In a rare rebuke to the overall behavior of a city administration, it observed that "we would be ostriches if we failed to take judicial notice of the heavy stream of First Amendment litigation generated by New York City in recent years . . . As a result of the relentless onslaught of First Amendment litigation, the federal courts have, to a considerable extent, been drafted into the role of local licensers for the City of New York." The court then listed seventeen examples in which federal courts had "preliminarily enjoined or found unconstitutional on First Amendment grounds some action or policy of the City."

Not all the legal conflicts were brought against Giuliani. In one bizarre case that stemmed from *New York* magazine's having placed tongue-in-cheek ads on the side of city buses claiming that the magazine was "possibly the only good thing in New York that Rudy hasn't taken credit for," Giuliani sent city lawyers to court to assert—unsuccessfully—that his privacy rights had been violated.

Of all the conduct of Mayor Giuliani personally and that of his administration that violated the First Amendment, no action was more notorious than his conflict with the Brooklyn Museum, and none resulted in so personally humiliating a defeat for Giuliani. Yet only a few months before the case began, the notion of Mayor Giuliani seeking to punish and perhaps destroy the Brooklyn Museum would have been unthinkable.

THE MUSEUM

Like a number of New York City's cultural treasures, the Brooklyn Museum is a nineteenth-century creation. From its inception, the museum had one thing in common with a number of New York's great institutions, including the Metropolitan Museum of Art, the Museum of the City of New York, and the Museum of Natural History: The city had constructed and owned the majestic landmark buildings in which all those collections repose; but the museums were privately run and had purchased and owned all the works in their collections. City aid was provided to all the institutions—27 percent of the funding of the Brooklyn Museum (about $7.2 million) came from the city in 1999—but all artistic decisions were made by the museums themselves. The city did not fund particular artists or exhibits but provided general funds to assist the institutions in paying for maintenance, security, energy, and some education programs.

By September 1999 the Brooklyn Museum was the second-largest art museum in the country and one of the city's premier cultural institutions. Its vast collection numbered more than 1.5 million objects; during 1998 and 1999 alone, it was visited by over a million people. The museum's core holdings included art of the Western world, extending from the civilizations of the ancient Middle East, ancient Egypt, and classical Greece and Rome to the present day, as well as extensive holdings in the art of Asia, Africa, the Pacific, and Central and South America.

Throughout the years the museum's temporary exhibitions had included the work of artists both well-known and largely unknown and works both classical and controversial. In 1999, for example, an exhibition of impressionist paintings was followed by an exhibition of eighteenth- and nineteenth-century Persian art largely unfamiliar to most Western audiences.

In 1990 and 1991 the museum had presented controversial exhibitions of art throughout history illustrating how works once viewed as politically, religiously, or sexually objectionable were considered mainstream today. The earlier one was called "The Play of the Unmentionable: The Brooklyn Museum Collection"; the later one, "Too Shocking to Show." Some objections

311

had been voiced to both exhibitions, but not by the city.

But if the exhibitions of the early 1990s generated some controversy, a show mounted in 1999 was incendiary. Entitled "Sensation: Young British Artists from the Saatchi Collection," it came to the museum following highly successful, and even more highly controversial, showings in London and Berlin. The exhibition included approximately ninety paintings, sculptures, photographs, and installations by approximately forty contemporary British artists from the collection of British collector Charles Saatchi. Saatchi was a leading figure in advertising who had, to the discomfort of some of his countrymen, become Britain's leading patron of contemporary art.

The artists contributing to "Sensation" included some of the most honored contemporary artists in Great Britain. Many had had their works displayed in prestigious art museums and galleries around the world. Three of them—Damien Hirst, Chris Ofili, and Rachael Whitehead—had each been awarded the prestigious Turner Prize, awarded annually to a British artist under the age of fifty for the outstanding exhibition or artwork of the year.

But no amount of prior recognition of its artists could shield the art in the "Sensation" exhibition from often overheated criticism. Damien Hirst's cross-sections of animals suspended in formaldehyde were a particular source of comment in

London, where the exhibition was displayed at the Royal Academy of Arts and drew enormous crowds. Even more was *Myra*, a portrait of English serial child-killer Myra Hindley created out of tiny handprints of children, which was denounced as outrageous by much of the English press and public.

Little was made in London, however, of the single work that would give rise to the greatest trouble in New York City, Chris Ofili's painting *The Holy Virgin Mary*. Ofili, a Nigerian-British artist, was represented by five paintings in the exhibition, each of which used elephant dung as a sort of decorative, textured, compositional material. The dung was not, as would often be charged, "smeared" or "splattered" on any of the pictures. In Ofili's image of the Virgin Mary, "resin-clad and decorated," as Dr. Arnold Lehman, the director of the Brooklyn Museum, would later write, "the shaped clumps of elephant dung are used as controlled compositional elements and as pedestal feet."

Ofili's *Virgin Mary* was a depiction of an African woman clad in a brightly colored outfit. A viewer of the picture would not have known, without being told, that the picture incorporated dung. Nor would the viewer have known, unless she was within a foot or two of it, that at various places on the painting were small photographic depictions of the most intimate parts of a woman's body. In fact, the uninitiated viewer who was unaware of its title would not likely have been able to identify the painting's subject as the Virgin Mary.

In the spring of 1998 Dr. Lehman had begun working to bring the "Sensation" exhibition to Brooklyn. Impressed with the quality of the work in the collection and desirous of attracting a large and diverse audience to the museum and of making a high-profile statement about the museum's commitment to contemporary art, Lehman spent months cajoling Saatchi to allow the pieces to be displayed at the museum and raising the funds to make that possible. During the course of his efforts, Lehman reported on various occasions to the museum's board of trustees, including showing it slides of some of the works involved and presenting to it the catalogue of the London exhibition. Representatives of the city were ex officio members of the board and thus were invited to all board meetings and received the minutes of each meeting. Susan Rothschild, the designated representative for Schuyler Chapin, commissioner of the city's Department of Cultural Affairs (DCA), regularly attended meetings of the board, as did other city representatives.

Throughout the period preceding the opening of the exhibition, the city was kept informed about it. In January 1999, a submission was made to DCA which included a description of the "Sensation" show and a statement regarding the fees that had been charged at prior special exhibitions. In early March Lehman met with DCA commissioner Chapin to discuss, among other things, the "Sensation" exhibition, and presented him personally with a copy of the London catalogue.

In April Lehman wrote to Chapin to inform him that "Sensation" was slated for an October opening; Lehman stressed the controversial nature of the exhibition and advised the commissioner that an admission fee would be charged and a requirement imposed that children under seventeen be accompanied by an adult. The same letter was sent to all other board members the next day, including Mayor Giuliani's representative. On April 14, 1999, Chapin responded with a cheery note:

> Thank you for your fascinating letter about "Sensation: Young British Artists from the Saatchi Collection." I seem to recall reading about this exhibit not too long ago in the *Times*. It certainly sounds as if you are shaking up New York's art world. I'm marking September 30th in my calendar for an event that will undoubtedly shake me out of my occasional late-middle-age lethargy!
>
> If I have any thoughts about funding I'll be back in touch.
>
> Congratulations!

On July 14, 1999, Dr. Lehman made a personal presentation to Mayor Giuliani and his staff about the museum's upcoming and future plans.

The "Sensation" exhibition was included in the presentation. The mayor was shown a slide of Damien Hirst's *The Physical Impossibility of Death in the Mind of Someone Living*, which featured a shark preserved in formaldehyde; the work was one of the signature pieces of the exhibition. The mayor was also provided with an illustrated report on the museum's planned activities. At no point during the entire period leading up to the opening of "Sensation" did the city or any of its representatives raise any objections to the proposals to bring the exhibition to the BMA, to charge admission for it, or to require that children under seventeen be accompanied by an adult.

Advertising for the exhibition, scheduled to open on October 2, 1999, was brash. HEALTH WARNING, the ads proclaimed. "The contents of this exhibition cause shock, vomiting, confusion, panic, euphoria and anxiety." (Critics would later constantly cite the tongue-in-cheek tone of these ads, drafted by the museum's advertising agency in an effort to capture the attention of a wide audience, to rebut any claim of the artistic value of the exhibition.)

Two weeks before the scheduled opening, the trouble began. On September 16, 1999, the *New York Daily News* introduced New York City to the forthcoming exhibition with a flamboyant four-column article. Under the headline BROOKLYN GALLERY OF HORROR: GRUESOME MUSEUM SHOW STIRS CONTROVERSY, the exhibition was described as a "shocking contemporary art exhibit that features real animals sliced in half, and graphic paintings and sculptures of corpses and sexually mutilated bodies." Particular "outrage," the article stated, had been voiced "over such works as a painting of the Virgin Mary splattered with elephant dung." Mayor Giuliani's press secretary, Sunny Mindel, was quoted saying that "assuming the description of the exhibit is accurate, no money should be spent on it."

On September 22, six days after the *News* article was published, a member of the mayor's staff suggested to a journalist that he ask Giuliani at his daily morning question-and-answer session with the press about his views of the forthcoming exhibition generally and, more specifically, about its inclusion of *The Holy Virgin Mary*. It was an unusual tip; opinionated as he was, the mayor had never before been asked his thoughts regarding any forthcoming art exhibition, at the Brooklyn Museum or anywhere else.

Giuliani had not seen the exhibition (and never would see it), and there is no reason to believe that he knew that each of Ofili's five paintings in the exhibition contained elephant dung for decorative reasons, or that that material is considered regenerative in Nigerian tribal culture. Earlier that morning, at his daily eight a.m. meeting with high-ranking members of his cabinet, the mayor had angrily denounced the exhibition as an anti-religious affront and instructed his aides to take all steps necessary to suspend funds to the museum. When asked about the exhibition at his later question-and-answer session, he was ready:

It offends me. The idea of in the name of art having a city subsidize art, so-called works of art, in which people are throwing elephant dung at a picture of the Virgin Mary, is sick. If somebody wants to do that privately and pay for that privately, well, that's what the First Amendment is all about. You can be offended by it and upset by it. You don't have to go to see it if somebody else is paying for it. But to have the government pay for it is outrageous. You don't have a right to a government subsidy to desecrate someone else's religion. And therefore we will do everything that we can to remove funding from the Brooklyn Museum until the director comes to his senses. And realizes that if you are a government-subsidized enterprise then you can't do things that desecrate the most personal and deeply held views of the people in society. This is an outrageous thing to do. And if people want to do it with their own money, they have a right to do it, and we have to defend their right to do it, even though we can sit back and say they are sick and they are disgusting. However, the government doesn't have to contribute taxpayers' dollars to this. This is not something that taxpayers have to underwrite. I would feel the same way if it were a desecration of Protestant religion or Jewish religion, Muslim religion. What the city is going to do is try to remove all the funding it possibly can from the Brooklyn Museum, and send them a message. Because taxpayers' dollars should not be used to support an exhibit where somebody has apparently done a collage, I am reading from the article in the *Daily News*, a collage in 1996 in which elephant dung is splattered on linen [and] is called *The Holy Virgin Mary*. Then it goes on to the bodies of two pigs which are preserved in formaldehyde solution [and] displayed in two glass tanks. I thought that's what they do in biology labs, not in museums of art. It's sick stuff. The city should not have to pay for sick stuff.

Later that day Giuliani's colleagues at City Hall implemented the new policy. Deputy Mayor Joseph Lhota called Robert Rubin, chairman of the Brooklyn Museum's board of trustees, and told him that if the museum did not remove *The Holy Virgin Mary* from the exhibition, the city would terminate all its funding. Robert Harding, the city's director of management and budget, instructed Schuyler Chapin to call museum director Lehman in the name of the mayor to warn him that if the museum did not cancel the exhibition, all city funding would cease immediately. When Chapin objected, protesting that no city money was even going to the "Sensation" exhibit, Harding repeated his instruction. Reluctantly, Chapin made the call to Lehman. To top it off, Deputy Mayor Randy Levine, speaking publicly to the press, added the observation that the museum received its "checks on a first-of-the-month basis . . . Those checks will be suspended unless this exhibit is canceled."

The messages were a bit mixed—was the problem limited to the single Ofili picture or to a wider group of the artworks?—but the ultimate message was unambiguous: remove the Ofili painting or else.

Pressure from City Hall increased the next day, September 23. On checking the 106-year-old lease of the museum, city officials concluded that under a literal reading of it, the museum might need the personal consent of the mayor to restrict admission to anyone, including children under seventeen. The 1893 lease provided that the museum should "at all reasonable times be free, open and accessible to the general public on such terms of admission as the Mayor and Commissioner shall approve" and that if the museum ceased "to be maintained according to the true meaning and intention" of the lease, the lease would be forfeited.

Delighted at this discovery, the mayor leapt further into the fray. "The people running the museum find this exhibit so horrendous and so disgusting that they are not allowing children in without the permission of their parents," he said. But the museum required the permission of the mayor to limit access, and that, the mayor would not give. "Last time I checked," Giuliani said, "I was the mayor, and I don't find closing down access to a public museum consistent with the use of taxpayers' dollars, and that's the whole problem here."

As phrased more legalistically in a letter later that day from Corporation Counsel Michael Hess to the museum, "In light of the fact that BMA has already determined that it would be inappropriate for those under 17 years of age to be admitted to the exhibit without adult supervision (a determination with which the City does not disagree), BMA cannot proceed with the exhibit as planned." The museum was thus advised that the mayor would not approve any parental supervision requirement despite the city's ostensible agreement with that requirement, and that as a result, the entire exhibit would have to be canceled.

Later on September 23, Deputy Mayor Randy Levine piled on with another threat, this one aimed at the museum's board. Offering the "Sensation" exhibition, he said, was "such a highly irresponsible act" that "there are serious questions as to the fiduciary responsibilities of the people who run this museum; and until they come to their senses, there's not going to be any public funding of it."

The next day, September 24, the mayor was at it again, adding his fire to Levine's. A museum that received public funding, he said, did not "have a right to put [its] hands in the taxpayers' pockets to support vicious, horrible, biased attacks on religion." The museum was being used "for shock value in order to commercialize" itself. As a result, the mayor said, under the lease "this board forfeits its right to run the museum, and the museum reverts to the city, and you can be darn sure that we will insist on those legal remedies." The exhibition was not being done for any "real artist's purpose," but only "to make money in the most crass way." And who was responsible for all this? The museum's board of directors. "Since they seem to have no compunction about putting their hands in the taxpayers' pockets in order to have pigs in formaldehyde and cows dissected and have their parts put out there and throwing dung on important religious symbols, I'm not going to have any compunction about having to put them out of business, meaning the board."

On September 24 I was scheduled to meet with Mitch McConnell, the Republican senator from Kentucky, who was leading the opposition to adoption of the McCain-Feingold campaign finance bill. Knowing of my qualms about the constitutionality of the bill, Senator McConnell had called to ask if I would testify before his committee in opposition to it. At that point, I thought at least a good part of the proposed legislation was probably unconstitutional under the First Amendment, but had not studied the subject enough to be confident that I was prepared to offer public testimony on it. Senator McConnell and I agreed to meet at his Senate office to discuss the matter.

On my way to Washington on the Metroliner, I called my assistant, Denise O'Neill, to ask if I had had any calls. Dr. Lehman, the Brooklyn Museum's director, and Mr. Rubin, the chairman of its board, had called to retain me, she said. I contacted Dr. Lehman immediately, was briefed by him on what had occurred (almost all of which had already appeared in the press), and agreed to meet with him and Rubin the following day, with the understanding that if it was necessary to go to court, I and my colleagues at Cahill Gordon would represent the museum.

I called my partner Susan Buckley, described the situation to her, and asked her to begin to prepare for a possible litigation against the city and Mayor Giuliani. Upon my return to New York, Susan and I discussed the full range of legal issues that the situation seemed to raise. As a First Amendment matter, the case seemed straightforward enough. The mayor was at it again, and once again well-established case law seemed to stand in his way. First Amendment law had long established that public officials could not retaliate against institutions because of their exercise of First Amendment rights, and this certainly seemed like nothing but retaliation. In fact, in a strikingly similar case, a Cuban-American museum had virtually been put out of business by the city of Miami because of what city officials viewed as the pro-Castro affiliations of many of its artists. A federal court there had held that the city's cancellation of the museum's lease for that reason was unconstitutional, even though the museum was a tenant in city-owned property on a lease that was terminable at will. From the start, Mayor Giuliani's conduct seemed, if anything, even more clearly unconstitutional. The Miami city officials had falsely denied their motivation; Giuliani, on the contrary, had been nothing but forthcoming about his own. He was, as I later told the court, "the least ambiguous trampler of the First Amendment that our law has yet seen." The content of the Ofili picture was the problem; the problem could be dealt with only by the removal of the picture; and according to City Hall, if the picture was not removed, all city funding would be withheld. If that wasn't unconstitutional retaliation, what was?

There were other ways to articulate the core First Amendment problem raised by the mayor's conduct. Many cases had concluded that government could not "prohibit expression of an idea simply because society finds the idea itself offensive or disagreeable" and that even in those narrow areas where the government might regulate speech on the basis of content, it could not do so with the purpose of suppressing any particular viewpoint. Once again, given Giuliani's rhetoric, how could his insistence on the removal of the Ofili painting be considered anything but an effort to suppress speech?

There was, however, one potentially serious First Amendment issue that lurked behind the surface of the case. The city was certainly not obliged to fund the arts at all. To what extent, then, could it successfully argue that it was therefore free not to fund art that might be viewed as offensive by a significant number of people because of its content? There had been one United States Supreme Court case in this area, *National Endowment for the Arts v. Finley*, a 1998 ruling that held that NEA grants could be made on a basis in which the peer review groups that recommended which artists should be given grants took into account notions of "decency" and "the diverse beliefs and values of the American public." The scope of that decision was unclear. While affirming the constitutionality of the statute, the Court did not address the question of whether grants could be denied to particular artists because their works were "indecent." In its ruling the Court itself had expressed concern about the possibility of the NEA's leveraging its power "to award subsidies on the basis of subjective criteria into a penalty on disfavored viewpoints." Even when subsidies were provided, the Court said, "the government may not 'aim at the suppression of dangerous ideas,' and if a subsidy were 'manipulated' to have a 'coercive effect,' then relief could be appropriate." In our view, that was precisely what Giuliani was doing.

Our chances of prevailing on our First Amendment arguments thus seemed excellent. Not only was the mayor acting in a way that seemed flatly at odds with deeply rooted First Amendment law, but he was leaving behind him a verbal trail of statements amounting to a confession that he was seeking to punish the museum for defying him. Better yet, Giuliani's disdain for First Amendment principles was well known in the courts. Unconstitutional conduct that would be unthinkable by any past mayor of living memory seemed to be the norm for Giuliani, a starting point that could not help assisting us.

But there remained one potential legal problem. For all the strength of our First Amendment case, what about the museum's 106-year-old lease? The mayor was relying on it to give him authority to expel the museum from its city-owned premises if it did not make the totality of its space available to the public at large—children included. On one level, this seemed absurd. Why should the museum, criticized because of the content of its exhibition, suffer by *limiting* access to children without being accompanied by their parents? Moreover, Lehman had already fully disclosed the museum's intention to do so to Commissioner Chapin, who had not objected, and to his board, which had as one of its members a representative of the mayor. How could the city now step in, feign surprise at what had occurred, deny permission for the museum to keep underage viewers out, and then require the entire exhibition to be closed?

None of this made sense (common sense, that is), but the law is sometimes less than sensible. The lease was old and could be read against us. Why take any unnecessary chances? In my first meeting with Bob Rubin and Arnold Lehman, I raised the question of whether the museum might reverse itself and consent, after all, not to restrict access. Lehman and Rubin quickly agreed, adding that they would like to put up a sign warning parents that portions of the exhibition might not be appropriate for children. And so, in a bizarre twist, the first on-the-ground effect of Giuliani's blustery threats made in the name of protecting the public from the art in "Sensation" was to allow children to be exposed to the very art the mayor so vehemently denounced.

Rubin told me that the board of the museum would consider the issue at its meeting scheduled for September 28, which would also consider the mayor's demand that the entire exhibition be canceled. In the meantime, he instructed me to prepare to go to court to defend the museum against the city and Mayor Giuliani. We did so

327

over the weekend, drafting a complaint for filing in federal court in Brooklyn.

On September 28 the museum's board met at four p.m. By this time, Giuliani had publicly focused even more clearly on the punishment he wanted most to inflict on the museum: Beyond merely stripping it of its city funding, he wanted to *evict* it from the premises it had occupied for over a century. At his morning press conference, he denounced the exhibition once again for taking "one of the most important symbols to Catholics and throw dung at it and have pictures of the private parts of women displayed all over it." What would happen next? As always, the mayor's answer was unambiguous:

> The corporation counsel told them what we're going to do, the lease tells us what we're required to do, which is to evict them and to stop dealing with them as a board. We'll do that over a period of time. We'll hold back their funds because they are not a properly constituted board at this point and then over a period of time there will be a substitute board put in place. The lease, which I invite you to read, says that the museum must be open to all public and private school students at all times (actually has the words 'public and private school students' in it) and that any restriction on that open admission has to be

approved by the mayor. Failure to get that approval results in forfeiture of the lease.

At the board meeting, Deputy Mayor Joseph Lhota attended for Mayor Giuliani, together with Corporation Counsel Michael Hess, whom I had, almost thirty years before, litigated against in the *Pentagon Papers* case. The coincidence was startling. Here was Hess once again representing a serial First Amendment violator and I—or so I thought—representing just the sort of victim of government misconduct that the Bill of Rights was drafted to protect.

Both Lhota and Hess spoke, warning the board members in the starkest terms not to proceed with the exhibition. To do so, they said, would be illegal. The week before, Hess had been quoted in the press stating that "a change in the board of the museum" to one that "would have better judgment as to what is appropriate for this type of museum" would be advisable. That morning, the mayor himself had announced that the city would "stop dealing with them as a board." Notwithstanding all these threats, Rubin, as chairman, proposed to the trustees that the exhibition, scheduled to begin on October 2, proceed, and urged the board to avoid what he characterized as a needless legalistic dispute with the mayor over the terms of the Museum's lease by abandoning the parental supervision requirement and replacing it with signs warning parents of the challenging nature of the exhibit. Over the sole dissenting vote of Deputy Mayor Lhota, the trustees voted to go ahead with the exhibition and to abandon the child-supervision requirement. Rubin further proposed, and the board by the same vote agreed, to take whatever legal steps were necessary to defend the rights of the museum.

It is easy, years after the fact, to underestimate the courage of Rubin and his fellow board members in refusing to accede to the mayor's demands. Museums are dependent for their survival upon significant contributions and grants, and New York City was not only providing the museum around $7 million each year—27 percent of its yearly budget—in operational funding, but had earlier promised another $28 million in capital funding. City officials had also indicated that even more capital funding would be provided in the future.

The potential financial harm to the museum was not limited to the sanctions the city might impose on it. When Giuliani first publicly attacked the museum, both the United States Senate and the House of Representatives had rapidly joined forces with the mayor, passing by voice votes denunciations of the museum and ordering, in nonbinding votes, a cutoff of all federal aid. (Only the later intervention of New York Senator Daniel Patrick Moynihan, who had been off the floor when the resolution passed, kept Congress from actually doing so.) But whatever the threat from Washington, the greater risk lay in City Hall in New York City. Mayor Giuliani was a fearsome enemy for any museum in the city to confront. That a museum board of lay citizens should have been willing to risk the mayor's continuing wrath remains an impressive act of defiance.

As the meeting progressed, I had more immediate concerns on my mind. While various speakers voiced their opinions, I reviewed the complaint that we had prepared over the weekend, a copy of which I had brought with me. It sought a judicial declaration that the city's acts and those of the mayor violated the First Amendment and an injunction against any such continued conduct.

We had decided to bring the action in the United States District Court for the Eastern District of New York, the federal court located in Brooklyn, immediately after the board voted to proceed with the exhibition. Our concern was that the city would file first in state court in Brooklyn, a potentially less hospitable forum for resolution of First Amendment issues. In New York City, mayors have considerable clout over who becomes a state judge, and many of those judges are far less skilled than federal judges in deciding constitutional cases. Had the city filed first in state court, it would have been difficult, and quite likely impossible, for us to persuade a federal judge to decide a later case filed on behalf of the museum. As the meeting of the board progressed, I kept looking at my watch. The clerk's office in the federal courthouse closed at five p.m., and if we wanted to file that day, it was necessary to do so by then.

At 4:55 p.m. the board voted to proceed with the exhibition. I left the room and called Susan Buckley at my office, who in turn was on the line with Robert Cawthra, our firm's managing attorney, who was waiting in the courthouse for the order to file. At 4:58 p.m. the complaint was filed. All cases in that court are immediately assigned, on a random basis, to a judge for all purposes, and ours was assigned to Judge Nina Gershon.

That night the city reacted to the board meeting and the filing of our complaint by announcing that it was suspending all aid to the museum. Seven million dollars had been allocated to the museum for the fiscal year 1999 by legislation adopted by the city council and signed by Mayor Giuliani. Now the museum was to receive none of it. The same was true of the additional $28 million in capital funding that the administration had indicated it would provide, as well as potential additional funding for the construction of a new facade for the building in which the museum reposed.

On September 30 I called Judge Gershon's clerk to ask for a meeting with the judge to discuss scheduling issues. We had learned that Judge Gershon was trying a case and were concerned that she might have difficulty seeing us promptly. Instead, she scheduled a hearing for 5:00 p.m. the same day. It was a favorable start. The worst judicial reaction to our complaint would have been either boredom or hostility; neither would likely have produced so quick a response from the court.

At the hearing, I argued that there would likely be few factual issues in controversy and that with a limited amount of exchange of documents and depositions, the case would be ready for a hearing on our motion for a preliminary injunction to stop the mayor from implementing his various threats against the museum. "From start to finish," I said, those threats had "been accompanied by a series of deceptive and false and pretextual statements" about the museum's lease. The first was the exchange about the museum's initial plan to limit attendance at the museum so as not to allow in individuals under seventeen without an accompanying adult. That we had dealt with, I explained, by the museum's "saying, well, all right, if the mayor insists, we will allow people under seventeen to attend, and we will put up warning signs in the museum." Then, I said, we had read in the newspapers that morning that the mayor had conjured up "another pretextual reason for seeking to punish the museum for the exercise of its First Amendment rights": the fact that Saatchi, the owner of the art, and Christie's, the prominent auction house, would profit from its being shown. All that, I argued, was an effort to "avoid the reality of what is at issue here, and what is only at issue here, a deliberate, unambiguous effort of Mayor Giuliani and the city to punish the museum for the exercise of [its] First

Amendment rights." I asked that the hearing be set quickly.

Hess responded by first telling Judge Gershon that the city had just commenced its own action in state court in Brooklyn seeking to eject the museum from its 106-year home. He handed me a copy of the complaint. It claimed that the museum had violated its lease with the city in three ways: by planning to charge an admission fee to the "Sensation" exhibition without the consent of the mayor or the parks commissioner; by failing to "educate and enlighten schoolchildren and the public"; and "by presenting an exhibition that furthers the commercial interest of private parties" rather than "public purposes." Accordingly, the city claimed, the museum was obliged to "deliver possession of the premises and the building thereon to the city."

At the end of the hearing, and with the city's acquiescence, Judge Gershon established a speedy schedule to ensure that she could promptly hear our motion for a preliminary injunction. Discovery was scheduled on an expedited basis. October 8 was set as the day for the hearing.

The next day, October 1, 1999, we raised the ante in the case. If Giuliani was prepared to seek to destroy the museum over a single picture of which he disapproved, we were ready to give *him* something to worry about as well. Our initial complaint, filed on September 28, had sued both the city and "Rudolph Giuliani in his official capacity." That meant that we were not seeking any damages from him personally but only from the city, since anything he had done was done on behalf of the city.

But if what Giuliani had done was as constitutionally outrageous as we were claiming, we did have a potential claim against him personally. It is difficult, but not impossible, to sue successfully city or state officials in their personal as well as official roles. Officials are generally immunized from personal liability even for unconstitutional acts they perform so long as they act in good faith. But if a city official *knowingly* violates someone's constitutional rights, he can be required to pay punitive damages for doing so. Here the law against retaliating against an institution for exercising its First Amendment rights was straightforward, and the mayor was likely aware of the law, if only because he had been sued so often and lost so often before. I also viewed it as improbable that Giuliani, whose vanity about his knowledge of the law was well known, would even consider claiming that he did not know the elements of First Amendment law. He himself had represented the *Daily News* when he was in private practice. If he was going to misuse the law in an effort to punish the museum, why shouldn't we use the full protections of the law to punish him? It would, not coincidentally, give us great satisfaction to do so as well.

We filed an amended complaint on behalf of

the museum, adding a new paragraph that read as follows: "BMA [the museum] is entitled to punitive damages against Mayor Giuliani as he acted maliciously and with intent to violate or with reckless or callous disregard for plaintiff's rights under the First Amendment of the Constitution of the United States." For months afterward, friends of mine who knew the mayor told me how angry that sentence had made him. It wasn't fair, they told me he had said, that his meager assets should be at risk. One lawyer for the city went so far as to ask me privately to drop the claim lest the mayor become still more upset at the museum. With the greatest pleasure, I respectfully declined to do so.

Not all the events of those days were so satisfying. At a time when the ultimate ruling in the case was very much in doubt, Philippe de Montebello, the director of the august Metropolitan Museum of Art, published an op-ed piece in the *New York Times* fawning over Mayor Giuliani for his "aesthetic sensibilities" in criticizing the exhibition. Citing the works of Cézanne, Delacroix, Picasso, and Manet as "good art" and the Brooklyn Museum's offerings as "bad art," de Montebello wrote that Giuliani had "shown astute critical acumen" in denouncing the exhibition as worthless. He concluded his article with a ritualistic tip of his hat to Voltaire, piously observing that like that great and brave defender of free expression, de Montebello himself would nonetheless "defend to the death" the Brooklyn Museum's right to offer the bad art that Giuliani had rightly denounced.

The article deeply offended me. De Montebello, whose museum had itself received over $16 million from the city in 2001, had praised Giuliani for his bravery—in common, of course, with his own—in rejecting "the clarion call for avant-garde art which cries out to be seen no matter what." In doing so, he lent support to Giuliani in an area in which he needed it the most—the contention that the "Sensation" exhibition was not really art at all. De Montebello's attack on the most vulnerable member of the artistic flock, undertaken when tigers were searching for prey, was an appalling breach of artistic fellowship—if, that is, there is such a thing. It was ugly pandering, not undone by the fact that the Metropolitan Museum itself later joined with a large number of other museums in a fine legal brief drafted by First Amendment expert Victor Kovner denouncing Giuliani's misconduct.

DISCOVERY

The high point of discovery was the deposition of Deputy Mayor Lhota, taken by Susan Buckley. Lhota had filed an affidavit with the court identifying which works of art in the "Sensation" exhibition the city believed had been inappropriate for the museum to display. Two pictures, including *The Holy Virgin Mary*, he wrote, were offensive to

Catholics; others were inappropriate for children; another (*Myra*) "inappropriately glorifies a heinous criminal." Susan pressed him on what standards he had used to make his choices, quickly establishing that the standards used by Lhota, and by extension the city, were the stuff of comic opera, not law.

> Q: In selecting the works that you deemed to be inappropriate, how did you go about doing that?
>
> A: I asked myself the following question: One, do they desecrate anyone's religion? . . .
>
> The second question is: Would I like my eight-year-old daughter to see this work of art? . . .
>
> And the third question that I asked was: Would anyone who believes in animal rights be offended?

There it was. According to the Giuliani administration, the art in a world-class cultural institution such as the Brooklyn Museum was to be reduced to a level fit for an easily offended animal-loving eight-year-old.

Was he serious? Susan pressed on with examples. Asked if Michelangelo's *David* was the sort of work of art that his eight-year-old daughter should see, Lhota replied that it was not. Could it be displayed at the Brooklyn Museum? Yes, said Lhota. When Susan showed him a picture of Jean Broc's graphic painting *The Death of Hyacinth*, he likewise agreed that it was not fit for his daughter but fit for the museum. The same was true, he acknowledged, of other "controversial" or "mature" works. Within twenty minutes of articulating a legal standard based upon his eight-year-old daughter's sensibilities, Lhota had conceded that the standard had not the slightest reality to it.

The second area Susan explored followed from the first: If the standards were as Lhota had set them forth, how could a museum know in advance which works were inappropriate? In response to this query, Lhota suddenly discovered the First Amendment. "This is not," he said, "something that . . . the city of New York would ever put in some kind of protocol, some kind of procedure." Was there anyone in city government to whom a museum could turn? Of course not, "since there are no government procedures . . . no government rules" and "no government regulations."

The bottom line, then, was this: Giuliani could, on the basis of indefensible and quickly scuttled ad hoc tests, conjured up after the fact, ban any work of art that was displayed in any city-owned building. There were no meaningful standards that could be articulated to determine which works of art were or were not appropriate and no place within the city government to go to learn, in advance, the city's determination of what was appropriate. According to the mayor, it was his prerogative to decide which works of art could be displayed based on his own subjective reaction to them. *David* was permissible; *The Holy Virgin Mary* was not. Museums would act at their peril in predicting which fare would or would not incur mayoral wrath.

Oral argument on our motion for a preliminary injunction began, before a courtroom overflowing with the press and public, at ten a.m. on October 8. In the meantime, the city had made a new motion of its own, seeking to persuade Judge Gershon to dismiss the federal case we had brought so as to permit its later-filed state court case to proceed. Under a 1961 United States Supreme Court case called *Younger v. Harris*, federal courts are obliged to abstain from deciding matters pending in state court under certain circumstances. One requirement for any such refusal of a federal court to decide a case properly brought before it is that an "important" state interest be involved. Another is that the state action be filed in good faith and not for purposes of harassment or retaliation.

After Leonard Koerner, a senior attorney in the New York City Law Department, began by arguing that Judge Gershon should defer to the city's ejectment action in state court, I responded by arguing that since the ejectment action was "a form of retaliation in and of itself," our federal action

340

should be permitted to proceed to decide that issue. The city itself, I said, had argued that the ejectment of the museum was prompted by the need for the government to be "able to respond in a meaningful way to art that is deeply offensive." What else was that, I asked, but asserting in more euphemistic terms that the city must be free "to retaliate against constitutionally protected speech?"

Judge Gershon turned quickly to the facts, asking if they were in dispute. I responded first, stating that while there were a few such issues, none was relevant and that, in fact, the city was not even arguing that they were. I then emphasized the facts we believed were most relevant—e.g., the museum's plans to offer the "Sensation" exhibition, the mayor's clearly stated objection to it because of the Ofili picture, and his decision to cut off the museum and otherwise punish it because it would not remove the Ofili work. I reviewed the mayor's threats, reading each one to the court, and focused on the revelations in the Lhota deposition the day before.

"We will all breathe a sigh of relief," I said, that Lhota had agreed that Michelangelo's *David* "would be appropriate in the Brooklyn Museum if we could pry it away from Florence." I then showed Judge Gershon, who could not avoid smiling, a 48"-by-30" blow-up photograph of *David* that we had prepared. When she responded that "the statue is quite a lot larger and more imposing," I observed, to laughter in the audience and another smile from the judge, "Yes, it looks like a shrunken *David*."

Sometimes an argument flows particularly smoothly, and as this one progressed—particularly with the benediction of two judicial smiles in the first five minutes—I felt increasingly better. After showing the court pictures of Broc's *Death of Hyacinth* and a nude print by Tom Hesselman, both of which Lhota had deemed appropriate for the museum, I turned to the heart of the case:

ABRAMS: Legally there is no doubt that art is protected by the First Amendment. There is no doubt that the art at the Brooklyn Museum is protected by First Amendment. There is no doubt that this exhibition is protected by the First Amendment, and I don't understand the city to be disagreeing with a word that I just said.

What the city did here, though, to this protected speech is to punish the museum for carrying it; and another proposition that the city doesn't address is that you can't punish anyone for simply exercising their First Amendment right.

It is true in all contexts. There are no exceptions.

What does the city say? The city relies

on the proposition that since it is a partial funder of the museum and since it is city property that the museum rests in, that the city may impose its own, or indeed the mayor may impose his own, definition as to what is or is not appropriate.

As for the issue of city property, they have the First Amendment inside out. The First Amendment does not stop at the door of the Brooklyn Museum. It is precisely because the property is owned by the city that the First Amendment does apply.

GERSHON: Well, you are not saying that the First Amendment wouldn't apply if the land wasn't owned by the city, right?

ABRAMS: I am saying that the First Amendment would apply if the city took action anywhere.

GERSHON: So what is the point you are making?

ABRAMS: The thing is that the city argues, "We own this property, therefore we are entitled for that reason to say we don't want offensive art on it." My answer to that is the fact that they own the property, if anything, makes it even easier to say the First Amendment applies. The answer to your question is you are absolutely right—even if they didn't own it, the First Amendment would apply.

Judge Gershon then turned to the religious side of the case. What difference did it make that the mayor's prime objection to the exhibition was the supposedly sacrilegious nature of the Ofili work? I responded:

I am glad you asked, Your Honor.

The centerpiece of the mayor's objection to the work shown at the museum related to a work by Chris Ofili which he, and then the deputy mayor yesterday, referred to as degrading to religion— attacking religion and the like.

There was a time, maybe two hundred years ago, in which this country recognized the notion of blasphemy. It is now not a word which is heard in American courts because for a variety of constitutional reasons, including the establishment clause [of the First Amendment], a city may not play the role that this city has undertaken here in order to protect religion, in order to do precisely what both the mayor and the deputy mayor have said that they are doing.

It is the ideas of this art, it is what they offer by way of disagreeable, painful, sometimes offensive ideas, that the mayor and the city are so upset about, and that is precisely what they may not use the funding process to deal with.

I ended my presentation:

Let me conclude with some thoughts on the impact of the mayor's conduct, if it is permitted to continue.

There is no principle—no limiting principle—which would limit [any mayor] from stripping any library even partially funded by the city of any book that the mayor viewed as offensive, disgusting, sick, anti-religion, or the like. There is no principle offered by the city. There is no principle, I believe, that can fairly be articulated. There is no principle that would protect against another mayor someday—perhaps pressured by the public, perhaps acting on his own behest, perhaps playing to the public's [basest] instincts—to use a bit of public funding as reason to take away more than a bit of our freedom. It cannot be. The First Amendment does not permit it to be that such funding means a loss of First Amendment freedoms, that if a museum or library takes any money from the public that the art it may carry and the books it may carry may, therefore, be selected thereafter by the mayor or his aides. And as for

Mr. Lhota's eight-year-old-daughter test, I will pass over it in silence.

Judge Gershon then asked about the constitutional issue always lurking in the case. Was I saying that the city was obliged to fund art that it finds offensive? I responded this way:

It is clear that the city doesn't have to fund the arts. It is also clear that when the city funds the arts that it can play a very major role in deciding what sort of art it funds. It can decide to fund art only about the history of New York City. It could decide not to fund photography art or abstract expressionism if it chooses.

But there is nothing in any case which says that once the city begins to fund the arts and treats a museum not as a spokesman for itself but as still an independent, autonomous entity, a public forum as it were, that the city can then switch and say "We don't like that picture" or "We don't like that concept for a picture."

It would be an unconstitutional policy for the city to say, "we will fund the arts, but we will not fund the arts with respect to this topic or this approach to a topic of which we disapprove." They can say, and they would be right in saying, "We won't fund obscene art because that is a crime," but once the city begins to fund, the First Amendment does kick in; and once the city starts to provide money to a museum, a library, and the like, they don't become the proprietors of the library. They don't become the moral censors, and they can't.

I was followed by Koerner, who quickly turned to the advertising of the exhibition and the commercial side of the museum's motivation.

How did this dispute occur? If you look at the exhibit and you look at how this subject has been advertised, it clearly is not your normal art subject. The advertisement itself warns that when people look at it, they may vomit, they may suffer from anxiety, people are not to go there who are physically ill. That was in their advertisement. In a memorandum in March from the director of the museum to Mr. Rubin, also an associate of the museum, it was emphasized that the entire subject matter had tremendous shock value, which could be useful to the museum, that persons [were] having trouble getting corporate sponsors, that no other museum would carry this particular subject and they are looking for ways to secure funding. The method by the securing of funding was to use Christie's auction house, which is trying to establish

347

a market for this particular art, and also, to secure funding from the owner of the private art collection, which in and of itself is unusual in the application.

Judge Gershon then interrupted, bringing Koerner back to the claims the city had made in its ejectment complaint.

GERSHON: You said, "We acted as a consequence of the nature of the exhibit." Does that mean that the charging of fees and the children, the issue with regard to children, are those now not in this case?

KOERNER: To this extent, yes, Your Honor.

GERSHON: Yes they weren't in the case?

KOERNER: Well, I am going to explain the fee is out and the admission of the children is no longer per se a ground, but it is extremely relevant in discussing whether this subject strayed from its original mission.

If the purpose of the museum is to cater to children in school and there is an announcement that children ought not to go to this subject, there is something inconsistent between the mission and the subject and that is part of the general argument that we are making about the subject.

GERSHON: If you wouldn't mind, I would

like to put that off a bit because I think it is a big part of your position and just at this point I would like to see what we are narrowing.

In the ejectment action the city asserts three grounds—one is the charging of a fee.

KOERNER: That is no longer a ground.

GERSHON: That is no longer an issue in this action or in the ejectment action?

KOERNER: That is correct.

GERSHON: Now, another issue in the ejectment action is that the exhibit furthers the commercial interest of private parties. While you have made some references to Saatchi in your brief in opposition to the motion for a preliminary injunction, my understanding is what you were saying is that is no longer an issue.

KOERNER: By itself it only creates an atmosphere for the general argument of the nature of the exhibit.

GERSHON: But that is also no longer a ground for the ejectment action?

KOERNER: Except insofar as it is used to supplement the proof that they strayed from the original mission, violated the condition of the lease and another would be the basis of the ejectment.

GERSHON: You are not saying, though, that the relationship between the museum

and Saatchi and Christie's really is a
basis in itself—a basis for ejectment?
KOERNER: That is correct, in and of itself.
GERSHON: All right.

Having disposed of two of the three grounds for
ejectment cited in the city's state court complaint,
Judge Gershon turned to the third, the city's claim
that the exhibition violated the mission of the
museum to educate schoolchildren. If the museum
presented an exhibition inconsistent with that
mission, Koerner argued, it was violating its lease.
Judge Gershon probed just how far that argument
went. Turning to publicly funded libraries, she said:

GERSHON: I don't think you would dispute
that the libraries must be filled with
works that are offensive to one group or
another, either on a political or social or
religious or other grounds, and I would
like to know what the city's position is
with regard to whether or not the city
would have the right to determine that
sacrilegious books have to be removed
from all public libraries.
KOERNER: It is the nature or the degree. A
book does not get the type of exposure.
Part of what the problem with this is,
it holds a significant portion of the
population within the city up for disparagement by disparaging their religion.

It was highly advertised. The subject matter clearly was not appropriate.

GERSHON: Well, are you suggesting that there aren't many, many books that hold many people up to disparagement, all types of groups?

KOERNER: But they do not have the impact on the community that something like this does. For example, if I might, if you turn the Brooklyn Museum into a pornography museum, the plaintiff's position would be that since we started funding it, we couldn't stop funding it because it would be protected by the First Amendment.

Koerner then turned to the exhibition itself.

We describe a number of the exhibits in this particular collection. There is the famous one with the elephant dung. There is another one with someone's head and a hole in that head with a bullet hole; a third with the Last Supper with a topless woman; another one with a dead dad, a nude man lying on the floor. Is that appropriate for children? Yes, that's its mission. It doesn't mean that we're suppressing the speech. What we're saying is there comes a point with the identity of the museum and the city's participation in it that it is just inappropriate as a matter of law and we reach that point in this particular case.

Finally, Judge Gershon turned to one of the critical issues in the case: who was to decide what art went in the museum, its director or the mayor?

> GERSHON: And I take it the city's position is that these decisions should not be made exclusively by Mr. Lehman or by the board of the museum; but who then is to make these determinations? On the record we have that the mayor has made them.
>
> KOERNER: Your Honor, it should have been made by the director of the museum. He did not discharge his responsibility under the lease. When it is not made by the museum, then it has to be made by the chief executive officer of the city and that is the mayor.
>
> GERSHON: Is it your position then that the court defers to the mayor's view? I mean, you are telling me that the exhibit is offensive. Clearly it is offensive to many people. This is not a question that either side has chosen to argue the merits of, and I'm not suggesting that they should have, but for purposes of the legal point, what is it that you're suggesting that the court should do?

KOERNER: I'm suggesting that unless the mayor's decision is irrational in light of the materials submitted to you, in light of the exhibit itself and the comments concerning the exhibit and in light of the mayor's obligation to interpret the conditions set forth in the lease and the enabling legislation—

GERSHON: He's not the only person who interprets, though—presumably there are two parties to the lease.

KOERNER: That's right.

GERSHON: And ultimately the court would—

KOERNER: And the court has to arbiter whether or not that mission of the museum was fulfilled by this exhibit; but in determining whether the mission was fulfilled, then you have to look at the evidence surrounding the exhibit and see whether the executive director discharged his obligation, and we believe that the evidence shows that he did not and, therefore, the mayor's judgment is a rational one in this context.

Obviously disturbed by the breadth of Koerner's argument, Judge Gershon pressed him on his claim that an exhibition could not be inappropriate for children.

GERSHON: But is it the city's position then that all works of art in the Brooklyn Museum have to be suitable for viewing by schoolchildren of all ages; every work of art in the museum has to be suitable for viewing by schoolchildren of all ages?

KOERNER: No.

GERSHON: So then what is the position?

KOERNER: The position is that when you have an exhibit, not one picture, but when you have an exhibit that is advertised solely for the purpose of shock, then that determines the character of the museum and so is inappropriate. A single picture is not going to affect the community surrounding the museum, but an entire exhibit which highlights a religious disparagement is going to affect the community.

At this point, Judge Gershon returned to the facts of the case before her.

GERSHON: Is it the city's position that the mayor, or whoever the city might delegate to perform this function, has the right to decide painting by painting which of the works in the museum should be removed on pain of losing its funding and its lease?

KOERNER: It has the right to decide whether the exhibit is consistent with the mission set forth in the lease.

GERSHON: Are you saying it would be the right of city officials on pain of losing its funding to enter the museum and, say, "Take that one off the wall"?

KOERNER: Insofar as the exhibit is concerned, if there are particularly offensive pictures in the exhibit.

GERSHON: Well, in this exhibit or any other exhibit in the museum.

KOERNER: If they're not consistent with the mission, yes.

I began my rebuttal by reading, once again, from the deposition Susan had taken the day before.

Q: You're not denying, Deputy Mayor Lhota, that the Brooklyn Museum was told that unless they took *The Holy Virgin Mary* out of the exhibition that their funding would be canceled?

A: I can't deny it because I told it to the chairman of the board.

Q: You made it quite clear to the Brooklyn Museum unless they removed this work from the exhibition, their funding would be canceled, is that true?

A: That's correct. I very specifically—not

to the museum, but to the chairman of the board.

I then said:

So, there is no question but that the power assumed by the city here was not limited to the exhibition as a whole, it was picture by picture. In fact, it was one picture which began this, it was one picture which if not removed was said by the deputy mayor, who serves in lieu of the mayor when he's out of town as the mayor, as [the basis of] the city policy.

I concluded this way:

Now, Mr. Koerner says that a book doesn't get the same exposure as an exhibition. I'm sure the people from various museums around town in the audience here would be glad to hear that. There are lots of books that have done enormous harm, real harm. The First Amendment protects them, but please, I should not hear that *Mein Kampf* is a book which has done less harm than this exhibition.

Now, where do we go from there. You asked a very important question. You asked what is the standard, what standard should be applied. With all respect, the answer was incoherent and then withdrawn. Part of the answer was that it was not for children, if works were not for children they could not be shown. That is not the same answer that Deputy Mayor Lhota—well, it is the same answer he gave at one point yesterday in saying that the test was his eight-year-old daughter. It is not what he said with respect to the three pictures I showed you, all of which he gave his and the city's approval for at a city museum. The fact is there is no standard. They're making it up as they go along. They're doing the best they can, but they cannot articulate any standard, let alone a constitutional one, that would govern in this city if the mayor and the city have their way here.

Judge Gershon then returned to the lease. Suppose, she asked, there had been some violation of the lease. Could the constitutional misbehavior of the city and the mayor that I had claimed still provide a basis for our claim?

It is my position that the city's prior complaints about lease violation have all been pretextual and that under First Amendment law we see through those pretexts and we say all they were ever really trying to do was shut down this museum, shut down this exhibition, get rid of that picture, etc., etc.

Even if they were still arguing the specific matters, I would tell you that the First Amendment is a defense to that. To the extent they're arguing now not those matters but the much broader proposition that this is supposed to be a museum which—I don't know how to phrase it—which doesn't have exhibits like this, which doesn't have exhibits which are "shocking," I have two thoughts. First, this is a serious artistic effort. It was well known that there would be people who would be unhappy. That was one of the things the director had to take into account and the board had to take into account, and there was a prediction because of what had happened in England of a shock factor and of opposition by some people. But that does not make it an illegitimate effort and it doesn't make it contrary to the lease.

We're not asking the court and, indeed, we say in our brief the court can't pass judgment on the quality of the art, but what they're saying is that this is not a bona fide exhibition at all, it's not really an exhibition, it's just a—and they fill in pejorative words. That is something that certainly cannot be said on the evidence before you and cannot be said constitutionally, it seems to me, except in circumstances so far from here, so different from what's before you, that a then very difficult issue would arise. But under this lease and under these facts, no.

I concluded as I had started. The case, I said, was about punishing speech. But it was about more than that, about nothing less than whether the museum could "continue to be a museum." Only the court, I said, could take steps to permit it to survive.

The court asked both sides to provide further written submissions and then adjourned for the day.

On November 1, I received a call from the judge's clerk saying that an opinion and order had been issued by the court which we could pick up at the courthouse.

We won a complete victory on every issue. After setting forth the nature and history of the museum, a description of its funding by the city, and a description of the controversy over the "Sensation" exhibit, the court turned to the abstention motion that the city had made. "The City," the court concluded,

> cannot oust the federal courts of jurisdiction over a fundamental First Amendment dispute by asserting in state court a landlord-tenant issue, especially one that, as will be seen, is purely pretextual. There is no federal constitutional issue more grave than the effort by government

officials to censor works of expression and to threaten the vitality of a major cultural institution, as punishment for failing to abide by governmental demands for orthodoxy. The defendants have not shown that the plaintiff, having properly invoked this court's jurisdiction, must instead assert its First Amendment claims as counterclaims to an ejectment action.

Judge Gershon then turned to the motion we had made for a preliminary injunction, first finding that the museum was "suffering and will continue to suffer irreparable harm if an injunction is not granted." The fact that the museum had thus far refused to yield to the mayor's demands, Judge Gershon concluded, "does not cure the irreparable injury and, of an already existing purposeful penalization for the exercise of First Amendment rights."

Starting with reference to one of the Supreme Court's greatest cases protecting civil liberties, *West Virginia State Board of Education v. Barnett*, a 1943 ruling concluding that the state of West Virginia could not require a child who was a member of the Jehovah's Witnesses to salute the flag in a public school if it was contrary to his religious beliefs, Judge Gershon invoked the powerful language of Justice Robert Jackson: "If there is any fixed star in our constitutional constellation, it is that no official, high or petty, can prescribe what shall be orthodox in politics, nationalism, religion, or other matters of opinion." It was in keeping with that principle, she wrote, that the First Amendment barred "government officials from censoring works said to be 'offensive,' 'sacrilegious,' 'morally improper,' or even 'dangerous.'" Each quoted word was supported by a ruling of the United States Supreme Court. She concluded her first paragraph on our likelihood of success with a quotation from Justice William J. Brennan's eloquent ruling for the Supreme Court holding a federal statute banning the burning of an American flag unconstitutional: "If there is a bedrock principle underlying the First Amendment, it is that the government may not prohibit the expression of an idea simply because society finds the idea itself offensive or disagreeable."

Her opinion continued with descriptions of the "many different contexts" in which "the Supreme Court has made clear that, although the government is under no obligation to provide various kinds of benefits, it may not deny them if the reason for the denial would require a choice between exercising First Amendment rights and obtaining the benefit. That is, it may not 'discriminate invidiously in its subsidies in such a way as to "aim at the suppression of dangerous ideas." '"Had the mayor aimed at the suppression of dangerous ideas? Judge Gershon's answer was straightforward:

The decision to withhold an already appropriated general operating subsidy from an institution which has been supported by the City for over one hundred years, and to eject it from its City-owned building, because of the Mayor's objection to certain works in a current exhibit, is, in its own way, to "discriminate invidiously in its subsidies in such a way as to 'aim at the suppression of dangerous ideas.'" By its own words, the City here threatened to withhold funding if the Museum continued with its plans to show the Exhibit. When the Museum resisted, the City withheld its funding and filed a suit for ejectment. While initially the City engaged in various claims of a violation of its Lease and Contract, unrelated to the content of the Exhibit, the City has now admitted the obvious; it has acknowledged that its purpose is directly related, not just to the content of the Exhibit, but to the particular viewpoints expressed. There can be no greater showing of a First Amendment violation.

Judge Gershon took pains to distinguish between any requirement that a taxpayer support a particular point of view (which the Constitution would not tolerate) and what was involved here—"barring government officials from invidiously discriminating against ideas they find offensive either to themselves or to members of the community." As for the 1998 ruling of the Supreme Court in *National Endowment for the Arts v. Finley*, Judge Gershon first noted that under the Supreme Court's interpretation of the NEA's funding procedures, Congress had "declined to disallow any particular viewpoints" and had not actually precluded "awards to projects that might be deemed 'indecent' or 'disrespectful.'" *Finley*, in any event, had dealt only with the consideration that could apply in the awarding of grants, not with what the law was where funding had "already been appropriated for general operating expenses."

As for the exchanges she had had with Koerner and me about the power of the city to "direct a publicly supported library to remove particular books on pain of a loss of financial support," Judge Gershon rejected the city's contention that works of art were more susceptible to subjective judgments of a mayor than were books. The "relative power of books and visual arts," she wrote, "is of course immaterial." In fact, "the communicative power of visual art is not a basis for restricting it but rather the very reason it is protected by the First Amendment."

The court rejected out of hand the only remaining argument of the city with respect to the lease, the claim that the exhibition violated the museum's mission. This position, similar to that taken by Miami in the case of the Cuban-American museum, was pretextual. There was no basis in the record for the city's accusation that "the museum has failed in its duty to educate," nothing in the lease or contract "which requires that every exhibit be suitable for schoolchildren of all ages," and nothing "which prevents the Museum from imposing reasonable restrictions on the access of schoolchildren to certain exhibits, in order to accommodate the Museum's undisputed right to display what Deputy Mayor Lhota called 'mature' works of art."

Finally, the court returned to the continued arguments by the city and Giuliani that they had a "duty" to withdraw support from the museum because the Ofili painting desecrated religion. Judge Gershon emphasized, citing a recent Supreme Court case, "that government [must] remain neutral with regard to religious expression, whether "it manifest[s] a religious view, an anti-religious view or neither." She concluded as follows:

> The suggestion that the Mayor and the City have an obligation to punish the Museum for showing the Ofili work turns well-established principles developed under the Establishment Clause on their head. If anything, it is the Mayor and the City who by their actions have threatened the neutrality required of government in the sphere of religion.

With that verbal spanking of the Mayor and the City, the court then entered an order barring the city and Giuliani, during the pendency of the case,

from inflicting, or taking any steps to inflict, any punishment, retaliation, discrimination, or sanction of any kind against the Brooklyn Institute of Arts and Sciences, doing business as the Brooklyn Museum of Art, as well as against any of the Brooklyn Museum of Art's directors, officers or representatives, as a result of the Brooklyn Museum of Art's displaying the Exhibit "SENSATION: Young British Artists from the Saatchi Collection" (the Exhibit), including but not limited to:

1) withholding or otherwise failing to provide the Brooklyn Museum of Art any sums of money appropriated, allocated, promised or otherwise payable to the Brooklyn Museum of Art;
2) denying, delaying, or otherwise discriminatorily treating pending or future funding requests of any type as the result of the Exhibit;
3) evicting or seeking to evict the Brooklyn Museum of Art from its premises at 200 Eastern Parkway, Brooklyn, or otherwise directly or indirectly interfering with the Brooklyn Museum of Art's occupancy and use of those premises, including

prosecuting against the Brooklyn Museum of Art the action styled *The City of New York v. The Brooklyn Institute of Arts and Sciences*, filed September 30, 1999 in the Supreme Court of the State of New York, Kings County, Index No. 35376/99;

4) interfering in any manner, directly or indirectly, with the composition of the Board of Trustees of the Brooklyn Museum of Art, other than those members of the Board of Trustees who are the designees of the defendants, or interfering with the Board of Trustees' exercise of its authority.

The mayor's response to the ruling was telling. He had invested a good deal of himself in the litigation both personally and politically and was deeply committed to defending his own conduct and vilifying those who disagreed with him. Now he turned abusive to Judge Gershon herself. Her decision, he said, was "intellectually dishonest." She was "totally out of control" and had "lost all reason." She was "biased" and "almost seemed to rush to a decision." "We hope," he said, "that we can get before a more objective group of judges who do not let their own ideology blind them to the fact, which is what the judge has done here. If you got before a group of judges that were not part of the politically correct, left-wing ideology of New York City [they] would look at this very, very differently."

Giuliani's comments were stunningly injudicious, even contemptuous. He was, after all, a graduate of the Harvard Law School, a former United States Attorney, someone who had practiced law at well-regarded law firms. In England, as I pointed out to the *New York Times* journalist who called me for a reaction to the mayor's comments, he would have been jailed for contempt of court.

The following month, a coalition of leading (and wholly apolitical) legal organizations called the Joint Committee to Preserve the Independence of the Judiciary cited seven intemperate attacks by the mayor during the previous two years, including his slurs of Judge Gershon, stating that they were a misuse of his authority. In response, Giuliani embraced the First Amendment. "What they are attempting to do is to stop me from exercising my First Amendment rights—to criticize judges if I think they are wrong."

With the preliminary injunction in effect, the city resumed its monthly payments to the museum and turned over to it the money it had withheld since September 22. The exhibition, which had opened on schedule on October 3, remained open to the throngs of visitors who waited patiently in long lines that snaked outside the vast structure that Giuliani had sought to close forever. Many of the visitors had never visited a museum before; they had Giuliani to thank for their interest.

The city filed an appeal from Judge Gershon's order and sought and obtained (with our agreement) an expedited briefing schedule and argument date. In the meantime, pretrial discovery continued, with increasingly insistent efforts on my part to schedule Mayor Giuliani's deposition. There were some down moments for us during this period, as the *New York Times* published front-page articles criticizing the museum for exhibiting a privately owned collection and taking money from Saatchi and Christie's. The museum responded, pointing out that private collections have routinely been shown, without criticism, at the most renowned museums around the world. Every such exhibition has the potential of indirectly increasing the value of the collection, but the issue for responsible museum professionals has always been the quality of the work presented. As for direct contributions to the museum by Saatchi, his cash commitment of $160,000 (with the possibility of reducing that amount to $100,000) had been made only after repeated appeals by the museum for support for an exhibition that was unusually difficult to fund. That contribution, like the $50,000 grant from Christie's (also made after repeated pleas by the museum), constituted less than 10 percent of the projected expenses for the exhibition, and had been cited as part of what Judge Gershon referred to as "an extremely full factual record" presented to her.

"The assertions in the [*Times*]," she wrote, "are, for the most part, in the record already before the court," one that had led the city to "abandon the issue." Later articles in art periodicals directed at the art world lent support to the museum's position but provided little solace for the pounding it had taken in the press.

None of this had any impact on the case. Both sides prepared and submitted their briefs to the court of appeals, rearguing virtually every issue decided by Judge Gershon. This time we had more time to prepare our brief, something that is not always helpful. In the interim, one of the many letters I had received from the public raised an interesting question about the tone of the brief we would submit to the court of appeals. The letter had included a passage from the diaries of Joseph Goebbels. In March 1943, Goebbels had written about "the so-called Exhibition of Young Art in Vienna," noting that Hitler, having expressed "violent disagreement" with cultural policies that had permitted the exhibition, had placed "Vienna's cultural affairs . . . under my direct supervision." Goebbels continued: "If the Viennese should object, all subsidies from the Reich are to be cut off. That would, of course, mean the ruin of Viennese cultural life."

Was there a way to use this, perhaps in the conclusion of the brief? I drafted a version that referred to it, trying to make clear that I was not comparing Giuliani to the Führer, but only making the point that subsidies for art could be (and had been) misused by evil governments. I redrafted the brief, this time explicitly disavowing any possible interpretation of the passage that would equate the two men. I finally yielded to the views of everyone I asked—Susan, our associates, and our co-counsel—that there was no way to use the quotation without suggesting a Giuliani-Hitler analogy that was not only obviously untrue but harmful to our case. Our brief concluded, instead, with an American reference:

> Mayor Giuliani is hardly the first person to be outraged by the art created during his lifetime. Manet's classic painting, *Luncheon on the Grass*, was criticized as indecent in its day for showing a nude woman surrounded by two fully dressed, contemporary Parisian men. Courbet's painting, *Sleeping Women*, shocked contemporary audiences because of its portrayal of two unclothed women lying on a bed in a sexually suggestive manner.
>
> The same has been true throughout the history of art. Both Pope Paul IV and Pope Clement VIII threatened to destroy Michelangelo's *Last Judgment* in the Sistine Chapel, which contemporary critics described as "filthiness"; when Veronese's *Last Supper* was painted, it was accused of being filled with "vulgarities." It has, in short,

been the norm, not the exception, for new art to be dismissed as "sick" art.

It is also not at all novel for a prominent public figure in this City to take umbrage at the display of art. No less a statesman than Theodore Roosevelt denounced the now-legendary exhibition held at the 69th Regiment Armory in this City in 1913. "The artists," he thundered, were "a bunch of lunatics." As for the art itself, "[t]he Cubists are entitled to the serious attention of all who find enjoyment in the colored puzzle pictures of the Sunday newspapers."

The critical difference, of course, is that no one made any effort to shut that exhibition down and that no one sought to punish anybody for displaying it. Roosevelt used his First Amendment right to criticize. If that were all that Mayor Giuliani had done, the First Amendment would have been vindicated, not violated.

The district court's order should be affirmed.

Oral argument in the court of appeals went well, especially when Koerner was being closely questioned by Judge Jon Newman, who expressed disbelief that the city would actually take the positions it was articulating. "What I want to know is," Judge Newman asked Koerner, "is it really the city's position that the Brooklyn Museum should take *all* of its articles and *move out* of the building *now*?" When Koerner answered that that was the position, Newman asked, "And you believe there is a reasonable chance that a state court judge would *consider* that?" Very quietly, Koerner responded, "I have no idea what a judge would do." Newman responded, in turn, "What do *you* want them to do?" Koerner answered, still more softly, "We want to terminate the lease and maybe negotiate with a new group that would have exhibits appropriate for schoolchildren."

"Is every book in the New York Public Library appropriate for schoolchildren?" Newman asked.

"No."

"Are *they* next?"

Koerner was, of course, not at fault for the impossible position he found himself in. Like Michael Hess, he was a lawyer representing an impossible client. But it certainly seemed, as the argument progressed, that our chances of success were overwhelming.

Some weeks later, while we awaited a decision from the court of appeals, and only a few days before Mayor Giuliani would finally have had to appear under oath to defend himself (probably in a publicly held deposition, one that the press had already applied to Judge Gershon to attend), I received a call from Hess asking for a meeting to discuss settlement. Not long afterward, we agreed on the entry of a permanent order that would bind the city and the mayor from retaliating in any way against the museum, from withholding any sums of money already appropriated to it, and from seeking to evict it or otherwise punish it in any way. The city agreed to restore all funding previously appropriated to it, including $7 million in annual operational funding and $28 million in capital funding. The city also agreed to provide additional capital funding of $5.8 million to enhance the entrance plaza to the museum. For our part, we agreed to drop any additional claims for damages, including our claim against Giuliani personally for punitive damages, and to waive counsel fees.

The most striking thing about the order that was finally entered dismissing the case was its repeated inclusion of Mayor Giuliani. Not only was the city barred from taking certain steps, but Giuliani personally, so long as he was mayor, was barred from doing so. Any violation of the order would have subjected him to contempt-of-court charges. We insisted on these provisions and we got them:

> The Mayor, for as long as he holds office as Mayor of the City of New York, agrees as follows:

> (a) He will not act to reduce the amount included in any expense budget of the City (or any amendment thereof) for

operational funding allocated to the Brooklyn Institute by an amount that is disproportionately greater than any reduction in operational funding included in such expense budget allocated to all Museum CIGs [Cultural Institution Group: the Metropolitan Museum, the American Museum of Natural History, and others].

(b) He will not act to increase the amount included in any expense budget of the City (or any amendment thereof) for operational funding allocated to all Museum CIGs by an amount that is disproportionately greater than any increase in operational funding included in such expense budget allocated to the Brooklyn Institute.

(c) He will not act to reduce any increase by the City Council of the City in operational funding allocated to the Brooklyn Institute in any expense budget of the City.

(d) He will take all actions within his control to cause the amounts included in the City's expense budget for the City's fiscal years beginning July 2000 and July 2001, for direct payment by the City of costs for energy consumption by the Brooklyn Institute and of costs, if any, for pension and any like benefits for individuals working at the Brooklyn Institute, to be determined in the same manner as in the expense budget of the City for the fiscal year ending June 30, 2000.

It was a humiliating end to the case for the mayor.

Why did Giuliani act as he did? Some observers believe that he began the whole process of fighting with the Brooklyn Museum for political reasons relating to his then-anticipated race with Hillary Clinton for New York's United States Senate seat being vacated by Daniel Patrick Moynihan. Those people still maintain that the mayor profited from his battle with the Brooklyn Museum by showing those on the rightward flank of the state body politic, particularly Catholic voters, that he was attendant to their interests.

I've never credited any of those arguments. While politics is never absent from the decision-making of political leaders, I remain convinced that the mayor was genuinely angry at the content of the exhibition, that he meant what he said about it, and that he thought he could carry the public with him in thinking so.

That doesn't mean that we would have failed in our efforts to obtain a punitive damage judgment against him. I still believe that Giuliani knew perfectly well that First Amendment law made his conduct lawless. About that, I think, he simply didn't care.

When the injunction was entered, I reviewed for the press the essence of what had occurred:

> A decision was made by the mayor that because one painting in an exhibition which the mayor had not seen was offensive to him, he would coerce the museum into dropping the picture or do all in his power to punish it—by stripping it of its funding, ejecting it from its premises, dismissing its board of directors and the like. Let me put it another way. Mayor Giuliani concluded it was for *him* to decide which art exhibitions are to be shown—and, in fact, whether one or another picture may appear in an exhibition. It was precisely as if he had instructed a partially city-funded library to take a book he found offensive off the shelves.
>
> This is intolerable under the First Amendment. Did the mayor really think that because the city owns the property on which the Brooklyn Museum stands that he could decide what art it could show? The First Amendment allows no such behavior. Did the mayor really believe that because this is a city which treasures its great cultural institutions—and profits from them—and therefore contributes to the Brooklyn Museum, that he could coerce the museum into taking a picture

down or even abandoning the whole exhibition? The First Amendment doesn't allow it. Did the mayor really think that because the lease on the museum requires it "in general to provide the means for popular instruction and enjoyment through its collections" that its decision to offer this exhibition empowers him to throw the museum out in the street? The lease doesn't allow that—and the First Amendment doesn't either.

Long after the event, and after Giuliani's post-September 11 enshrinement as what the *New York Times* referred to as a "civic saint," he returned to the Brooklyn Museum case in his best-selling book, *Leadership*. His depiction of the case was one in which he had taken a reasoned and principled position on a matter about which "people could in good faith have a difference of opinion." It was his opponents, he said, who had behaved "hysterically." They, the "New York elite" and the "politically correct," did not understand something that he did. It was that there had been "an important First Amendment issue at stake."

CHAPTER 8

CAMPAIGN FINANCE REFORM AND THE FIRST AMENDMENT

L ate in the year 2000, I was invited to give a speech at All Souls Unitarian Church, on New York City's Upper East Side, about a variety of First Amendment issues. The senior minister there, Forrest Church, is a subtle and wise man who has written, among a number of fine books, *The American Creed*, a study of the Declaration of Independence.

I spoke that evening about a range of First Amendment cases, winding up with a lengthy description of the then recently decided Brooklyn Museum case. The audience listened intently, smiled at the right places, and nodded appreciatively as I proceeded. I was pleased with my performance.

When I had finished my prepared remarks, the audience was given a chance to ask questions, and the very first one was a home run. It went something like this: "You've told us about a number of cases—the Brooklyn Museum case, the Pentagon Papers case, and lots of others—and you've set forth views on a number of First Amendment issues. This is a very liberal church, and I'm sure that all of us agree with everything that you've said. All that is easy enough for us and for you. But can you give us one example of some First Amendment position that you've taken with which we would not agree?"

I paused. It was a good question, far better than the norm for after-speech queries. After reflecting for a few seconds, I responded by saying that one view that I had come to that I suspected they would take exception to was that substantial parts of the then pending McCain-Feingold campaign finance legislation were probably unconstitutional. I could hear an audible intake of breath around the room, as people looked disbelievingly at me. A few frowned and shook their heads. I had certainly come up with a potent example of a First Amendment position of which they disapproved.

I tried to clarify my stand. I told them that there was obviously a problem with large corporations and unions giving millions of dollars to political parties. At the least, I said, such contributions left the impression that favored treatment might follow. But that impression might not suffice as a basis for the sort of legislation that was being proposed. The statute that was being considered, as I understood it, banned *all* such contributions, regardless of amount, and might thus be viewed as embodying a sort of overkill that could ultimately doom the statute as a whole.

Political parties had First Amendment rights, too,

I explained. McCain-Feingold might go too far in limiting their ability to seek funds to permit them to engage in political activities. There were ways, however, that the problem of unlimited corporate and union contributions might be addressed. One was more stringent reporting standards, requiring, for example, immediate Internet disclosure of every contribution a party received. Another might be to place caps on the amount of corporate or union contributions. A third might be increased public funding of campaigns, thus making it easier for less well-funded candidates to run.

Most of all, I warned my listeners that while their concerns about the malfunctioning of the current system were understandable and that problems with the system were real, they should take care before endorsing any new regime of regulation of speech. This was especially true if the statute contained a ban on advertisements that commented on public policy issues and the positions of candidates on those issues. Censorship was unacceptable, I said, even in the interest of campaign reform.

I then described two of my favorite First Amendment cases, the first of which was the 1966 Supreme Court ruling in *Mills v. Alabama.* There, an Alabama statute had been adopted that barred newspapers from publishing on Election Day editorials urging voters how to cast their ballots on issues submitted to them. The stated purpose of the law, enacted at a time when most people obtained most of their information from newspapers and most communities in Alabama had only one newspaper, was to protect the public from confusing last-minute charges when, "as a practical matter, because of lack of time, such matters [could] not be answered or their truth determined until after the election is over." Yet despite the narrow time period in which the statutory ban applied (Election Day only), the Court unanimously held the law unconstitutional.

"Whatever differences may exist about interpretations on the First Amendment," Justice Hugo Black had written, "there is practically universal agreement that a major purpose of that Amendment was to protect free discussion of governmental affairs." That, Black observed, "includes discussion of candidates." A statute banning a newspaper, even for a day, from encouraging people to vote one way or the other thus must be held unconstitutional. That was a great decision, I explained to the audience, as it protected free speech principles against well-meant but unconstitutional efforts to ensure the purity of the electoral process.

The other case was commenced by a Miami labor leader, Pat Tornillo, who was a candidate for the Florida House of Representatives. The *Miami Herald* had published editorials criticizing Tornillo; the union leader had responded by demanding that the *Herald* publish, verbatim, replies he had written to each editorial. Under a Florida "right of reply" law, the newspaper would have been obliged to do just that. Instead, the paper went to court, seeking a judicial declaration that the statute was unconstitutional. When the case reached the Supreme Court in 1974, it concluded—also unanimously—that despite the force of Tornillo's argument that the First Amendment was served by more rather than fewer views being expressed in the press and despite the dangers raised by the consolidation of newspapers, the statute violated the First Amendment. Any "compulsion" upon a newspaper to publish what it chose not to, the Court concluded, was unconstitutional. The "intrusion" of the statute "into the function of editors" thus could not stand. There, too, I said, even though voters might have had more information as a result of the statute, the Court had concluded this was simply not an area in which a state legislature could substitute its views for that of the publisher.

My audience was unmoved. How, they asked again, could I be against campaign finance reform? How could I justify a system in which the wealthy had more voice in promoting who was elected than those who were less well off?

I have often thought about that evening. Years before, I had spoken in a local synagogue in defense of the right of Nazis to march in Skokie, Illinois. I was sure that my audience in All Souls would have marched in defense of the Nazis' First Amendment rights. I knew as well that if I had defended the right of nude dancers to perform in bars, or pornographers to peddle their sordid stuff, my listeners would have likewise agreed with me. If I had said that even when national security interests are arguably at issue, First Amendment interests should never be sacrificed, they would have assented. If I had recounted for them examples of my many arguments made through the years on behalf of journalists maintaining that they should not have to reveal their confidential sources even when doing so would have been of potential benefit to defendants who were at risk of being *executed*, they would have nodded approvingly. But when I insisted that we had best take care not to limit speech about public issues and candidates during an election campaign, they recoiled.

They were not alone in that reaction. Campaign finance reform not only was a popular issue then (as now) among liberals but seemed an essential one to most people whose political and social views I tended to share. Many of our most renowned newspapers were passionate in supporting what they viewed as reform in an area sorely in need of it. By one count, over a five-year period the *New York Times* and the *Washington Post* published one editorial every five and a half days advocating some version of what became the McCain-Feingold bill.

Opposition to any such legislation was viewed in my world as reactionary, regressive, and ultimately illegitimate. That the Supreme Court, in its own opinion about campaign finance reform in *Buckley v. Valeo* in 1976, joined in by no less a liberal icon than Justice William J. Brennan, had concluded that "the concept that government may restrict the speech of some elements in our society to enhance the relative voice of others is wholly foreign to the First Amendment," my friends found unpersuasive. As for the arguments made by opponents of campaign finance reform based on First Amendment principles, the people making the arguments more often than not had First Amendment credentials that were anything but sterling. So why, my friends asked, should they take the criticism seriously?

My own answer was simple enough and all the less appealing because of that. It was fundamentally a matter of the correctness of the First Amendment arguments, arguments, I told them, that were supported by organizations such as the ACLU and constitutional scholars such as Dean Kathleen Sullivan of Stanford Law School and Professor Akhil Amar from Yale. It was not what my friends wanted to hear.

My own first exposure to the interplay between campaign finance legislation and the First Amendment had shaped my views with respect to such legislation. In early September 1972 the American Civil Liberties Union and the New York Civil Liberties Union had submitted for publication to the *New York Times* a proposed advertisement entitled "An Open Letter to President Richard M. Nixon in Opposition to His Stand on School Segregation." The advertisement denounced the president for "taking steps to create an American apartheid by supporting legislation barring federal courts from ordering busing as a remedy for *de facto* school segregation." After criticizing Nixon for making "scapegoats of the federal courts and attack[ing] the rule of law itself," the advertisement urged readers to let opponents of the Nixon administration "hear from you," and stated that "they deserve your support in their resistance to the Nixon administration's bill." There then followed a listing of an "Honor Roll" of 102 members of the House of Representatives who had opposed the administration and the states from which they came. The advertisement was submitted to the *Times* a bit less than two months before the federal election to be held in 1972.

The Federal Election Campaign Act of 1971 was then in effect. Like every previously or subsequently adopted statute limiting spending in the period before elections, it contained provisions that were designed to avoid "loopholes" that undermined the impact of the legislation. In this respect, the statute was similar to the 1974 law that would govern for the next twenty-nine years and the McCain-Feingold bill, which would be signed into law in 2002. Whatever Congress sought to do to limit the amount of money raised and spent around the time of federal elections, those who had money or raised money or sought to spend money always seemed to have an answer, a way out, an escape. These loopholes, proponents of the laws concluded, had to be closed.

Under Title I of the 1971 act, limitations on spending by candidates for federal office had been imposed. To effectuate those limitations and avoid circumvention of the monetary limits set forth in the statute, the law provided that any newspaper or other publication that wished to publish any advertisements "on behalf of a candidate" was obliged first to obtain a certification from a candidate that the cost of the advertisement (which would be included in the amount attributed to the candidate) did not exceed his total spending limitation for media advertising. (One of the implementing regulations of the statute defined an expenditure "on behalf of a candidate" as one that identified the candidate and supported or advocated his or her election.)

Both the ACLU and the NYCLU viewed as unconstitutional any law that imposed upon them the duty of obtaining such a statement from candidates before their own advertisement opposing Nixon's segregation policy could be published. Both organizations refused to obtain the certifications— 102 of them, one for each of the representatives in their "Honor Roll"—and thus did not provide to the *Times* the materials required by the statute and its regulations. The *Times* accordingly refused to publish the advertisement, and the two civil liberties groups promptly went to court (with the *Times*, represented by me, appearing as *amicus curiae*— friend of the court—on their behalf) to challenge the constitutionality of the statute.

We appeared in mid-September 1972 before a three-judge panel in the District of Columbia, composed of Chief Judge David Bazelon of the court of appeals and district judges William Bryant and Barrington Parker. Each of the judges asked sharp, sometimes accusatory, questions of the lawyers from the Department of Justice, headed by Nixon Attorney General John Mitchell, which defended the constitutionality of the statute. How, the judges repeatedly asked, could a statute that put the press at risk of criminal prosecution for publishing an advertisement criticizing the President and praising members of Congress possibly be constitutional? Of me, the court wanted to know only two things: How soon did the *Times* need the protection of an injunction against application of the statute, and what should the injunction say? It was a delightful way to spend an afternoon in Washington.

The three-judge court quickly entered an injunction barring the enforcement of the statute against the *Times*. On November 14, 1973 the court wrote an opinion holding the requirement that had "charged the media with first-line responsibility to enforce, by refusal to publish, the requirements of the Act" to be unconstitutional. The opinion of the court, by Judge Parker, acknowledged that the purpose of the law was to avoid an obvious potential loophole: A candidate for Congress, say, could sidestep the monetary limitations placed upon him or her by having a third party place an ad that in effect advocated his or her election. But placing the media in the position where it could be subject to criminal penalties if it published such an advertisement, Parker wrote, imposed a "severe and unnecessary burden" upon the media, one that itself "discouraged free and open discussion of matters of public concern." The statute, therefore, could not stand as it was written; the civil liberties groups were free to submit other such advertisements; and the *Times* and other newspapers were free to publish them without fear of being prosecuted criminally for having done so.

The case seemed an easy one, and the three-judge court certainly exhibited no difficulty in reaching its conclusion. Apart from its direct impact on the press, however, the statute raised a broader First Amendment question: How, after all, could the ACLU be effectively frustrated from publicly honoring members of Congress that it had concluded had served the cause of civil liberties by voting against particular legislation? And if that praise occurred close to an election, was that not all the more reason to protect the speech rather than subjecting it to criminal prosecution?

Thirty years later, the McCain-Feingold law was adopted, once again to close what was viewed by its sponsors as loopholes in the enforcement of existing campaign finance legislation. Even more than past legislation, it treated speech by or about candidates for a public office as subject to the strictest limitation by Congress. But unlike the 1971 law, no advocacy "on behalf of a candidate" was required in order to bring the federal electoral apparatus into play; a mere reference in a corporate or union-funded TV advertisement to the name of a member of Congress who was running for reelection or to the candidate's opponent was now considered a criminal act, which could subject the ACLU and any other corporation or union to fines and its leadership to prison terms. So sweeping were the terms of McCain-Feingold that television ads in its sponsors' home states of Arizona and Wisconsin scheduled to run within sixty days of elections involving Senator McCain or Senator Feingold could not even mention the popular name of the law drafted by the senators.

This was not by any means the only provision in the new law, or even its most significant or controversial provision with regard to campaign finance issues. At its heart, the legislation severely restricted any national, state, or local political party committee and its agents from soliciting, receiving, or transferring what is known as "soft money"—money subject to state regulation in each of the fifty states but which had not been previously subjected to federal limitations as well. McCain-Feingold regulated not just the national political parties, but also state parties, which were powerful and frequently effective participants on their own in state politics. In California, for example, over six million people had voted in a referendum in November 2000 to *enhance* the role of political parties in state politics. The law, called Proposition 34, imposed limits on direct contributions to candidates but offered them benefits in exchange for their voluntary acceptance of campaign spending limits. At the same time, however, Proposition 34 was also designed to allow political parties to spend more, not less, in state and local elections. The law contained a specific finding that "political parties play an important role in the American political process and help insulate candidates from the potential corrupting influence of large contributions." One explicit purpose of the ballot measure was to "strengthen the role of political parties in financing political campaigns by means of reasonable limits on contributions to political party committees and by limiting restrictions on contributions to, and expenditures on behalf of, party candidates."

In particular, Proposition 34 allowed higher limits ($25,000 annually) on contributions to political parties for candidate-related expenditures, no limits on contributions made to political parties for other purposes, and no limits on political party contributions to (or expenditures on behalf of) candidates for state office. In contrast, the centerpiece of the McCain-Feingold law prohibited state and local parties from spending their funds on what the new law called "federal election activity"—a broadly defined phrase encompassing voter registration, voter identification, get-out-the-vote activity, and the sort of generic campaign activity that occurs whenever there is a federal election. Because California (like most other states) holds its elections for statewide and local office simultaneously with federal elections, McCain-Feingold thus largely banned the California parties from using their funds to engage in these activities. Thus, McCain-Feingold effectively trumped the California law that allowed state parties to raise more money for purposes relating to state elections.

This conflict permitted a challenge to be raised against the new law based not only on the First Amendment rights of political parties and those that wished to contribute to them, but on principles of federalism—the right of states to conduct their own elections free of federal control. The latter was a serious challenge, I thought, but not one I would have chosen to make on my own. In the name of federalism, the Supreme Court, under the leadership of Chief Justice William E. Rehnquist, had significantly limited the powers of the United States vis-à-vis those of the states. Whether the Court was right or wrong (more often the latter, I thought), the cause of federalism, as construed by the Rehnquist Court, was not one that would have led me to contribute hundreds of thousands of unbilled hours of my firm's time to vindicate. The provisions that troubled me most in McCain-Feingold and that ultimately led to my personal involvement in the challenge to its constitutionality related to its quite deliberate suppression of speech.

In 1976, in one of its most controversial rulings of the twentieth century, the Supreme Court in *Buckley v. Valeo* had concluded that Congress had significant power to limit the amount of contributions to candidates but far less power to limit expenditures by donors to further their political ends. First Amendment protection for the first category, the Court concluded, was far less substantial than for the second. In the course of taking a hard look at congressionally imposed limits on expenditures, the Court had held unconstitutional expenditure limitations of $1,000 per person that were "relative to a clearly identified candidate." That language was so broad—so overbroad, in fact—that the Court limited its scope to avoid having to strike down as unconstitutional a statute that so limited any speech "relative to" a candidate. It did so by reading the statute narrowly to apply only to "communications that in express terms advocate the election or defeat of a clearly identified candidate for federal office." But what did "express terms" mean? What was required to "advocate" someone's election?

The Court clarified those words by offering a number of examples: advertisements containing words such as "vote for," "elect," "support," "cast your ballot for," "Smith for Congress," "vote against," "defeat," and "reject" constituted *express* advocacy that could be regulated by Congress. Advertisements that did not contain such language could not be regulated.

This bright-line test had obvious advantages. It was clear and predictable, thus avoiding the self-censorship that vague criminal statutes routinely provoke. By focusing on the language actually used rather than the subjective intentions of the speakers that used it, *Buckley* had barred the government from engaging in probing and hence potentially chilling investigations into the motivations of speakers. But the test was also easy to evade, since advertisements could easily enough be drafted that avoided the specific language cited by the Supreme Court but still packed an electoral wallop. An ad could refrain from saying "Vote for Jones" but still leave no doubt that Jones was the preferred candidate because of his views.

The *Buckley* Court understood that any list of words it might offer by way of example could not account for every case of electorally motivated advocacy that might in some manner affect an election. The Court explained that the distinction between regulated express advocacy and all other speech "may often dissolve in practical application" because "candidates, especially incumbents, are intimately tied to public issues involving legislative proposals and governmental actions.

Not only do candidates campaign on the basis of their positions on various public issues," the Court concluded, "but campaigns themselves generate issues of public interest." Nevertheless, the Court explained, the vagueness problem inherent in the statute could not be solved by anything but a bright-line test:

> Whether words intended and designed to fall short of invitation would miss that mark is a question of both intent and of effect. No speaker, in such circumstances, safely could assume that anything he might say upon the general subject might be misunderstood by some . . . In short, the supposedly clear-cut distinction between discussion, laudation, general advocacy, and solicitation puts the speaker in these circumstances wholly at the mercy of the varied understanding of his hearers and consequently of whatever inference may be drawn as to his intent and meaning.
>
> Such a distinction offers no security for free discussion. In these conditions it blankets with uncertainty whatever may be said. It compels the speaker to hedge and trim.

In adopting a bright-line test—referred to (and often ridiculed by) McCain-Feingold proponents as *Buckley*'s "magic words"—the Supreme Court recognized that "it would naively underestimate the ingenuity and resourcefulness" of speakers who choose to "skirt the restriction on express advocacy" to believe that they "would have much difficulty" in doing so. Nonetheless, the Court concluded, the First Amendment required that speakers be permitted to do just that as the price of preserving robust debate about candidates and issues. "So long as persons and groups eschew expenditures that in express terms advocate the election or defeat of a clearly identified candidate," the Court concluded, "they are free to spend as much as they want to promote the candidate and his views."

McCain-Feingold rejected all this reasoning. Its scope was breathtaking. Within sixty days of a federal election or thirty of a primary or convention, unions or corporations (including not-for-profit organizations such as the ACLU and the National Rifle Association) could not even *mention* the name of a candidate for federal office in any advertisement broadcast on television, radio or cable in an area in which the candidate was running for office. For the presidential race, that meant the geographic limit was nationwide in scope; for a senatorial race, the limit was statewide; and for a contest for election to the House of Representatives, the speech was banned in the district of the representative. Noncorporate entities would also be held to act criminally if they used any corporate money to run such ads. Under the law, the subject of the advertisement was irrelevant; what mattered was whether or not it cited the name of a candidate.

The ACLU, as a not-for-profit corporation, would thus have been directly in the line of fire of the new statute if it had broadcast in 2004 some equivalent of its 1972 advertisement that I had defended on behalf of the *New York Times*; it would act criminally if, as it planned to, it urged President Bush in a televised advertisement within sixty days of the 2004 election not to propose any expansion of the Patriot Act, or criticized him for proposing the law in the first place. So would, say, the NRA or the NAACP every time either one of them referred, however fleetingly, to any federal candidate in advertisements broadcast in that two-month period. The NRA had, in fact, frequently run a thirty-minute televised ad denouncing gun control in the last weeks of the 2000 campaign. In passing, it made one reference to then-vice president Al Gore, who was running for president at the time on the Democratic ticket. Under the new law, the reference to Gore would have been criminal.

McCain-Feingold's impact on unions was one that I found particularly distressing. The AFL-CIO routinely ran advertisements throughout the year urging members of Congress, identified by name, to vote for or against particular legislation and praising or denouncing those representatives depending on their stand with respect to the union position on the legislation. Often, the same ad would be run both before the sixty-day period and during it. Sometimes, the same ad would mention individuals who were running for reelection and those who were not. Under McCain-Feingold, all names of individuals running for Congress had to be omitted during the latter part of the campaign season.

One advertisement, broadcast within sixty days of the 1998 election in the district of Oregon congressman David Wu, seemed to me to epitomize the constitutional vice of the new law. The advertisement, paid for by a group favoring term limits, sought to pressure Wu to support term limits by saying the following:

> The people of America should be running our government. That's the way it was set up in the first place. The problem is the special interests and the paid lobbyists who control the Washington politicians. The answer is term limits. Term limits replace Washington insiders with new people who reflect community interests, not politics as usual. Molly Bordonaro has signed the pledge to limit her terms in Congress. David Wu refused. Call David Wu and tell him to sign the U.S. Term Limits Pledge.

Under McCain-Feingold, the term limits group would have been subject to criminal penalties for broadcasting the ad. I simply could not reconcile myself to the notion that a group that sought to influence what a sitting congressman would say and do about a public issue such as term limits could be criminally punished for doing so, even if the advertisement could have some impact on the imminent election.

I had the same reaction to an advertisement paid for by a pro-life group that was broadcast in Wisconsin in 1998 and 2000:

America was outraged when two New Jersey teenagers checked into a Delaware hotel and delivered and disposed of their newborn baby in a Dumpster. Most Americans couldn't believe that this defenseless human life could be so coldly snuffed out. But incredibly, if a doctor had been present that day in Delaware and delivered the infant all but one inch from full birth and then killed him, it would have been perfectly legal. Instead of murder or manslaughter, it would have been called a partial-birth abortion. Killing late in the third trimester, killing just inches away from full birth. Partial-birth abortion puts a violent death on thousands of babies every year. Your Senators, Russ Feingold and Herb Kohl, voted to continue this grisly procedure. Contact Senators Feingold and Kohl today and insist they change their vote and oppose partial-birth abortion. Their number in Washington is 202-224-3121.

This advertisement was broadcast in the 1998 election, in which Senator Feingold was a candidate, and again prior to the 2000 election, in which Senator Kohl was a candidate. When I asked Senator Feingold about the ad, he testified that the framers of the ad might not really have been focused on "insisting" that the two senators "change their vote," since their positions were well known. "I do question," he said, "whether an ad like this as it was used in this context is really about banning late-term abortion or whether it is simply a way to win an election."

To me, this turned the First Amendment on its head. The ad was about a topic of critical public concern. So far as I was concerned, it should not even matter if it arose out of mixed motives—a desire to comment on issues *and* to impact the election—or even from a desire to impact an election by discussing one or another issue. I could not accept that a First Amendment that stated that "Congress shall make no law . . . abridging the freedom of speech" could be reconciled with legislation that made such speech criminal.

McCain-Feingold's proponents viewed advertisements such as these as hidden ("sham," they called them) candidate ads, end runs around the effort of the statute to enforce a regulatory regime that restricted election spending. They were not totally wrong. Many ads broadcast toward the end of a political campaign that did not expressly urge a vote for or against a candidate certainly made the candidate seem either admirable or unattractive. Many, but by no means all, were undoubtedly drafted with that in mind. But everything I knew about the First Amendment impelled me to defend such speech, not to accede to its criminalization. Ads about issues and candidates, I believed, could properly be treated as nothing but pure First Amendment speech, speech entitled to the highest level of legal protection.

Another factor led me to become personally involved in challenging the new law. As the 1990s wore on, I was becoming increasingly concerned that political liberals (I considered myself one) were too often trading in their First Amendment beliefs to further political or social causes they favored. It was, I thought, a devil's trade, which permitted liberals to be true to their normal ideological bent only by sacrificing their libertarian principles.

In 1997 I had participated in a symposium in the *Nation* magazine entitled "Speech and Power," in which the magazine raised the question of "whether liberals and progressives" should "rethink their beliefs about free speech." The symposium was needed, the *Nation* wrote, because the First Amendment was being wielded "to thwart progressive reforms such as caps on campaign spending, public access to the airwaves, and regulation of cigarette advertising." And there was worse news yet. In all these battles, "the wrong side kept winding up with the First Amendment in its corner."

My contribution had been barbed. I had grown accustomed to conservative indifference or hostility to free speech; for liberals to abandon their historic defense of it seemed to me a desecration. Liberals, I complained, seemed "pleased with a First Amendment that protects radical hawkers of leaflets" at the same time that they despaired "of a First Amendment that protects wealthier, more powerful speakers. Unhappy with who is speaking these days and how much they are speaking, liberals are promiscuously signing on to a variety of positions that simply ignore the core of First Amendment jurisprudence."

Is that what liberalism had come to? I knew, I wrote, how difficult it was to read First Amendment lectures written by George Will. But the First Amendment was not, I pointed out, the sole property of liberal Americans. It was not the New Deal redrafted and expanded so as to apply to speech. It certainly was not a promise that democracy would work as the *Nation* and its readers would undoubtedly prefer.

The First Amendment, I concluded, "protects all who wish to speak—do I really have to say this?—from *governmental* decision-making about what and how much they may say. It is rooted in distrust of government, concern about historic misuse of governmental power. It is not—it is the opposite of—granting power to the government to decide who may speak about what."

A few years later, writing in the *Columbia Journalism Review,* I took another step toward disassociating my views from those of my usual allies. I argued that, even as typical attacks from the right (efforts to ban "dangerous" books, to amend the Constitution to permit flag burning to be criminalized, to limit federal funding of the arts) proceeded, the real news about the First Amendment was that increasingly its attackers were coming from the left. I reminded my readers that the First Amendment, as Yale Law School professor J. M. Balkin had written, had historically "been the friend of left-wing values, whether it was the French émigrés and Republicans in the 1790s, abolitionists in the 1840s, pacifists in the 1910s, organized labor in the 1920s and 1930s, or civil rights protesters in the 1950s and 1960s." Now, I argued, the tide had turned.

"New issues—conservative ones—have led to reconsideration by many conservatives of the First Amendment. The right to spend money to support one's political favorites, to engage in commercial speech, to say things that 'hate speech' codes might punish, and to protest outside abortion clinics all resonate with conservatives."

Liberals should take care, I argued, to resist the temptation to opt for narrowed First Amendment protections. "It is not hard," I wrote, "to understand what it is about First Amendment law that has led to the current liberal disenchantment. The wrong people are speaking; they have too much money behind them; they are saying too much. But when that sort of thinking becomes a basis for legislation, it is at war with the First Amendment."

I concluded by referring to the 1997 forum sponsored by the *Nation*. Instead of bemoaning that the "wrong side" was winning First Amendment battles, I observed, perhaps the *Nation* should ask itself a question. Did it ever occur to them, I asked, to rethink their political positions to avoid being on the wrong side of the First Amendment?

Given my views, when Senator Mitch McConnell called and asked if I would be one of two lawyers who would lead his effort at challenging the constitutionality of the law, I expressed interest in doing so. McConnell had personally led the opposition to the enactment of McCain-Feingold and similar legislation for over a decade and had been mocked and savaged for doing so. His own commitment to the First Amendment had included a rare Republican vote against amending the Constitution to allow prosecution for burning the American flag. While I was pleased that he had taken that position, I would have reached the same conclusion even if it were his only foray into defending First Amendment principles. I raised the possibility of my involvement with Ike Kohn, the chairman of our firm's executive committee, who in turn discussed it with our colleagues on the committee. They agreed that we should proceed to represent Senator McConnell on a pro bono basis.

The last time I had requested that the firm become involved on a pro bono basis from the very beginning through the end of a highly charged case with potential political as well as First Amendment implications had been over a score of years before. Ironically, our client then was the *Nation*, which had been sued for copyright infringement by the publisher of former president Gerald Ford's memoir for publishing an article containing between three hundred and four hundred words from it prior to its publication. The case raised significant issues about the interrelationship between the First Amendment and the Copyright Act and the nature of what is known as "fair use" in copyright law. We had lost that case at trial, won it by a 2-1 vote in the court of appeals, and then lost in the Supreme Court in a 6-3 opinion written by Justice Sandra Day O'Connor. In the interim, I had successfully represented indigent defendants on death row in Parchman Prison in Mississippi in two cases in the Supreme Court. Those cases as well were handled by my firm on a pro bono basis, but neither was handled by us all the way from the lowest court through the Supreme Court. Now we were about to start down that path again, and I was eager to learn from Senator McConnell who would join me in leading our team.

At our next meeting, Senator McConnell told me the name of my new partner. It was Kenneth Starr.

I had been publicly critical of efforts of the Office of Special Counsel (OSC) led by Starr to bring President Clinton down, as I had been of the impeachment of President Clinton by the House of Representatives. I had appeared on television news programs to denounce what I viewed as excesses of Starr's office, including its First Amendment-threatening efforts to suppress criticism of it by using a grand jury to inquire into what communications had occurred between Clinton White House aide Sidney Blumenthal and journalists. The notion, articulated by OSC attorneys, that those communications could be viewed as potential obstructions of justice seemed to me to be both perverse and constitutionally threatening, and I said as much.

At times, I had been briefly involved professionally against the OSC, advising Barnes & Noble when it received an OSC subpoena directing it to turn over records of what books Monica Lewinsky had purchased, and a television network when it was subpoenaed to turn over outtakes (material taped but not broadcast). I had also advised Steve Brill about certain legal issues as he prepared for his then new magazine, *Brill's Content,* an article entitled "Pressgate," a powerful critique of press acquiescence in and silence about what Brill concluded was the misbehavior of Starr's office in persistently leaking information to the press.

Yet, through it all, I remembered a different Ken Starr—Ken Starr before he became *Ken Starr.* When he was solicitor general of the United States during the Reagan administration, we had occasionally met. I had always been impressed with the breadth of his knowledge, his willingness to listen to views other than his own, his personal decency. When he was a judge on the Court of Appeals for the District of Columbia, I had been taken with the lucidity of his writing and his commitment to First Amendment values.

I had come to know him briefly on a personal level as well. At one dinner party that my wife, Efrat, and I attended, he was seated next to her and she, a native of Israel who had been born and educated there and who had served in the Israeli Air Force, successfully persuaded him to accept an invitation he had received from one of the great universities in that country. When I was appointed the William J. Brennan Jr., Visiting Professor of First Amendment Issues at the Columbia University Graduate School of Journalism, he had attended the reception at the Supreme Court, and we had spoken easily and at length about pending cases. And so, when a three-judge court in Washington had determined to appoint a new special counsel to look into the alleged transgressions of President Clinton (a decision I deeply regretted because the displaced counsel was Robert Fiske, one of the most distinguished and trusted lawyers in the nation), I was pleased it was Ken Starr who had been appointed.

When Senator McConnell advised me that it was Starr I would be working with, I voiced no objection and set about the task. It was, in fact, an easy one. Starr was a thoughtful legal analyst and an imaginative strategist. He became and remains a good friend.

Most of my friends and some clients could accept none of this. How could I, they repeatedly asked me, represent Senator McConnell at all, let alone against John McCain, an individual so principled that he was prepared to take on his own political party in the service of campaign finance reform? How, they asked me, could I abandon a cause so worthy and associate with such less-than-worthy allies, who were seeking to maintain an inherently corrupt political system? And how, of all people, could I associate myself with Ken Starr?

The *New York Times Magazine* rarely publishes an article prompted by a subject as little newsworthy as a lawyer's agreeing to represent a client. When my association with Starr on behalf of Senator McConnell was announced, however, it quickly commissioned a piece about my retention, which it ran under the headline "Fighting with the Right." It was in question-and-answer format, beginning with the question of whether I had "taken a lot of heat from [my] friends on the left" and concluding with queries about whether I was "comfortable with Republicans now" and (tongue in cheek) whether I had plans to join the conservative think tank at the American Enterprise Institute. I had taken some heat, I responded, thinking specifically of some friends at the *Times* itself, but my view was that the proper question was not whether I was being used by the right but whether I was correct in my position vis-à-vis the matter. As for the AEI, I assured the inquiring *Times* reporter that I would never fit in there.

Fortunately, I could not afford to spend much time worrying about what my friends thought of my apostasy. From the start Starr and I faced the challenge of providing some degree of leadership to the disparate group of litigants that had chosen to challenge the constitutionality of McCain-Feingold. My problem was not that most of the lawyers we were working with were conservatives (although their frequent references to Federalist Society and AEI meetings they were about to attend might have led Hillary Clinton to be surer still of the vast right-wing conspiracy she had identified) but that they were all but impossible for us (or anybody) to lead.

The plaintiffs included not only Senator McConnell, the National Association of Broadcasters (represented by me and my colleagues at Cahill Gordon), and the Southeastern Legal Foundation and various conservative public interest groups associated with it (represented by Starr and his colleagues at the Kirkland & Ellis law firm). There were also the American Civil Liberties Union and the National Rifle Association, the AFL-CIO and the National Chamber of Commerce. There were the California Democratic and Republican parties. And there were plenty more—eighty-two plaintiffs in all from all corners of the political spectrum, in eleven separate lawsuits, all of them represented by lawyers who, like Starr and myself, were not lacking in ego.

McCain-Feingold was signed into law by President Bush on March 27, 2002. Within hours, we commenced litigation challenging the constitutionality of the law. Within weeks, a total of 101 parties on both sides were involved. The three-judge court that was appointed to hear the case established a schedule providing for five months for discovery and another month for cross-examination of witnesses. Oral argument was scheduled for December 3 and 4.

The five months of work were exhausting. Tens of thousands of documents were produced by each side to the other; sworn answers to questions posed by one side to the other were submitted; depositions were conducted around the nation.

For me, this period had two highlights. One involved the two days deposition that I took of Senator McCain himself; the other related to the extensive work Susan Buckley, our associate Brian

Markley, and (to a far lesser extent) I did with regard to certain studies relied upon by the proponents of McCain-Feingold.

The McCain deposition was combative, often abrasive. For all the favor with which he was routinely treated in the press for his supposed candor, McCain was no more accustomed to being required to respond to questions directly than most other politicians. Like most powerful people and almost all politicians, the senator, described in the *Almanac of American Politics* as "the closest thing American politics has to a national hero," resisted the notion of being subject to rules that called for flat, declarative responses to straightforward inquiries.

McCain reminded me of no one so much as the man whose deposition I had never been able to take in the Brooklyn Museum case—Rudolph Giuliani. Each was a talented public servant who did little to conceal his continuing presidential ambitions. Each had served his country heroically when his time of testing had come. Each was a moderate or even liberal Republican (much as he might wish the L-word away for political reasons) who took the career of Theodore Roosevelt as his public model. But I thought each was viewed far too uncritically. Giuliani's exemplary leadership on September 11, 2001, had led too many observers to overlook his shortcomings as mayor; McCain's unending efforts to court favorable press coverage had succeeded so well that he was treated on television as an expert on just about every issue, foreign or domestic, with which the nation was confronted. Each, as well, had a darker side, rooted in his unalloyed self-assurance in his own virtue and his contempt, sometimes reflected in fury, for those who disagreed with him. Both Giuliani and McCain made enemies easily, since both viewed their political and ideological adversaries as inherently being enemies. I have met few public servants as committed as these two men, and hardly any I would feel less comfortable with in the ultimate public office to which they both so obviously aspire.

For all the skirmishing between McCain and me, two themes emerged clearly from our exchanges. One was that the new law could not be justified as an anticorruption measure based on any notion of actual corruption—quid-pro-quo corruption, that is, in the sense of votes being traded for money. The second was that the very idea of suppressing speech based not on the reality but only on the "appearance" of corruption was deeply troubling.

I began by questioning Senator McCain closely about a statement that he had made on his Web site that a recent "rise in pork barrel spending [was] directly related to the rise of soft money, as Republicans and Democrats scrambled to reward major donors to their campaigns." When I asked him which Republicans and Democrats had done the scrambling, he responded that he had "no idea" and that he would not "ever speculate on such things." The statute, he said, had been designed to "eliminate" the "widespread belief" that there was an "appearance of corruption" in Washington.

Unsatisfied, I kept asking for names. Each time, he could not or would not answer. On his Web site Senator McCain had set forth ten examples of "pork barrel spending" supposedly prompted by "special interest unlimited campaign contributions." But when I pressed for details, Senator McCain offered none.

> Q: Can you identify for us which senators, if any, would not have proposed or supported these items, but for the existence of soft money?
> A: No, of course not.
> Q: Is that because you are unable to do so, or because you don't choose to do so?
> A: No, it's not my responsibility to do so, so I've never contemplated it in the past nor would do so now.

I pressed on, asking for specific information.

> Q: Well, I will ask you then now, Senator, to identify for this record in this litigation in which you are appearing as a [party], to identify for us which senators, if any . . . would not have proposed

or supported these items, but for soft money contributions?

A: Of course not.

Q: You will not do so?

A: Of course not.

Q: Your observation that you acknowledged having made that "the rise in pork barrel spending is directly related to the rise of soft money, as Republicans and Democrats scramble to reward major donors to our campaigns" leads to this question. Which Republicans and which Democrats scrambled to reward major donors with respect to the particular pork list that I read to you?

A: I have no idea, nor would I ever speculate on such things, Mr. Abrams.

I tried again, choosing one of the examples on Senator McCain's list.

Q: Taking one of them, by way of example, on the first page of this exhibit, you said, "The following examples will give you an idea of what laced this most recent trichinosis attack. Twenty-six million dollars to compensate the Dungeness crab fishermen, fish processors and fishing crews negatively affected by restrictions on fishing in Glacier Bay National Park in Alaska." Do you know,

Senator McCain, if anyone inserted this provision in the appropriations bill because the person had received soft money?

A: No.

Q: And would you [give] the same answer if I went through each of the other examples cited by you in this document?

A: Sure.

Although in two days of testimony, Senator McCain could not offer a single example of actual corruption brought about by soft-money contributions, the far more amorphous area of the "appearance" of corruption seemed more promising. He referred to multimillion-dollar contributions by large corporations to political parties, arguing that the public had concluded that only those with large sums of money could affect the legislative process. But the statute did not bar only large soft-money contributions; it barred *any* such contributions. That it did so solely based on what co-sponsor Senator Russ Feingold referred to in his own deposition as "the possibility of the appearance of corruption" rather than its reality made the case even fuzzier.

McCain himself had, for example, just written a book entitled *Worth Fighting For.* The *New York Times,* on the very day of McCain's deposition, had featured an article about a book party celebrating the publication of the memoir, sponsored by Frederick Smith, the chairman and CEO of Federal Express. That company was the largest all-cargo air carrier in the world and an entity that frequently appeared before the Senate Commerce and Transportation Committee, which McCain had previously chaired and came to chair again when the Republicans regained control of the Senate.

Was there, I asked, an appearance of impropriety about that? Was there an appearance of corruption in the CEO of the nation's largest all-cargo air carrier's paying for a book party for the ranking member and likely future chair of the Senate Commerce Committee? McCain responded with irritation: "Absolutely not."

Of course, my point was not that McCain was corrupt or even that his conduct necessarily appeared to be so. The first was untrue; the second was a matter of opinion. But that was precisely my point. Where actual corruption was not involved, the idea of suppressing or criminalizing speech because of the foggy notion of the "appearance" of corruption was dangerous, far more so than McCain or his allies would acknowledge.

What seemed from the start far more central to the ultimate resolution of the case was the answer to a single question: How much "genuine" advocacy about issues and candidates—as opposed to specific advice about whom to elect—would be caught in the new statutory net cast by the statute? If the Court decided to retain its own formulation of express advocacy in the *Buckley* case, the statute should surely fall. A law making it a crime even to mention the name of a candidate for federal office within sixty days of an election certainly could not be squared with *Buckley*'s protection of all speech that did not constitute express advocacy—unambiguous statements urging people to vote for—of a particular candidate.

We would see, soon enough, what the Supreme Court had to say about *Buckley*. But even if we lost on that front, proponents of McCain-Feingold still had a difficult problem regarding the sixty-day ban in the statute. The legal issue here was over-breadth—i.e., whether the statute criminalized a substantial amount of speech that all would agree was protected by the First Amendment.

It was in this area that two studies prepared by the Brennan Center for Justice at the New York University School of Law seemed to become so significant. Both studies, frequently cited by members of Congress in support of McCain-Feingold, sought to respond to the concern that a statute that made criminal *any* advertisement broadcast within sixty days of a federal election that was funded even in part by corporate money and that even mentioned a candidate for federal office would be banning too much speech that did not involve genuine advocacy to elect anyone to office. This was a particular problem under McCain-Feingold, since its key provision criminalized such activities as a mere reference to a

416

candidate, a plea that a member of Congress vote for a particular bill, or any criticism of a sitting president in the months before an election.

The two Brennan Center studies, entitled *Buying Time 1998* and *Buying Time 2000*, provided the answers the proponents of the new law were seeking. The Brennan Center had been involved in all aspects of the passage of the statute. It had participated in drafting it, in lobbying for it, and in defending it. Now it was producing studies designed to supply the empirical data that might ensure that the statute was held constitutional.

The studies themselves were based on data obtained and analyzed by Professor Kenneth Goldstein with the help of his political science students at Arizona State University (for the 1998 report) and the University of Wisconsin (for the 2000 report). The students were shown storyboards of political ads broadcast during 1998 and 2000 which contained the text and selected frames of the video of the ad (usually six or so frames per thirty-second ad); they were then asked to "code" the commercials based on their content. In brief, the reports concluded—based on the assessment of the students about whether the "purpose" of the advertisements was to inform about an issue or to generate support for a candidate—that the vast majority of advertisements aired in the sixty-day window before election day—93 percent in 1998 and over 99 percent in 2000—were not what the Brennan Center viewed

417

as "genuine issue advocacy" but were instead what it characterized as "sham issue advocacy." Thus, the argument went, since so little speech truly worthy of constitutional protection would have been condemned under BCRA, no overbreadth problem arose.

I had a long relationship with the Brennan Center. I had been personally friendly with Justice Brennan and had chosen his name for the chair I hold at the Columbia Graduate School of Journalism. I had attended planning sessions for the establishment of the Brennan Center, had received an award from it, and had been active in ensuring that my firm made a yearly contribution to it.

For months, Susan Buckley and I reviewed the materials turned over to us by the Brennan Center from their files on the studies—their grant applications, their internal e-mails, and the mass of data reflecting the preparation of the studies. Susan and I then questioned under oath the authors of the studies and those who oversaw their preparation. When we were through, each of us had reached the same conclusion.

The Brennan Center's work was indefensible. From the start, the Brennan Center and those it retained were so dedicated to advancing campaign finance legislation that fundamental scientific standards had been sacrificed. A grant for the studies had been sought for the express aim of fueling "a continuous and multi-faceted campaign reform forward." The scholar who sought it—

Professor Goldstein—had represented that his study would be "designed and executed" to achieve the cause of "reform." So far had those in charge deviated from normal academic rectitude that they had promised their funders that they would abandon all research after an introductory stage if it appeared that the result would not "enhance the case for reform"—if, that is, the answers were coming out *wrong*.

As for the studies themselves, the most important claim of *Buying Time 1998* was that "only" 7 percent of issue advertisements that the Brennan Center deemed to be "genuine" that had been broadcast during the 1998 election cycle would be barred by the new law. But we had learned that—in the words of Brennan Center president and CEO Joshua Rosenkranz in an internal e-mail—the 7 percent figure was "not just misleading," but "flat-out false." In an extraordinary concession the authors of *Buying Time 1998* had acknowledged that using the same approach that the Brennan Center employed to report its findings in 2000 (and the same approach used by yet another scholar it commissioned to analyze the 1998 data), over 14 percent of the ads broadcast in the last sixty days of the 1998 campaign were "genuine," by Brennan Center standards, yet still would now be illegal. No law could be deemed constitutional that made criminal so much concededly First Amendment-protected speech.

Our analysis had taught us still more. Based on

the Brennan Center's own data (and documents produced by Professor Goldstein), we knew that the 14 percent figure was itself significantly understated. So-called "coding sheets" produced by Professor Goldstein and filled in by his students as they evaluated the advertisements demonstrate that a full 64 percent of advertisements aired during the last sixty days of the 1998 election were "genuine," but still would have been prohibited by McCain-Feingold. The critical question asked of the coders was, "In your opinion, is the purpose of this ad to provide information about or urge action on a bill or issue, or is it to generate support or opposition for a particular candidate?" Students were given three choices: (1) provide information or urge action; (2) generate support/opposition for candidate; or (3) unsure/unclear. If the student chose answer 1, the ad was determined to be a "genuine issue ad"; if the student chose answer 2, the ad was determined to be an "electioneering" ad. According to the coding sheets, the students determined that at least ten of the group-sponsored advertisements that aired thousands of times during the last sixty days of the 1998 election and referred to a federal candidate were "genuine" issue advertisements. Nevertheless, *Buying Time 1998* reported that there were only two such ads. Incredibly, someone—either Professor Goldstein (who claimed no knowledge of the facts), someone else who wrote the 1998 study (the authors also claimed no knowledge of what happened), or some unnamed person at the Brennan Center—*recoded* eight of these advertisements from "providing information" to "generating support or opposition for a candidate." According to the Brennan Center's and Professor Goldstein's own data and crediting the student coders' original assessments, 64 percent of the ads that would have been barred in 1998 were "genuine."

The eight recoded ads offered useful examples of speech that would be caught in McCain-Feingold's web. Three of them related to term limits; two were AFL-CIO ads relating to protecting Social Security; one praised a senator for his stance against granting excessive power to trial lawyers; another criticized a candidate for the Senate for his position on criminal justice issues; and the last criticized two senators (one running for reelection, one not) for opposing a federal ban on partial-birth abortion. All these advertisements were precisely the sort of speech that the First Amendment most clearly protects.

So, it turned out, were many ads that the Brennan Center's student coders characterized as "designed to generate candidate support." The David Wu advertisement set forth above, pressuring Wu to support term limits, was illustrative. The student coders determined that the "purpose" of that advertisement was to generate support for a candidate; my own interpretation was that its "purpose" was to pressure a vulnerable candidate to sign on to the term-limits agenda. But what did it matter who was right? Or if there was any "right" answer at all? No analysis that took account of the First Amendment, I thought, could permit such speech to be treated as a criminal act.

The numbers mattered. If even 14 percent of ads covered by the statute that would now be deemed criminal were viewed as "genuine" by the Brennan Center itself, no constitutional legerdemain could save the statute. If the actual number was 64 percent, even jurists sympathetic to McCain-Feingold's aims could hardly find its provisions to be constitutional. And if many of the ads adjudged by the Brennan Center not to be "genuine" turned out, like the David Wu ad, to be the sort of advocacy that must be fully protected by the First Amendment, there could be little basis even to begin to defend the statute against First Amendment challenge.

So we thought, anyway. When the three-judge district court panel rendered its ruling, we were less than fully pleased. We had won more than we had lost, but we had still lost too much. The panel could agree on little except its members' obvious disdain for one another. The single jurist from the court of appeals, Judge Karen Henderson, agreed with us that most sections of the law were unconstitutional; district court judge Colleen Kollar-Kotelly agreed with the government that virtually the entire statute was constitutional; district court judge Richard J. Leon agreed with each of his colleagues on certain issues. After one perused the over sixteen hundred pages of angrily conflicting opinions (the longest decision ever rendered in the District of Columbia), we knew this much: The core soft-money provisions of the law were basically held to be unconstitutional by a 2-1 vote, and the political parties could continue to receive soft money so long as they did not spend it on television advertisements that attacked or opposed candidates. The sixty-day advertising ban was held unconstitutional by another 2-1 vote; but an alternative definition that criminalized the broadcast of ads at any time by organizations such as the ACLU, the NRA, and the AFL-CIO that attacked or "promoted" a candidate was upheld by yet another 2-1 vote, with one of its provisions designed to protect against unconstitutional vagueness itself having been held unconstitutionally vague.

We were ready for the Supreme Court. Or so we thought.

THE NUMBERS

As we prepared for the argument, the math was easy enough. From reading prior opinions of the Court, four of its members seemed oriented in favor of sustaining major provisions of the new law. Justices Stevens, Souter, Ginsburg, and Breyer had all indicated in past rulings their concern about abuses in the current system and their disinclination to permit First Amendment arguments to trump Congress's power to deal with those abuses. Justices Scalia, Thomas, and Kennedy, in contrast, had repeatedly voiced concern about subordinating First Amendment interests to regulatory concerns in this area. Chief Justice Rehnquist's views seemed less predictable: He had been chary of affording much in the way of free-speech protection to corporations but had grown increasingly skeptical about congressional overstepping of what he viewed as constitutional boundaries in a variety of circumstances. As for Justice O'Connor, her views in this area were uncertain. What everyone did know was that she had increasingly come to be recognized as the most powerful woman in the nation as her votes tipped the ever-more-divided Court one way or the other in case after case. It had been she who cast the critical vote saving affirmative action at the University of Michigan, she who had done the same in the Texas case concluding that homosexuals could not be found guilty of criminal behavior for engaging in sodomy, she who in one case after another had determined the fate of constitutional law in the United States. "Every night as I go to sleep," Starr had told me, "I ask myself what argument might persuade her." I did as well.

As I prepared for the argument, which was scheduled for September 8, 2003, two recent developments in the case were much on my mind.

As regards the Brennan Center study, there had been a complete turnabout of the parties. The more we reviewed the data compiled by the scholars the Brennan Center had retained to support McCain-Feingold, the more it seemed to help us. If even 14 percent of the ads broadcast in the last sixty days of the 1998 election had been what the Brennan Center pro-regulation scholars acknowledged as "genuine," the statute surely should not withstand a challenge based on its overbreadth. And if, as we argued was the case, 64 percent of those ads had been "genuine," even as tabulated from Brennan Center data, how could the statute possibly withstand First Amendment attack?

The impact of our attempt to use the Brennan Center data to aid our own cause quickly became apparent to our opponents: In its briefs to the Supreme Court, the Solicitor General's Office, representing the United States, placed little reliance on the Brennan Center's work designed to identify which advertisements had been "genuine." We, in turn, argued that while the published results of the Brennan Center were indeed unreliable, the data it compiled demonstrated that McCain-Feingold could not be squared with the First Amendment.

There had been another change of emphasis during the briefing of the case in the Supreme Court. Moving away from much of the emphasis on other legal issues in its briefs in the lower courts, the government now was placing primary reliance on a 1990 ruling of the Court in a case called *Austin v. Michigan Chamber of Commerce*. In that case, the Court, by a 6-3 vote, had upheld the constitutionality of a Michigan law barring corporations from using what the Court had referred to as their "vast aggregations of wealth" to fund candidates running for office. Corporations, the Court had said, could use funds from their political action committees, or PACs, to support candidates but not treasury funds of the corporations themselves. Corporate executives could contribute to PACs directed by their companies but could not use a dollar of money of the corporation itself to support candidates. The Michigan statute, the majority of the Court insisted, was not a ban at all but simply a requirement that a corporation confine its expenditures to what it had raised through its PAC.

Austin undoubtedly posed difficulties for us, ones we had sought to sidestep by pointing out that the speech involved there had been express advocacy as defined in *Buckley*—a call, in so many words, for voters to elect a specific candidate as a state representative. Such speech, we argued, had not received protection under *Buckley* itself, and *Austin* should thus not be read to permit regulation of speech that *Buckley* appeared to protect.

There was another way to respond to *Austin*, and that was to have the Court overrule it. Of the six justices who had made up the majority in *Austin*, four (Justices Marshall, Brennan, White, and Blackmun) were no longer on the Court; only Chief Justice Rehnquist and Justice Stevens remained. The three dissenters in *Austin*—Justices Scalia, Kennedy, and O'Connor—all remained on the Court. If only, we thought, the chief justice would change his mind.

ARGUMENT

The Court set four hours aside for argument of the case, an extraordinary amount of time, matched in recent years only, so far as we knew, by the four hours scheduled for *Buckley v. Valeo* a quarter of a century before. It returned from its summer recess to hear the argument on the day it specially designated for the hearing. After sometimes awkward and always agonizing negotiations among our many lawyers, we agreed that Starr and Bobby Burchfield, the lawyer for the Republican National Committee, would represent the challengers to Title I of the statute, dealing with soft-money contributions, and that I would argue together with Larry Gold, counsel to the AFL-CIO, against the constitutionality of the advertising ban contained in Title II. The defense of the statute would be set forth by Ted Olson, the solicitor general of the United States (a position Starr himself once held); by Paul Clement, his chief assistant; and by Seth Waxman, President Clinton's solicitor general, now representing Senator McCain and the other sponsors of the bill.

By the end of the morning's argument about the constitutionality of Title I of McCain-Feingold, we had strong reason to believe that the chief justice was oriented in our direction. His questions to Olson and Waxman had been probing and his references to the First Amendment implications of the challenged statute strongly suggested that he was persuaded that the law could not withstand First Amendment scrutiny. By the end of the day, he would make explicit that he had indeed changed his mind about the *Austin* case in favor of providing more First Amendment rights to corporations.

When I rose to argue to the Court shortly after 1:30 p.m., I was cheered by the events of the morning. If the chief justice had moved to our side of the line, we had four very likely votes. So, of course, did the defenders of the statute—which would leave, as had so often occurred in recent years, Justice O'Connor to cast the decisive vote.

I began by trying to make plain how much easier our case was than that involving the soft-money ban. The Court had often said, I reminded it, whenever Congress had sought to bar or limit expenditures—people or entities spending their own money to advance their political views by, say, buying their own advertisements rather than contributing the money to a political party or group—that the power of the government to impose limits was particularly restricted. This was especially relevant to McCain-Feingold, I said, because its ban on certain ads was based on their content, a particularly suspect legal category. An ad mentioning a candidate who was running for office was criminal; one that did not was not.

I had spoken for about forty-five seconds when Justice O'Connor interrupted me. Did I, she asked, "take the position that no effective regulation of electioneering communications was possible"?

It was a difficult question to answer with the speed Supreme Court advocacy requires, speed that was necessary because new questions were sure to be asked by others before I was finished responding to this critical one. For one thing, I could not immediately tell whether she meant the words "electioneering communications" in the lay sense of all communications about elections, or in a more technical one—any communications broadcast on television within sixty days of an election that met the requirements set forth in the new law. At the same time, she had used the term "effective regulation." Even I had not argued that the regulation imposed by the law in effect prior to the McCain-Feingold bill had been terribly effective. The protection of all speech other than "express advocacy," as defined in the *Buckley* case, had meant, as the Court itself had predicted in *Buckley*, that only a small amount of speech would be regulated, and that speech that did not contain language that directly urged viewers to vote for or against a particular candidate could be freely made. I had only the briefest second to get my

429

answer out: "I take the position that 'election-eering communications' as defined in the statute is so overbroad that the totality of what is encompassed in it is not regulatable. Electioneering communications includes within it 'express advocacy,' what is now or what had been subject to regulation, and to that extent, it is subject to regulation."

Justice O'Connor asked no further questions of me and only one, later in the day, of my opponents. (Of them, she wanted to know how the statute could be constitutional when it barred reference even to the name of a statute such as McCain-Feingold.) If the only question we had coming into the argument was how Justice O'Connor would vote, we knew little more by argument's end than we did at the beginning. When Chief Justice Rehnquist made it clear, however, that he had changed his view on the *Austin* case, the road was open for Justice O'Connor, who had dissented in *Austin*, to ensure that the dissenters in 1991 had become the majority today. If she were to join Justices Kennedy, Scalia, and Thomas (who had joined the Court after 1990 but had repeatedly made plain his grave First Amendment concerns about regulation of speech about elections), she would have turned the tide for us on *Austin*. We would not know until the decision itself any more about Justice O'Connor's views.

I would quickly learn, however, how strongly the four members of the more liberal group of jurists felt about the case, as each of them questioned me intensively, sometimes with barely concealed hostility. Prior to the argument itself, I had retained some residual, if romanticized, hope that at least one of the four (each of whom had often voted in favor of First Amendment positions in the past) might be reluctant to conclude that the ACLU or, say, the AFL-CIO could be barred from broadcasting any advertisement even mentioning President Bush in the last few months of a political campaign. It quickly became apparent that my hopes—they were nothing more than that—were unavailing.

Justice David Souter followed O'Connor's question with one asking me if I thought anything beyond express advocacy—the "magic words" referred to in *Buckley*, which proponents of McCain-Feingold had repeatedly mocked—could be regulated. Attempting to defend *Buckley*, which guaranteed us victory if it were applied to McCain-Feingold, I responded that only express advocacy could be regulated. Justice John Paul Stevens, a longtime defender of campaign finance reform efforts against First Amendment challenges, then asked if the *Buckley* distinction between advertisements directly advocating the election of an official with words such as "vote for" or "vote against" and ads about issues made sense. Why, he asked, "should a speech urging expressly to elect a particular candidate . . . President of the United States, why should that speech be entitled to less constitutional protection than a speech urging the ratification of the Panama Canal Treaty?"

It was a fair question, which went to the heart of the distinction made in *Buckley* between express advocacy and all other advocacy. Although justifying that distinction was difficult, and my own views would have impelled me to seek full First Amendment protection for all such expenditures, defending *Buckley* was a strategic priority for us since some jurist (Justice O'Connor, perhaps?) might be reluctant to reverse it. *Buckley* had concluded that speech containing the so-called magic words was "unambiguously campaign related." I rephrased that language, arguing that direct advocacy of an individual's election is "such a final act of saying, vote for the candidate, not for this reason, not by suggestion" that the Court had decided to treat it more as a contribution to a candidate (and thus subject to regulation) than as a simple expenditure by the speaker (and thus not subject to regulation). Justice Stevens pursued me, asking how I could defend treating direct advocacy of whom to vote for as "second-class speech." As I struggled to support the Court's obviously vulnerable opinion in *Buckley*, Justice Scalia, in a bemused tone, threw me a lifeline. "Maybe," he said, "it's more likely to induce gratitude and hence more likely to lead to the, quote, appearance of corruption." Yes, I said gratefully, yes.

More questions followed about *Buckley*, and I finally addressed the question implicit in all of them: if the Court abandoned *Buckley*, should it opt for more regulation or less, more First Amendment protection or less? "If you were to move" away from *Buckley*, I said, "I would certainly urge you to move in the direction of affording more protection to the direct advocacy that Justice Stevens asked me about rather than less protection" for, say, the AFL ad that we had provided to the Court which had simply urged a named member of Congress to vote against Most-Favored-Nation treatment for China.

Now Justice Stephen Breyer entered the fray. From the time he had joined the Court in 1994, Justice Breyer had seemed unpersuaded that the First Amendment should be read at all as broadly as its advocates such as myself would have preferred. He had articulated views about how the First Amendment should be taken into account in cases involving campaign finance reform in past judicial opinions and, in particular, in a speech he delivered at New York University Law School in October 2001. The First Amendment, he had argued then, was not simply a "negative" protection against governmental action. Notwithstanding the negative phraseology of the amendment ("Congress shall *make no law* abridging . . . the freedom of speech"), Breyer insisted that it should be read as part of the Constitution's general effort to further "democratic self-government," one "open to participation" by all. So read, the First Amendment offered support for "both sides of the constitutional equation" when issues like campaign finance reform statutes were before the Court.

To me, this approach to the First Amendment was potentially calamitous. The First Amendment I knew was not some sort of charter for good government (although that was often a result of free speech), but a protection against oppressive government. It was negative not only in its language but in the sense (as I had argued in the *Nation*) that it was rooted in distrust of government and concern about historic misuse of governmental power.

Totalitarian governments throughout history have justified their suppression of speech on the grounds that by limiting speech they were actually furthering the cause of democracy. "The defenders of every kind of regime," George Orwell had written, "claim that it is a democracy." "Not only is there no agreed definition" of democracy, Orwell wrote, "but the attempt to make one is resisted from all sides." The clarity of the First Amendment, I thought, should not be abandoned in favor of highly debatable, utterly unpredictable, and deeply subjective judgments as to whether legislation actually advanced "democratic self-government." Supreme Court Justice Potter Stewart had put the point well in a 1973 opinion that warned of the "dangers that beset us when we lose sight of the First Amendment itself and march forth in blind pursuit of its 'values.'" That, I thought, was a splendid response to Justice Breyer.

The reality, however, was that my own opinions about Justice Breyer's First Amendment views were not exactly what interested him, as he made clear in his first question after my reference to the now illegal AFL ad opposing most-favored-nation treatment for China:

Q: But it's not that they can't run the ad. I mean, the unions can run the ad. The corporations can run the ad. The ACLU can run the ad. They all can run the ad. It's just that they have to pay for it out of a PAC . . . So why is that . . . if the disclosure regulations, the new ones, the new provisions in the law on independent expenditure—

A: Yes.

Q: —are constitutional, if they are constitutional, then it's pretty hard for me to see any additional burden on any of these organizations to make this expenditure on the ad you are worried about through a PAC. What's the problem of saying, go through the PAC, and what we achieve by that is limiting the amount of money that any one individual can give, and what we lose by it is nothing . . .

A: My first response is that you lose a lot of speech.

Q: Why?

A: Why? Because much less money will be obtained.

Although I urged upon Justice Breyer that serious burdens would be imposed on the AFL or any organization by requiring it to speak about issues and candidates only through its PAC, I made no headway at all with him or with any of the three other liberal jurists. I pointed to the fact that an organization like the ACLU has no PAC and wants none since it does not view itself as a political organization. I argued that PAC money could only be spent for political purposes, and that for the ACLU to be obliged to characterize falsely every ad that it broadcast as being for such purposes was itself misleading.

Justice Ruth Bader Ginsburg, a former general counsel at the ACLU, rejected my argument immediately. "Why," she asked, "couldn't the ACLU call its PAC the Nonpartisan Issue-Oriented PAC?" The name wasn't the problem, I said; the reality was that PACs had to have and disclose their "political purposes," and the ACLU had no such purposes.

More broadly, I returned to the critical limitations placed by the law on all PACs, which ensured that their voices would be muted. PACs, I said, had far less money than the corporations that set them up, because they required additional fund-raising from a far smaller base of people. The NRA, to take an example, had four million members but in previous campaigns had been able to appeal for funds to spread the NRA message to eighty million gun owners in the country. Since a PAC can seek funds only from its own members, I argued there would be an enormous diminution in the amount of speech the NRA could engage in if it were limited to its own membership. Justice Breyer questioned the accuracy of my contention:

Q: I'm not quite clear on that. Why is that—I thought all they had to do was, if they want to raise money for these kinds of ads, sixty days before the election, mentioning the candidate's name, is in their advertising, they say, please send your check to the NRA Election Time PAC. Do they have to do more than that?

I thought they had to open a bank account, they have to appoint somebody a treasurer, they have to make disclosure. And it's a slight difference there between over $250 rather than over $10,000. And that's it.

A: And they're only allowed to solicit from their membership.

Q: In other words, you can't go and ask—

> if I start a PAC or anybody here starts
> a PAC, you can't go and just ask the
> general public to belong?
>
> A: No.

I sought, as my time quickly evaporated, to return to the topic of the quantity of ads that could no longer be shown under the new law. Judge Henderson, one of the three judges who had heard the case in the district court, had indicated that between 14 percent and 64 percent of the ads were, by any standard, "genuine." The other two judges had used or at least referred to the 14 percent figure, a number that by itself should have doomed the statute.

Justice Souter noted that many of the ads were hybrids, ones that "really do address issues" but that contained "also a very clear implication about what they want you to do in the ballot booth." Since the participants in the Brennan Center study, he observed, were not given a chance to respond that an ad was both issue-oriented *and* election-oriented, wasn't the whole study flawed?

Of course, that had been precisely our argument at the district court. What sort of study, we had asked, was it that forced participants to treat an advertisement as only electoral or only issue-oriented when many ads had components of both? Now Justice Souter was asking me the same question, but the pro-McCain-Feingold thrust of his query was whether the flaws in the Brennan Center study should not lead the Court to ignore it completely. I responded that the failure of the study to be entirely fair (it surely had not been that) should not be held against us. When significant numbers of students concluded that an ad was "genuine," notwithstanding its reference to a candidate, credit should at least be given for that. Chief Justice Rehnquist then interjected a friendly related question. "This was the defendants' evidence," he asked, "wasn't it?" "Yes," I responded appreciatively, "it was the defendants' evidence."

By the end of the argument, I was reconciled to the fact that our chances with the four liberal jurists were hopeless. We found ourselves, as so many litigants in the Supreme Court had before us, in the hands of Justice O'Connor.

THE DECISION

On December 10, 2003, the Supreme Court announced its decision in *McConnell v. Federal Election Commission*. On virtually every significant issue we lost by a 5-4 vote. Our calculations had been right. The chief justice and Justices Kennedy, Scalia, and Thomas were for us; the four more liberal jurists—Justices Stevens, Souter, Ginsburg, and Breyer—had voted against us. The previously inscrutable Justice O'Connor had joined with Stevens and his allies to offer a solid, if slim, victory to the defenders of McCain-Feingold.

The Court's opinion, written by Justices Stevens and O'Connor, focused, almost in its entirety, on Title I of the act—the total ban on soft-money contributions. Tracing congressional efforts "to purge national politics of what was conceived to be the pernicious influence of 'big money' campaign contributions" from corporations back to 1907, the majority opinion treated McCain-Feingold as a "modest" effort at reform. Every constitutional objection to the core of the new law was rejected, every First Amendment argument rebuffed. The Court did not rely on any actual corruption's having occurred as a result of soft money contributions; the government had acknowledged that it could cite no such example, a concession consistent with that Senator McCain had made to me in his deposition. For the majority, the "appearance of corruption" was sufficient, and the Court found plenty of that.

When the Stevens-O'Connor opinion reached Title II, about which I had argued, its opinion was so terse that it contained almost no analysis. McCain-Feingold had not really banned any corporate or union speech at all, the opinion stated, since those entities could still speak through PACs. So much, then, for our hopes that Justice O'Connor, consistent with her dissent in *Austin*, would provide a fifth vote to reverse it. The opinion made no reference to the burden of using PACs, the inappropriateness of PACs for certain organizations such as the ACLU, and the reality that a requirement that PAC money alone be used by unions and corporations would ensure that far less speech would be available to the public. Nor did it respond to a basic question that had been phrased with particular felicity in the NRA's brief: If the purpose of McCain-Feingold was truly to prevent official corruption, real or apparent, why were PACs permitted? Such a statute, the NRA argued, "makes no more sense than a bribery statute requiring corporations to pay for their bribes using funds from PACs."

McCain-Feingold was not overbroad, the majority curtly concluded, because advertisements that ran within the thirty- and sixty-day period were the "functional equivalent of express advocacy." Why? The "vast majority of ads" in the months before elections "clearly" had an "electoral purpose" and therefore should be treated as if they had directly advocated the election of a candidate *even if they had not done so at all*. Just a year before, in a case in which the Court had held un-constitutional a statute that had banned virtual pornography, computer-generated images of people engaged in sexual activities who appeared to be but were not minors, Justice Kennedy's opinion for the Court had concluded that "the Government may not suppress lawful speech as the means to suppress unlawful speech." "Protected speech," he had observed, "does not become unprotected merely because it resembles the latter." Justices Stevens,

Souter, Ginsburg, and Breyer had joined that opinion. Now the four of them plus Justice O'Connor were concluding that lawful speech *could* be criminalized because of its supposed "purpose."

In reaching its decision, the majority opinion abandoned the express advocacy test of *Buckley*. For all its limitations, *Buckley* itself had sought to construct a rough compromise designed to vindicate both First Amendment and regulatory interests. As rewritten in the *McConnell* case, however, *Buckley* became totally speech-destructive. Quickly, almost casually, the opinion dismissed First Amendment interests altogether.

In concluding that the "vast majority" of advertisements mentioning candidates in the last sixty days of the 1998 and 2000 campaigns had the "purpose" of influencing those elections, the Stevens-O'Connor opinion studiously avoided even mentioning the flawed Brennan Center study that members of Congress had so often cited. Instead, it referred to a study by the Annenberg Public Policy Center, which opined about the "purpose" (but not the specific language) of most ads broadcast close to elections, and to a report submitted to the Court by an author of one of the Brennan Center studies and a colleague, which used the same data the Brennan Center had used and was therefore subject to all the same criticism that study had received.

The Stevens-O'Connor opinion referred particularly to one ad that our opponents had relied upon, a vicious personal attack on a candidate that had nonetheless not contained any of the so-called magic words from *Buckley*. The opinion made no reference to the numerous ads that had been shown on television during the 1998 and 2000 campaigns that were, by any standard, "genuine" issue ads that would now be banned by McCain-Feingold. Nor did it cite any of the ads before the Court that dealt with genuine issues but were apparently viewed as constitutionally expendable because their supposed purpose, as distinct from their language, was electoral.

The ads described earlier in this chapter—the David Wu term limits ad, and the late-term-abortion ads of National Right to Life—were illustrative of the type of ad that the Stevens-O'Connor opinion chose to ignore. Their language was clearly about issues. The intentions of those who paid for the ads may or may not have been electoral in nature, and the ads themselves may have therefore been broadcast out of mixed motives. But even if they were, how could banning them be deemed consistent with the First Amendment?

The opinion concluded with a note of intended reassurance. Corporations and unions had significant protections against the imposition of criminal liability on them in the future. They could use PAC money to pay for any ad they wished. Or they could "simply avoid any specific reference to federal candidates" in their ads the waning days of the campaign.

This latter proposed solution seemed to me to demonstrate better than any critical commentary just how far the majority of the Court had deviated from the fundamental principles of the First Amendment. Urging vulnerable parties to avoid risk by omitting the name of a candidate from ads was inviting surrender. The Brooklyn Museum, after all, had been told by city officials that it could proceed with its show if it dropped only one painting. The *New York Times* had been told that its salvation in the Pentagon Papers case was to "simply avoid any specific reference" to classified material. To offer to parties who wished to speak in a particular way and who justifiably feared criminal prosecution for doing so the solution that they abandon the very speech they wished to engage in was not to offer any First Amendment protection at all.

The dissenting judges hit hard at the weaknesses of the Stevens-O'Connor argument. Justice Kennedy's fifty-eight-page opinion for himself and (on almost all subjects) the other three dissenters argued that Title I violated well-established First Amendment principles. As for Title II, relating to the advertising ban, the opinion urged that the *Austin* case should be reversed, since it had made "the impermissible content-based judgment that commentary on candidates is less deserving of First Amendment protection than discussions of policy." *Austin*'s conclusion that corporations were entitled to less First Amendment protection than others, Kennedy

444

urged, was itself unconstitutional. Nor were PACs acceptable substitutes for actual corporate speech. The availability of a PAC, he wrote, still does not avoid the conclusion that a "corporation *as a corporation* is prohibited from speaking."

Kennedy offered a telling hypothetical to illustrate the overbreadth of McCain-Feingold.

> Suppose a few Senators want to show their constituents in the logging community how much they care about working families and propose a law, 60 days before the election, that would harm the environment by allowing logging in national forests. Under the McCain-Feingold law, a non-profit environmental group would be unable to run an ad referring to these Senators in their districts. The suggestion that the group could form and fund a PAC in the short time required for effective participation in the political debate is fanciful. For reasons already discussed, moreover, an ad hoc PAC would not be as effective as the environmental group itself in gaining credibility with the public. Never before in our history has the Court upheld a law that suppresses speech to this extent.

On the broader issue of whether the mere fact that an ad "may, in one fashion or another, influence an election" can permit its criminalization,

Kennedy was unambiguous: "I should have thought," he wrote, "influencing elections to be the whole point of political speech."

Justice Scalia's separate dissent focused on the actual purpose of McCain-Feingold. It had been drafted, he concluded, to prevent not the appearance of corruption but criticism of government itself. Congress did not like so-called attack ads, particularly by outside groups; they irritated incumbents, deprived them of the chance to decide what issues to focus on, and required them to spend more on their campaigns. The legislative history of McCain-Feingold, Scalia demonstrated, was filled with statements to that effect. No law could appropriately seek to avoid public criticism, Scalia argued, except at the expense of the First Amendment. He began his dissent this way: "This is a sad day for freedom of speech."

For me, Justice Thomas's dissent had special relevance. For well over thirty years I had sought to protect the right of the press to publish as it wished without being prevented in advance from having its say or punished for doing so after the fact. Every significant First Amendment loss, whether or not it directly involved the press, had the potential to limit press freedoms as well. Justice Thomas's opinion spoke directly to that issue.

How, he asked, could the logic of the Court's ruling be limited so as not to apply equally to media companies? In McCain-Feingold, Congress had chosen to exempt the print press from the

446

definition of "electioneering communications" and not to extend that definition to any "communication appearing in a news story, commentary, or editorial distributed through the facilities of any broadcast station." In its written submission to the district court, however, the United States had suggested that the regulations could also have been applied to the print press if Congress had chosen to do so.

Justice Thomas's opinion urged that the logic of the Court's ruling now placed the entire press at risk of being subject to "outright regulation" by Congress. Every justification for the regulation of speech by other corporations, he argued, could in theory be applied to media corporations as well. Candidates could be just as grateful to media companies, he pointed out, as to other corporations. Because "editorials and commentaries published in newspapers certainly can influence elections," what, then, was "to stop a future Congress from determining that the press is 'too influential,' and that the 'appearance of corruption' is significant when media organizations endorse candidates or run 'slanted' or 'biased' news stories in favor of candidates or parties?"

The opinion closed with another warning to the press. The *Tornillo* case, one of the two I had cited to my audience at All Souls Church three years before, could now be considered at peril. *Tornillo* had concluded that, notwithstanding that the print press had become, in certain ways, "noncompetitive and enormously powerful and influential in its capacity to manipulate popular opinion and change the course of events," a state could not "intrude into the function of editors" by interfering with "the exercise of editorial control and judgment." Now, Thomas argued, "supporters of such laws need only argue that the press's 'capacity to manipulate popular opinion' gives rise to an 'appearance of corruption,' especially when this capacity is used to promote a particular candidate or party." Freedom of the press, Thomas asserted, could thus well be "next on the chopping block," since "no principle of law or logic" prevented application of the Court's reasoning in that setting. The press, Thomas concluded, "now operates at the whim of Congress."

Some would undoubtedly argue that Justice Thomas's opinion, like many other Supreme Court dissents, was simply the overheated response of a single justice to a majority opinion that he viewed as intolerable. "Dissenting opinions," Judge Henry Friendly once observed, "are not always a reliable guide to the meaning of the majority; often their predictions partake of Cassandra's gloom more than her accuracy."

Still, it is not at all fanciful to expect some lawyer in the not too distant future to urge the Supreme Court to sustain Congress's adoption of additional "reform" legislation with regard to the print press, arguing that *Tornillo* was wrongly decided, or, in any event, decided in a way that should not limit Congress in its continuing quest to cleanse the electoral process. More likely still, Congress may well adopt new legislation designed to limit even further advertisements that appear on television. McCain-Feingold, after all, bans only ads that mention the name of a candidate for office. When efforts are made to "circumvent" that statute by *not* mentioning the name of a candidate but still taking positions that might be deemed helpful to one candidate or harmful to another, will new legislation be brought to bear by a determinedly regulatory Congress?

I can well imagine a reform lawyer of the future defending new statutes limiting freedom of expression during political campaigns, laws that might put at risk not only the *Tornillo* case but *Mills v. Alabama*, which I initially described to my All Souls audience. *Mills* had involved a ban on certain editorials on Election Day to help voters avoid being too influenced by confusing last-minute changes. Just one day, Alabama's lawyer had argued. Just one day, and for such a good cause. In *Mills*, the Supreme Court had unanimously said no to such arguments, affirming that discussions of candidates were at the core of the First Amendment.

In the *McConnell* case the plea had been comparable. We are doing so little, defenders of the statute maintained, and for such a good cause. Only within sixty days of an election, only if the name of a candidate is mentioned, only if the other statutory requirements are met, the McCain-Feingold supporters argued, are we limiting speech at all. That the speech being limited was the very speech the Court in *Mills* had concluded was so central to the First Amendment was of no moment to the five jurists who voted to sustain McCain-Feingold.

Do I exaggerate? Did Justice Thomas when he concluded that the decision was "the most significant abridgement of the freedom of speech and association since the Civil War"?

On some levels, the impact of McCain-Feingold in the 2004 election remains ambiguous. To the extent the law was adopted to limit the amount of money spent on elections, it certainly failed at that. In 2004, campaign spending *increased* by about $1 billion from the amount expended in 2000, to about $4 billion. At the same time, corporate and union spending decreased significantly, one of the results sought by the framers of the legislation (and one, as I had predicted in response to a question of Justice Breyer, that was by no means offset by PAC spending). Simultaneously, however, the spending of almost $500 million by so-called 527 groups (named after the section of the Internal Revenue code that permitted their formation) played a far greater role in the election than had previously been thought imaginable, a problem, as Senator McCain and others view it, likely to lead to still further efforts at "reform"—

or, as I view it, at diminishing the amount of speech.

It is in the area of limitations on corporations and union-sponsored advertisements that McCain-Feingold has particularly vindicated the fears of the Supreme Court dissenters. To comply with the new law in the months before the 2004 election, the Chamber of Commerce of the United States, a pro-business group, had to abandon its plans to broadcast advertisements supporting class-action reform legislation which mentioned the names of senators and congressmen whose votes the Chamber coveted. At the same time, and for the same reason, the AFL-CIO was forced to forego its efforts to broadcast advertisements criticizing federal overtime regulations issued by the Department of Labor in which the union wished to identify names of members of Congress that it sought to pressure to vote their way. As for the ACLU, it ultimately broadcast advertisements denouncing the Patriot Act but refrained, as McCain-Feingold required, from criticizing (or even mentioning) President Bush as it did so.

To me, this is nothing less than outright suppression of speech of the most odious nature. I have personally seen the same First Amendment-destructive impact of the new law. Michael Moore's controversial movie *Fahrenheit 9/11* was advertised in the early summer with a segment featuring President Bush gravely warning terrorists and then, as the camera pulled back, proceeding only a second later to hit a golf shot with the club he held in his hand. Showing this disquieting and damning sequence in an advertisement for the movie was illegal in August, 2004, under McCain-Feingold, since the distributors of the movie were forbidden to include Bush's name or likeness in any ad broadcast within thirty days of the Republican convention. And so Susan Buckley and I advised Lions Gate, the movie's distributor, that for all of August as well as for most of September and all of October, the sequence could not be shown. When a conservative group called Citizens United (one that had supported our battle against McCain-Feingold) filed a complaint with the Federal Election Commission claiming—without the slightest basis—that it had reason to believe that advertisements for Moore's documentary would continue into August, we responded with language that any devotee of censorship would savor: no, we said, Lion's Gate had no intention of running the ads in August. That was enough for the federal agency, which promptly ruled in our favor.

Shortly after that encounter, I received a call from Alex Gigante, the general counsel of Penguin Group (USA), which was about to release a book by Senator John Kerry. Kerry was clearly listed as its author, his picture on the cover. "Is there anything in the new campaign finance law that could be problematic?" Gigante asked me. "Yes," I said. "There is one thing: you can't advertise the book on radio or television at all for the entire month of July leading up to the Democratic convention, for almost all of September, and for every day of October." That antidemocratic achievement, I said, was directly attributable to McCain-Feingold.

Gigante listened to me in disbelief and then asked the unavoidable question: "Is that law constitutional?"

"Not under my First Amendment," I told him. "Not under mine."

CHAPTER 9

AT HOME AND ABROAD

Not long after our Pentagon Papers victory in 1971, I traveled to England, France, and Israel. In all three nations I met with judges, attorneys, and journalists, and was told that it would have been unthinkable to permit a newspaper to publish such material in their countries. Even journalists were stunned by the outcome of the case in the United States and not at all sure that it was a good idea.

The difference in approach here and abroad to issues concerning freedom of speech remains startling. How many of the cases described in earlier chapters in this book could have been won in, say, England? The answer may well be *none*. Not one of them would have resulted in a certain victory for the equivalent of the First Amendment side, and most of them plainly would have been decided to the contrary. All the cases involving prior restraints on the press described in chapters 1 and 2 would have been decided against the press—not just the Pentagon Papers case itself, but the *Nebraska Press Association* ruling as well. Publication of classified national security information not only would have violated British criminal law, but would have been subject to a prior restraint before publication. British law, as the distinguished British barrister and human rights attorney Geoffrey Robertson has written, ensures that "the British equivalent of the Pentagon Papers would never see the light of day." As for publication after an indictment and before the trial of the prior criminal record of a defendant, that would constitute a contempt of court leading to the likely jailing of the editor responsible for it. That was true forty years ago; it remains true today.

The cases described in chapter 3, relating to punishment of the press for telling the truth about sensitive matters, would all have been determined in England against the journalists involved. Statutes that barred publication of one or more pieces of truthful information—the name of a judge, the name of a juvenile, the voices on an intercepted wiretap—would have been deemed the subjects of legitimate criminal punishment.

Each of the three libel cases described in chapters 4 through 6 would likely have been decided against the press. England has no equivalent of the requirement established in *New York Times Co. v. Sullivan* in 1964 that a plaintiff can prevail in a libel action relating to matters of public interest only by proving a level of fault in the preparation of the challenged article. The cases described involved ultimate press victories based on the failure of the plaintiffs to prove precisely that. In *Newton*, Mr. Las Vegas failed to prove that material about him was broadcast with actual malice—that is, with knowledge of its falsity or with serious doubts as to its truth. In *Karaduman*, the Istanbul businessman failed to prove the statements about him were published with gross irresponsibility. Only the *Lasky* case might have been decided in England as it was here, since the jury determined that Lasky had failed to prove that the information broadcast about him was false. But even with respect to that issue, the law leans far more strongly in favor of journalists here than in England. One of the critical determinations of the Supreme Court in *New York Times Co. v. Sullivan* was that a plaintiff has the burden (what the English call the "onus") of demonstrating that statements made about him were false. That is why Lasky was obliged to prove that what ABC had said about him was false, rather than ABC being obliged to prove that what it said was true. In England, no such burden rests upon a plaintiff. It is the speaker or publisher that must demonstrate that what was said was true, a difference of emphasis that may sound like legal legerdemain but that has enormous real-world consequences in a courtroom.

The Brooklyn Museum case is probably the closest call of all. While an English equivalent of Mayor Giuliani might have lost his argument on the grounds that he did not have the power to cut off funding for a museum, that result is not a certainty. What does seem certain is that even a Giuliani defeat in England would not have been based on principles rooted in the nature of free expression itself. Judge Gershon's careful analysis of the law relating to free speech would have seemed alien indeed to a British court. The same would be true of any challenge to any new English equivalent of the McCain-Feingold law. (England already has one that permits less speech than does ours.) English courts do not have the power to strike down laws enacted by Parliament as unconstitutional, and while English courts are now obliged under the Human Rights Act adopted in 1998 to abide by the European Covenant on Human Rights (a document that provides significant free speech protection, although less than here), there is no chance at all that the constitutionality of a campaign finance statute such as was enacted in this country would have posed a close call for any English or European court.

To state that we have a different body of law than exists in England and other democratic nations is not, of course, to imply that our law is necessarily wiser than what exists abroad. We protect so-called "hate speech," speech that denigrates the race or religion of others. We don't like the speech or deny that it can do harm, but we protect it under the broad legal umbrella provided by the First Amendment. There is an inevitable trade-off in doing so. By broadly protecting such speech, we avoid the risks of suppressing valuable speech that could be argued to be unacceptably offensive to others—Salman Rushdie's *The Satanic Verses,* for example, which was banned in most of the Muslim world. We avoid the sort of speech-destructive efforts routinely made abroad to ban books such as Oriana Fallaci's recent impassioned attack on Islamic radicalism. Perhaps most important, we avoid legitimizing direct governmental censorship of speech based upon its content.

In England, Canada, France, Germany, and virtually every other democratic nation in the world, hate speech is banned. International treaties and conventions call upon nations not only to bar racial and other forms of discrimination but to ban *speech* advocating such behavior as well. The United States duly signed the International Convention on the Elimination of All Forms of Racial Discrimination, but President Jimmy Carter did so by adding a legally binding reservation declaring that "nothing in this Convention shall be deemed to require or authorize legislation or other actions by the United States which would restrict the right of free speech protected by the Constitution."

Are we right to continue to insist on safeguarding freedom of speech to such an extent? For our particular culture, I think we are. It may be the case that in India permitting the denigration of one religion by believers in another will inevitably lead to communal strife. It may be that in postwar Germany permitting people to deny the reality of the Holocaust was an unacceptable risk to take. Both countries may thus have acted consistently with their needs in criminalizing such speech. Other circumstances in other nations may justify less protection of freedom of expression than we have embodied in the First Amendment.

But the history of suppression of speech abroad has led me to conclude that, as Supreme Court Justice Byron White put it in *Miami Herald v. Tornillo*, "we have learned, and continue to learn, from what we view as the unhappy experiences of other nations" that have allowed "government to insinuate itself into the editorial rooms" of the press. The same is true of nations—often the same nations—that have permitted governments to decide what individuals may or may not say. "The right to think," Justice Anthony Kennedy observed last year, "is the beginning of freedom, and speech must be protected from the government because speech is the beginning of thought."

We are not alone in the world in protecting free expression. Indeed, in one recent case in which I was involved, an international court provided at least as much protection in a matter relating to freedom of the press as any American court would have. The case arose in 2002 before the International Criminal Tribunal for the former Yugoslavia in The Hague. In the midst of preparations for the trial of Serbian leader Radoslav

Brdjanin, who was accused of war crimes in Bosnia, the prosecution sought the testimony of Jonathan Randal, a former *Washington Post* reporter who had interviewed the defendant about his views regarding ethnic cleansing. Randal resisted testifying in the absence of a demonstration by the prosecution that his testimony was essential to the case, and that the substance of it could not be obtained in any other manner. Geoffrey Robertson represented Randal. I represented a group of forty journalists and journalistic organizations from around the world that supported Randal, a group that I believe I fairly characterized to the tribunal as probably the largest and most diverse group of its kind ever to join a single brief. After an argument before jurists from France, Guyana, Sri Lanka, Turkey, and the United States, the court unanimously ruled that Randal could not be required to testify in the absence of a demonstration by the prosecution of the centrality of the information he had and the unavailability of that information from other sources.

It was an extraordinary victory, not least because it provided protections for war correspondents that went far beyond those afforded journalists in many, if not most, reported decisions in the United States. So far as I know, it is the only ruling of an international tribunal to address the issue, and it is thus all the more significant as a possible precursor of future rulings. But it remains rare for rulings abroad to provide anything like the level of legal protection for journalists or others involved in communicating their views that is provided in the United States.

Except in one area. Increasingly, in countries that are fairly regarded as democratic, journalists are not required to identify their confidential sources of information. In a number of European nations including Germany, France, and Austria, there are no circumstances in which journalists may be required to break their word to their confidential sources by identifying them. In many other nations ranging from Japan to Canada to New Zealand, the rule is that confidential sources are protected, with exceptions being few and narrow. In Sweden, for example, not only are confidential sources protected, but it is a breach of law for journalists to reveal their sources.

A typical ruling abroad with regard to this subject was that of the European Court of Human Rights, which concluded in 1996 that:

> Protection of journalistic sources is one of the basic conditions for press freedom, as is reflected in the laws and the professional codes of conduct in a number of Contracting States and is affirmed in several international instruments on journalistic freedoms. Without such protection, sources may be deterred from assisting the press in informing the public on matters of public

interest. As a result the vital public watchdog role of the press may be undermined and the ability of the press to provide accurate and reliable information may be adversely affected. Having regard to the importance of the protection of journalistic sources for press freedom in a democratic society and the potentially chilling effect an order of source disclosure has on the exercise of that freedom, such a measure cannot be compatible with the [European] Convention unless it is justified by an overriding requirement in the public interest.

In the United States the situation is bleaker. While forty-nine of the fifty states have provided total or partial protection for confidential sources, and many federal courts have done so as well, a number of courts in recent years have provided little or no protection at all. Worse yet, a spate of "leak investigations," in which journalists have been targeted to reveal the identities of individuals who provided them, in confidence, with information, have posed increasing threats to the ability of the press to do its job.

As I conclude this book in late 2004, two clients of mine—Judith Miller of the *New York Times* and Matt Cooper of *Time* magazine—have been ordered jailed in Washington, D.C., because they refused to reveal the identities of government officials who provided them with information in confidence. At the same time, the Bush administration has sought to obtain the telephone records of Ms. Miller and another *Times* journalist, Phil Shenon, in a different leak investigation in Chicago, an effort that would, if successful, reveal scores of sources who provided information who have nothing to do with the government's investigation. Other efforts have been made by the federal government in places from Providence, Rhode Island, to San Francisco, California, to require journalists to disclose their sources.

These cases may be close ones from a legal perspective in light of the Supreme Court's decision in 1972 in the first case described in this book, the confidential source ruling of the U.S. Supreme Court in *Branzburg v. Hayes*. But it is not the *Branzburg* case that has led to this new threat to the ability of journalists to gather information. It is a purposeful decision made by federal prosecutors, usually authorized by the attorney general's office itself, that the disclosure in one leak investigation after another of who provided information to the press is more important than the press's ability to gather news and report it to the public. American lawyers rarely fare well when they try to persuade our courts to adopt rulings from abroad. But I would feel a lot more comfortable about the future if our judges would weigh carefully the conclusion of the European Court of Human Rights, expressed in 2003, that "the protection of journalistic sources is one of the cornerstones of freedom of the press."

Any comparison of foreign and American approaches to free speech leads me inevitably back to the question of why I changed my mind so radically about the amount of legal protection that the First Amendment should provide from my original views on the subject. Unavoidably, part of my shift in attitude stemmed from what I was saying on behalf of my clients. Lawyers don't have to agree with their clients, to condone (not to say approve of) their conduct, or to share their ideological preferences. But it is not uncommon for lawyers to persuade themselves of their clients' virtues. Sometimes that is harmful: A lawyer who is too close to a client may be the same fool the client would be if he were representing himself. On other occasions, such advocacy is both genuine (the lawyer *means* it) and useful (the lawyer can speak with special zeal on behalf of the client). I think my own evolution was the latter, not self-induced, but the product of what I had learned.

But my change of mind was rooted in even more than that.

I began to practice in this area at about the same time President Richard Nixon began to take on the press and, more important, to threaten constitutional liberties. When Nixon served as president, it was unnecessary to cite John Adams's sponsorship of the Alien and Sedition Acts to exemplify the risks that an administration might pose to constitutional government. Nixon was a self-proving risk, and his constitutional misbehavior in office led me to understand far better than I had previously the need for broadly interpreted protections of the Bill of Rights.

I came to the view, as well, that what I had previously dismissed (as some people still do) as mere self-serving rhetoric of journalists about the need for a free and unthreatened press was in fact firmly rooted in reality. Journalists made their share of mistakes, and continue to do so, but I concluded that they genuinely served the public in a manner that should only rarely be subject to any legislative or judicially imposed sanctions. The libel cases discussed in this book are illustrative of why the press should remain as free as our law permits. The behavior of a figure such as Wayne Newton prior to and in the very process of being licensed by a state in which he was both "worshipped" (as his counsel put it) and enormously powerful was of genuine public import. So was *Newsday*'s effort to set forth in terms all could understand the path of heroin from the poppy fields of Turkey to the bars of Long Island. So, as well, was the elegiac portrayal thirty years after the fact of the on-the-ground impact of McCarthyism in a small West Virginia town.

Many of the printed articles or televised segments that I have defended in the courts have served the public exceptionally well. *Time* magazine's valiant cover story depicting the ever-ominous and indefatigably litigious Church of Scientology as a "cult of greed" led to a seemingly endless and paralyzingly expensive litigation. Nina Totenberg's exposé on National Public Radio of Anita Hill's charges against Clarence Thomas led to a prolonged Senate "leak investigation" seeking to expose her sources. Both stories were in the best tradition of journalism, and the authors of both needed the strongest legal protection to protect them. *Time* defeated its Scientology foes, and the Totenberg investigation was ultimately abandoned. But they were both deeply threatening to the journalists involved, and only the high level of First Amendment protection that exists in the United States ensured victory for them. The same is true of other cases described in the preceding chapters. Had First Amendment law been weaker, the members of the Brooklyn Museum's board would have had a far tougher decision to make about resisting the enormous pressure that Mayor Giuliani placed upon them. Had anything but American-level First Amendment protections existed, the *New York Times* could have been shut up and shut down because of its publication of the Pentagon Papers.

While my work has led me to the view that sweeping First Amendment protections are essential to protect us against efforts—in bad faith or good—to limit speech, that does not mean that I believe that the institutional press or the multitude of speakers that now fill the Internet with information are free from error or that what is published and otherwise communicated does no harm. A free press is not necessarily an accurate or wise one. Precisely because speech matters so much, it can do great harm, and in fact sometimes does so. Our approach under the First Amendment has wisely, I think, generally been to risk suffering the harm that speech may do in order to avoid the greater harm that suppression of speech has often caused.

Protecting freedom of speech in as sweeping a fashion as the First Amendment does, however, makes it all the more important that we also both protect and honor thoughtful critics of the press and of others who exercise their First Amendment rights. We are not obliged to honor those who substitute ideologically rooted fervor for rigorous analysis. But some critics are entitled to special kudos.

Renata Adler has published two books containing pungent and powerful criticism of the performance of some of the leading journalistic organizations in the nation. In *Reckless Disregard*, she takes on both *Time* magazine and CBS for their coverage of the events that led to the prominent libel litigations commenced in the 1980s by former Israeli defense minister (and now prime minister) Ariel Sharon and by former general William Westmoreland. In *Canaries in the Mineshaft*, she takes on the *New York Times* for some of its recent coverage. I have represented all three of these institutions on a variety of matters, including one that involved the publication of some of the journalism that Adler savages. I know how angry her books have made the authors of each of the offerings she has criticized, and how strongly all of them believe that her criticism is wrong-headed and unfair. I will leave that debate to another forum. What is more important, I think, is that Adler be honored for writing the most scintillating press criticism in the nation over the past few decades.

Here she is, setting the stage for her analysis, in *Reckless Disregard*:

> With few and small exceptions—*The Nation*, say, or the *National Review*—an American no longer expects from his source of news a political viewpoint that comports with his own. His expectation, as in no other country and at no other time in history, is rather this: that, *given* the technology of news gathering and dissemination, given also the scale, the news is going to be, honestly and within human limits, factual. Whether it is a tabloid reporting a sensational murder or a network reporting a political coup somewhere, there is a trust that what is being reported (with the aura of authenticity not just of the printed word but of tape recordings and photographs) is factually true. And the contemporary American journalist aspires, in theory and

as a professional matter, to meet that honorable, essentially moral expectation. The difficulty is that most facts, at least those with which journalism is concerned, are what they are; and, in spite of bromides to the effect that there is no such thing as objectivity in journalism, statements of fact are either true or not. Their implications, political and other, are, of course, another matter; but the "truth" of the facts in question tends to be unitary—tends, in an almost religious sense, to be one. No one disputes this with respect to those subjects on which so much of reporting, at all times, depends: the Yankees won on a certain day or they did not, and by a certain score; the people whose deaths are reported in the obituary section held certain positions and are dead, or not. Stock closing prices, earthquakes, invasions, election returns. It is only with stories of another kind that the unitary standard seems to waver and meditations about objectivity begin. The reporter, meanwhile, not only wants to find out and report the facts; as a competitor, he wants to report them before anybody else. And the difficulty with that form of competition is that once a journalist has been the first to publish certain "facts" amounting to a "story" all other journalists tend to go after the *same* story, wanting only to tell more of it, sooner. At the same time, there has arisen in the profession an almost unimaginable solidarity; it is exceptionally rare for a story in one publication to contradict, or even to take the mildest exception to, a story published in another. Whether by temperament, or for whatever other reason, whatever rivalry exists, however intense it may be, is the rivalry of a pack going essentially in one direction. There is simply no notion, for instance, among journalists of a counter-scoop—and journalists are notoriously vindictive when the work of any of their number is criticized in print.

That is serious stuff, which remains thoughtful, incisive, and provocative, whether or not one still agrees with it in the aftermath of the noisy and contentious addition of Fox News to the ranks of news providers.

So has the writing of Professor Jay Rosen of New York University, who crafted a revealing essay about the press treatment of the speech that the then newly elected president Vaclav Havel of Czechoslovakia gave in Washington on his first official visit in 1990. Havel had been jailed for years under Communist rule for his writing, and Washington—bipartisan Washington—was delighted to welcome him. Near the end of Havel's address to Congress, Rosen recounted, he observed that the people of Eastern

Europe could offer to the West lessons of their "bitter experience" under Communist domination. That experience, Havel said, had left him certain of this proposition: "Consciousness precedes being, and not the other way around, as the Marxists claimed."

Havel's words, Rosen wrote, led members of Congress to break into hearty applause—but hearty applause without the slightest understanding of what they were applauding. The press was amused. The *Boston Globe* wrote about the speech as follows: "Whaaaat? A real, live philosophical notion? Discussed in front of our congresspeople? What gives? Hey, folks, the man is an intellectual." The *Washington Post* editorial about the speech referred to it as "impressive and humbling"; it observed that Havel "is not kidding about this stuff," and head-lined its editorial "Let's Hear It for Hegel." And a *Washington Times* article put it this way: "I don't think ten men in the chamber knew what he was talking about, and in fact, I don't know what he was talking about."

One thing was missing from the bemused press commentary about the speech: No reporter, not one, even tried to *explain* what Havel was talking about. Journalists, Rosen observed, who had mastered matters of complex economics and of sophisticated weapons systems, laughed at Congress, even laughed a bit at themselves—but made not the slightest effort to understand what Havel was saying or to tell their readers what Havel's words might have meant. The portrait of

Havel offered by journalists to its readers was thus that of "a speaker of alien discourse."

The answer, Rosen argued, "has less to do with a lingering anti-intellectualism in the press than with its resistance to a certain kind of discourse. To raise the issue of 'consciousness' is to speak frankly of the inner life, rather than outward events. Journalists tend to dismiss such talk, but not because they are godless technocrats unmoved by deeper questions. They are simply more interested in the game of power, and they consider ideas about the nature of 'being' irrelevant to their journalistic task."

That, too, is serious criticism of the press written at a level that should shame most press critics.

There remains another sort of response to free speech—suppression. I began this book with a discussion of censorship around the world in the twentieth century, and I close with one example. Early in the 1990s I was asked to speak at a law school in Kuala Lumpur, Malaysia. My topic was freedom of speech, a somewhat anomalous topic in a nation that is not known throughout the world as being a leading protector of it. Malaysia did not approach its neighbor in Singapore in its degree of repression of speech (I have yet to be invited there), but it remained an authoritarian nation in which free speech as we understand it is hardly the rule. One example of this was the banning in that nation of Salman Rushdie's work *The Satanic Verses*.

I spoke to the Malaysian students for about an hour about American cases. The Pentagon Papers case, in particular, startled them. "Wasn't the *New York Times* afraid that it would lose its license?" one student asked. When I explained that the *Times* had no license and that it would be unconstitutional—a difficult concept to explain—for the government to require one, they were nonplussed.

Then they asked about what really interested them. Had I read *The Satanic Verses*? Yes, I lied. Had I liked it? Yes, I said. Was it blasphemous? No, I said, adding that in the United States there was no legal doctrine of blasphemy, anyway. No book could be suppressed because it was critical of, even hostile to, religion. They liked that answer.

I turned the questioning back on them. "*The Satanic Verses* is banned here," I said. "If I had brought it into your country, I could have been arrested. How do you even know about it?" Their eyes shone as they answered: "CNN," they said, "CNN."

I gave that talk ten years ago, in pre-Internet days. If students then knew about Rushdie's book notwithstanding the position of their government, today they could probably read it despite their government's opposition. That is real, ultimately irresistible, progress. You don't have to be a First Amendment voluptuary to believe that.

ACKNOWLEDGMENTS

Litigation is a team sport and no book by me about my cases can conclude without my offering my warm thanks to the team at my law firm, Cahill Gordon & Reindel, LLP, that toiled so diligently on the cases depicted in these pages. Naturally enough, the team changed through the years. Some of my partners with whom I worked closely have retired or passed on, and many of my associates have moved on to other endeavors. That is the way of the world. All of them were essential to the legal efforts described in this book, and all made inestimable contributions to our successes.

The team was not limited to lawyers. From the secretaries and proofreaders who worked with us days, nights, and weekends to the telephone operators who placed (and shielded me from) calls, from the librarians who obtained books and other research materials to the paralegals who assisted us in all aspects of our work, an enormous number of deeply committed and extraordinarily talented people gave their all in all the cases described. I will always be in their debt.

As for this book itself, I offer my special thanks to Susan Buckley, Bill Goldman, Connie Bruck, and especially to my devoted children, Daniel and Ronnie, for reading it all and providing much needed encouragement and advice. I appreciate the enthusiastic and talented assistance of Jaynie Randall in the preparation of the endnotes. Without the cajoling of my agent and friend, Karen Gantz Zahler, to write the book and then her advice about writing it, no book would have been written. And only with the counsel and assistance of my editor, Rick Kot, would the book read as it does.

I owe special thanks to Kate Preston, who not only typed every word of this manuscript in-numerable times over the past two years, but advised me on numerous painful choices of voca-bulary, and to my assistant, Denise Fox O'Neill, who helped and often led me to structure my life at the office so I could survive the day-to-day perils of existence and still complete this manuscript.

Finally, I owe more thanks than words can convey to my wife, Efrat, and to my two children. They were the ones who paid the real price when I was away from home for extended periods, whether in Washington, Las Vegas, or even New York. A lawyer who is as consumed with his cases as I am is too often not really home even when he sleeps in his own bed. This book is for them.

NOTES

EPIGRAPH

vii   **"security of the Nation":** The quotation is from the trial court decision in the Pentagon Papers case. *U.S. v. New York Times*, 328 F. Supp. 324 (S.D.N.Y. 1971).

INTRODUCTION

xi   For all references to *New York Times* articles in this chapter, see *Political Censorship* (Robert Justin Goldstein, ed., 2001).

xii   **"by no means clear":** Emerson's piece may be found at Thomas I. Emerson, "Colonial Intentions and Current Realities of the First Amendment, 125 *University of Pennsylvania Law Review* 737 (1977), p. 37; Chafee's views are set forth in Zachariah Chafee, Book Review, 62 *Harvard Law Review* 891 (1949), p. 898.

xiii   **Bill of Rights:** The Court's declaration appears in *Duncan v. Louisiana*, 391 U.S. 145, 153 (1968).

xiv   **As for the First Amendment:** Michael Kent Curtis discusses the English and colonial background to the adoption of the First Amendment in Michael Kent Curtis, *Free Speech, 'The People's Darling Privilege''* (2000) in chapter 1.

xiv   **Sedition Act:** Geoffrey R. Stone offers a striking commentary on the Act on pages 33-34 of *Perilous Times: Free Speech in Wartime* (2004).

xv   **Not until 1925:** *Gitlow v. N.Y.*, 268 U.S. 652 (1925) contained the first indication that the First Amendment would apply to the states. *Near v. Minnesota*, 283 U.S. 697 (1931) represents one of the first major victories of First Amendment claims vis-à-vis a state statute.

xix   **"perfectly logical":** Justice Holmes's admonition appears in *Abrams v. U.S.*, 250 U.S. 616, 630 (1919) (Holmes, J. dissenting). An exhaustive and evocative description of the case is set forth in Richard Pollenberg, *Fighting Faiths: The Abrams Case, The Supreme Court and Free Speech* (1987). Justice Brandeis's famous quotation comes from *Whitney v. California*, 274 U.S. 357, 376 (1927) (Brandeis, J. concurring). For Holmes's opinions, see *Abrams v. U.S.*, 250 U.S. 616 (1919) (Holmes, J. dissenting); *Gitlow v. N.Y.*, 268 U.S. 652, 672 (1925) (Holmes, J. dissenting).

xx   **Several cases from the 1940s:** The cases

referred to are: *Bridges v. California*, 314 U.S. 252 (1941); *Pennekamp v. Florida*, 328 U.S. 331 (1946); and *Craig v. Harney*, 331 U.S. 367 (1947). Justice Brennan's opinion for the Court in *New York Times v. Sullivan* is at 376 U.S. 254 (1964).

xxiv **author of a forthcoming book:** Professor Bickel's book was published in 1957. Alexander M. Bickel, *The Unpublished Opinions of Mr. Justice Brandeis* (1957).

xxiv **Declaration of Independence:** Justice Thomas's writings on the Declaration include Clarence Thomas, "Toward a 'Plain Reading' of the Constitution: The Declaration of Independence in Constitutional Interpretation," 30 *Howard Law Journal* 983 (1987).

xxvi **political scientist who had written:** Mason's biographies of Justices Brandeis and Stone are Alpheus Thomas Mason, *Brandeis: A Free Man's Life* (1996); and Alpheus Thomas Mason, *Harlan Fiske Stone: Pillar of the Law* (1956).

CHAPTER I: THE PENTAGON PAPERS CASE

This chapter focuses on *U.S. v. New York Times Co.*, 328 F. Supp. 324 (S.D.N.Y. 1974), *remanded* 444 F.2d 544 (2d Cir. 1971); *reversed* 403 U.S. 713 (1971).

3   **agreeing to hear one of the cases:** The case eventually heard by the Court about journalists' confidential sources was *Branzburg v. Hayes*, 408 U.S. 665 (1972).

18   **as James Reston later wrote:** Reston recorded his own recollection on page 39 of James Reston, *Deadline: A Memoir* (1991).

20   **"The two of them":** Haldeman's own account of the Nixon administration's response appears in H. R. Haldeman, *The Ends of Power* (1978), p. 155. Additional material is quoted from Charles W. Colson, *Born Again: What Really Happened to the White House Hatchet* (1976), p. 57, and Richard Reeves, *President Nixon: Alone in the White House* (2001), p. 333.

20   **"based on factors":** Prados and Parker summarize the absence of any basis for the case on pages 149-50 of *Inside the Pentagon Papers* (2004).

22   **as one author put it:** Paul Hoffman's apt analogy capturing the *Time*s's dire situation is on page 102 of Paul Hoffman, *Lions in the Street* (1973).

25   **"prevent all such previous restraints":** Justice Holmes's extremely narrow description of the purpose of the First Amendment is on page 462 of *Patterson v. Colorado*, 205 U.S. 454 (1907). The 1931 opinion adverting to the publication of sailing schedules is *Near v. Minnesota*, 283 U.S. 697 (1931). Justice

Harlan's opinion rejecting prior restraints is in *Curtis Pub. Co. v. Butts*, 388 U.S. 130, 149 (1967).

30 **Mitchell told Nixon:** The text of the entire Nixon-Mitchell June 15, 1971, telephone call is set forth in John Prados and Margaret Pratt Porter, *Inside the Pentagon Papers* (2004), pp. 111-13.

33 **Reston was dining:** I first learned of the Reston-McNamara dinner in Harrison E. Salisbury, *Without Fear or Favor: The New York Times and Its Times* (1980), p. 245. See also John F. Stacks, *Scotty: James B. Reston and the Rise and Fall of American Journalism* (2002), p. 305.

37 **the solace of a *Washington Post* story:** The immortalizing article is Sanford J. Ungar, "Court Upholds FDA on Seizure of Detergent," *Washington Post*, Aug. 3, 1971, p. B1.

50 **phrased it in a more literary way:** Harrison E. Salisbury, *Without Fear or Favor: The New York Times and Its Times* (1980), pp. 303-4.

CHAPTER II: TO THE SUPREME COURT AND AFTER

The references in this chapter to the Pentagon Papers case refer to transcripts, briefs, and the opinions rendered in *U.S. v. New York Times Co.*, 403 U.S. 713 (1971).

52 **"extraordinary"**: David Rudenstine's observations appear on pages 224-25 of *The Day the Presses Stopped: A History of the Pentagon Papers Case* (1996).

62 **widely acclaimed book:** Griswold's book mentioned in the text is *The Fifth Amendment Today: Three Speeches* (1955).

81 **An article in the *William & Mary*:** Professor Sims's piece may be found at John Cary Sims, "Triangulating the Boundaries of the Pentagon Papers," 2 *William & Mary Bill of Rights Journal* 341 (1993).

85 **"Although the assessment states":** Mardian's memorandum assessing the impact of publishing the Pentagon Papers is on file with the author. Griswold's 1989 op-ed article is available at Erwin N. Griswold, Editorial, "Secrets Not Worth Keeping; The Courts and Classified Information," *Washington Post*, Feb. 15, 1989, p. A25.

86 **Much did change as a result:** Comments from Charles Nesson, Secretary Vance, Fred W. Friendly, and Professor Benno Schmidt were part of the research for Floyd Abrams, "The Pentagon Papers a Decade Later," *New York Times Magazine*, June 7, 1981, p. 22.

90 **"I appear here today":** The reference to the *Nebraska Press Association* case is to *Nebraska Press Ass'n v. Stuart*, 427 U.S. 539 (1976).

95 **"asking us to ride herd":** Judge Robb's

case reference here was in the *Washington Post*'s portion of the Pentagon Papers Case, *U.S. v. Washington Post Co.*, 446 F. 2d 1322 (1971).

96 **"Law . . . can never make us as secure"**: Bickel's poignant commentary on the nature of law is found on page 60 of Alexander M. Bickel, *The Morality of Consent* (1975).

98 **"the First Amendment tolerates"**: Justice Brennan's comments on prior restraints are on page 725 of his concurrence in the Pentagon Papers case.

CHAPTER III: TRUTH AND THE FIRST AMENDMENT

The primary cases discussed in this chapter are *Landmark Communications Inc. v. Virginia*, 233 S.E. 2d 120, (Va. 1977), *reversed*, 435 U.S. 829, (1978) and *Smith v. Daily Mail Publishing Co.*, 443 U.S. 97 (1979).

101 **The "way we cover news"**: David Broder's insights appear on page 19 of David S. Broder, *Behind the Front Page* (First Free Paperback Edition 1987). The quotation from Walter Lippmann is from his book *Public Opinion*, initially published in 1922. The quotation appears on p. 229 of the paperback version published in 1965.

102 **"overarching public interest"**: The Supreme Court's characterization of the

value of truth-telling appears in *The Florida Star v. B.J.F.*, 491 U.S. 524 (1989).

107 **The first of these cases:** The full reference for *Schenck v. U.S.* is 249 U.S. 47 (1919). Holmes's later dissents, cited in the text, include *Abrams v. U.S.*, 250 U.S., 616 (1919).

118 **corporations have free-speech rights:** The Court considered these issues in *First National Bank of Boston v. Bellotti*, 435 U.S. 765 (1978).

136 **1974 case of *Davis v. Alaska:*** The complete citation for *Davis v. Alaska* is 415 U.S. 308 (1974).

150 **Most recently, in 2001, the Supreme Court:** *Bartnicki v. Volper*, 532 U.S. 514 (2001). The quotations from Justice Scalia's opinion in *Florida Star* are at 491 U.S. at 541-542.

CHAPTER IV: WAYNE NEWTON AND THE LAW

The Wayne Newton case is the focus of this chapter. The ruling of the Ninth Circuit is at *Newton v. National Broadcasting Company*, 930 F. 2d 662 (9th Cir. 1990), *cert. denied*, 502 U.S. 866 (1991).

154 **"Las Vegas today":** Otto von Friedrich's observations of Las Vegas are taken from p. 289 of Otto von Friedrich, *City of Nets*

(1997). A recent book describes Senator McCarran more fully. Michael J. Ybarra, *Washington Gone Crazy: Senator Pat McCarran and the Great Communist Hunt* (2004).

201 **Newton admirers:** The references in the text to Newton and his acolytes appear in Ed Koch, "Wayne Newton Recalls Resort's Troubled Past," *Las Vegas Sun*, Aug. 18, 2000, and Carolyn Carpenter, "Wayne Newton," *Las Vegan Magazine*, available at www.lasvegan.net/lvn_issues/issue_0500/newton.html.

CHAPTER V: THE HEROIN TRAIL

An earlier depiction of this case before my firm's involvement is *Karaduman v. Newsday, Inc.*, 435 N.Y.S. 2d 556 (N.Y. 1980). There is no written opinion about the trial, and no appeal was taken.

204 **Newsday published the result:** The book form of "The Heroin Trail" articles is The Staff and Editors of *Newsday*, *The Heroin Trail: The First Journalistic Investigation to Trace Heroin Traffic from Turkey to France to Its Ultimate Consumer—The Young American Addict!* (1974).

CHAPTER VI: MCCARTHYISM AND LIBEL

The case of *Lasky v. American Broadcasting Co.*

led to no posttrial opinion and no appeal. A pretrial ruling in the case is set forth in 606 F. Supp. 934 (S.O.N.Y. 1985).

252 Victor Lasky's publications mentioned here are: *JFK:The Man & The Myth* (1963); *Arthur J. Goldberg, the Old and the New* (1970); *RFK Myth and Man* (1971); *The Ugly Russian* (1965). Additionally, see Ralph de Toledano and Victor Lasky, *Seeds of Treason: the True Story of the Hiss-Chambers Tragedy* (1950).

289 **Robinson had himself written:** Edward G. Robinson's autobiography is Edward G. Robinson with Leonard Spigelgass, *All My Yesterdays: An Autobiography* (1973).

CHAPTER VII: THE BROOKLYN MUSEUM CASE

The case discussed in this chapter is *Brooklyn Institute of the Arts and Sciences v. City of New York*, 64 F. Supp. 2d 184 (E.D.N.Y. 1999).

306 **When recent college graduates:** The data from a poll of recent college graduates appears on p. 13 of the January 2003 issue of *Harper's* magazine. Giuliani was honored as *Time* magazine's Person of the Year in 2001.

307 **In three separate lawsuits:** A sample of the First Amendment litigation during the Giuliani administration is catalogued in Victor A. Kovner, Edward J. Davis & Matthew A. Leish,

"The Mayor Versus the First Amendment: Will the Fight Last a Full Fifteen Rounds?" 18 *Communications Lawyer* 1 (2000).

309 **"it seems as if I could teach":** Professor Adler's comments are in Associated Press, "NYC Mayor Hot Topic at Law Schools," Dec. 2, 1999. The quotation from the Second Circuit on the attacks on the First Amendment during Giuliani's tenure as mayor appears on page 85 of *Tunick v. Sifir*, 209 F. 3d 67 (2000).

309 **In one bizarre case:** The litigation involving *New York Magazine* is *New York Magazine v. Metropolitan Transit Authority*, 136 F. 3d 123 (2d Cir. 1998).

324 **a Cuban-American museum:** The case involving the Cuban-American museum in Miami is *Cuban Museum of Arts and Culture, Inc. v. City of Miami*, 766 F. Supp. 1121 (S. D. Fla. 1991).

325 **one United States Supreme Court case in this area:** The full citation to the *Finley* case is *National Endowment for the Arts v. Finley*, 524 U.S. 569 (1998).

336 **"aesthetic sensibilities":** De Montebello's op-ed piece is found at Philippe de Montebello, "Making a Cause Out of Bad Art," *New York Times* op-ed, Oct. 5, 1999, Sec. A, p. 25.

340 **Under a 1961 United States Supreme Court case:** The full reference for *Younger v. Harris* is 401 U.S. 37 (1961).

360 **greatest cases protecting civil liberties:** The complete citation for the *Barnett* case is *West Virginia State Board of Education v. Barnett*, 319 U.S. 624 (1943). Justice Brennan's opinion on the constitutionality of flag burning is *Texas v. Johnson*, 491 U.S. 397 (1989).

366 **"intellectually dishonest":** Giuliani's comments and reaction are included in D. Barrett & M. Haberman, "Rudy: Museum Judge Too Far Left To Be Right," *New York Post*, Nov. 5, 1999; G. Smith, "Judge to Rudy: Give Back Museum Funds," *Daily News*, Nov. 2, 1999, p. 7; P. Hurtado, "Win for Museum," *Newsday*, Nov. 2, 1999, p. A07; D. Barstow, "Mayor Says Judge Rushed Decision in Museum Case," *New York Times*, Nov. 3, 1999, p. B3.

369 **The letter had included a passage:** The letter containing quotations from Goebbels is on file with the author.

377 **His depiction of the case:** Giuliani's account of the Brooklyn Museum case is found in Rudolph W. Giuliani, *Leadership* (2002), pp. 225-26.

CHAPTER VIII:
CAMPAIGN FINANCE REFORM AND THE FIRST
AMENDMENT

The campaign finance case refers to *McConnell v. Federal Election Commission*, 540 U.S. 93 (2003) *reviewing* 251 F. Supp. 2d 176 (D.D.C. 2003), 251 F. Supp. 2d 948 (D.D.C. 2003).

380 **two of my favorite:** *Mills v. Alabama* may be found at 384 U.S. 214 (1966). The case involving the *Miami Herald* is *Miami Herald Pub. Co. v. Tornillo*, 418 U.S. 241 (1974).

384 **"the concept that government":** Justice Brennan's views and those of other members of the Supreme Court joining its *per curiam* opinion in *Buckley v. Valeo* are at 424 U.S. 1 (1976).

387 **The Times accordingly refused:** The case described involving the advertisement placed in the *Times* by the ACLU and others is *ACLU v. Jennings*, 366 F. Supp. 1041 (1973), vacated by *Staats v. ACLU*, 422 U.S. 1030 (1975).

391 **In the name of federalism:** Judge John T. Noonan of the Ninth Circuit Court of Appeals powerfully critiques the Court's recent federalism decisions in *Narrowing the Nation's Power: The Supreme Court Sides with the States* (2002).

400 **"Speech and Power":** The piece in the *Nation* I refer to appears in Speech and Power Symposium, July 21, 1997. The *Columbia Journalism Review* article is Floyd Abrams, "Look Who's Trashing the First Amendment," *Columbia Journalism Review* Nov/Dec 1997, pp. 53-57.

404 **copyright infringement:** The copyright case

involving President Ford's memoirs is *Harper & Row Publishers, Inc. v. Nation Enterprises*, 471 U.S. 539 (1985). The death row cases mentioned are *Minnick v. Mississippi*, 498 U.S. 146 (1990) and *Johnson v. Mississippi*, 486 U.S. 578 (1988).

407 **rarely publishes an article:** The *Times* article mentioned is "The Way We Live Now: Questions for Floyd Abrams: Fighting with the Right," *New York Times*, April 7, 2002, p. 17.

424 **critical vote saving:** The University of Michigan case is *Grutter v. Bollinger*, 123 S. Ct. 2325 (2003); the Texas sodomy case is *Lawrence v. Texas*, 539 U.S. 558 (2003).

426 **1990 ruling of the Court:** The full citation to *Austin v. Michigan Chamber of Commerce* is 494 U.S. 652 (1990).

433 **Breyer entered the fray:** Justice Breyer's speech may be found at Stephen Breyer, Madison Lecture: "Our Democratic Constitution," 77 *NYU Law Review* 245 (2002).

434 **"defenders of every kind of regime":** Orwell's quotation is taken from *In Front of Your Nose: Collected Essays, Journalism & Letters of George Orwell* (Orwell & Angus, eds. 1968), pp. 132-133.

434 **put the point well:** Justice Stewart's concurrence may be found at *CBS v. Democratic National Committee*, 412 U.S. 94 (1973).

441 **The Court had held unconstitutional:** The pornography Internet case mentioned is *Ashcroft v. Free Speech Coalition*, 535 U.S. 234 (2002).

448 **"Dissenting opinions":** Judge Friendly's exhortation is on page 132 of *Local 1545, Brotherhood of Carpenters and Joiners v. Vincent*, 288 F. 2d 127 (2d. Cir 1960).

451 **To comply:** Information in this and the following two sentences was provided in interviews with Steve Bokat (Chamber of Commerce) on Oct. 21, 2004, Larry Gold (AFL-CIO) on Nov. 24, 2004, and Nadine Strossen (ACLU) on Sept. 24, 2004.

CHAPTER IX: AT HOME AND ABROAD

455 **British law:** Geoffrey Robertson's description of English law is taken from Geoffrey Robertson and Andrew Nicols, *Media Law* (4th ed. 2002), p. 20.

457 **"hate speech":** For illustrations of the American approach to hate speech, see *Brandenburg v. Ohio*, 395 U.S. 444 (1969), *National Socialist Party of America v. Skokie*, 432 U.S. 43 (1977), and Floyd Abrams, "Hate Speech: An American View," 22 *Israeli Yearbook on Human Rights* 85 (1993) (on file with author).

458 **The United States duly signed:** The reference is to the International Convention on

the Elimination of All Forms of Racial Discrimination, 660 U.N.T.S. 195 and to President Carter's reservation, S. Exec. Docs. C, D, E and F, 95th Cong., 2d Sess. vii (1978).

459 **"The right to think":** Justice Kennedy's opinion mentioned here is *Ashcroft v. Free Speech Coalition*, 535 U.S. 234 (2002).

460 **sought the testimony:** The *Randal* case before the International Criminal Tribunal for the former Yugoslavia is *Prosecutor v. Brdjanin and Talic*, Decision on Interlocutory Appeal, IT-99-36-AR73.9 (ICTY Appeals Chamber 2000). An interesting discussion of the case is found in Nina Kraut, "A Critical Analysis of One Aspect of *Randal* in Light of International, Economic, and American Human Rights Conventions and Case Law," 35 *Columbia Human Rights Law Review* 337 (2004).

461 **Germany, France, and Austria:** The German statutes are Section 53 of the German Criminal Procedure Code and Section 383 of the German Civil Procedure Code. The French statute is Article 109(2) of the French Code of Criminal Procedure. The Austrian statute is Article 31 of the Media Act 1981. Article 281 of Japan's Code of Civil Procedure allows witnesses to refuse to divulge "occupational secrets" unless the information is necessary for a fair trial. In *Sasaki v. The Hokkaido*

News, Inc., 930 *Hanrei Jihô* 44, Sapporo District Court, May 30, 1979, the court held that Article 281 applied to journalists and their sources. Furthermore, in the *Hakata Railway Station* case, 1969 (Shi) No. 68, Supreme Court, November 26, 1969, the Supreme Court of Japan recognized that the interest in news-gathering activity fell within the ambit of Article 21 of Japan's constitution. A Canadian court recently quashed a search warrant for material identifying a journalist's confidential source based upon the public interest in fostering the journalist-informant relationship. *National Post v. Canada*, (2004) O.J. No. 178 (Ont. Superior Ct. of Justice). Cases providing protection for confidential sources in New Zealand include *Broadcasting Corp. of New Zealand v. Alex Harvey Industries Ltd.*, (1980) 1 NZLR 163 (Ct. App., Wellington), and *European Pacific Banking Corp. v. Television New Zealand Ltd.*, (1994) 3 NZLR 43, 48 (Ct. App., Wellington). The Swedish law is Chapter 3, Article 1 of Sweden's Freedom of the Press Act. The European Court of Human Rights case is *Goodwin v. United Kingdom*, [1996] 22 E.H.R.R. 123.

461 **"Protection of journalistic sources":** The quotation is from *Schmit v. Luxembourg*, [2003]. E.C.H.R. 51772/99.

466 **paralyzingly expensive litigation:** The Scientology case referred to is *Church of*

Scientology v. Time Warner Inc., 238 F. 3d 168 (2d Cir.), *cert. denied*, 534 U.S. 814 (2001).

468 **"With few and small exceptions"** The quotation from Renata Adler's *Reckless Disregard* (1986) is from pages 16 and 17.

470 **So is the writing:** Professor Jay Rosen's essay is "Vaclav Havel in Washington: The Media Encounter That Never Was," *Deadline: A Bulletin from the Center for War, Peace and the News Media,* vol. 5, nos. 3-4, summer 1990.